Relationships Among Country Risk, Investor Expectations, and Financial Variables in Central Europe

A Study of Transitioning Economies

RELATIONSHIPS AMONG COUNTRY RISK, INVESTOR EXPECTATIONS, AND FINANCIAL VARIABLES IN CENTRAL EUROPE

A Study of Transitioning Economies

Edward M. Jankovic

With a Foreword by
Pan G. Yatrakis

The Edwin Mellen Press
Lewiston•Queenston•Lampeter

Library of Congress Cataloging-in-Publication Data

Jankovic, Edward M.
Relationships among country risk, investor expectations, and financial variables in Central Europe : a study of transitioning economies / Edward M. Jankovic; with a foreword by Pan G. Yatrakis.
p. cm.
Includes bibliographical references and index.
ISBN-13: 978-0-7734-1306-1
ISBN-10: 0-7734-1306-5
1. Europe, Central--Economic policy--Case studies. 2. Capital market--Europe, Central--Case studies. 3. Investments, Foreign--Europe, Central--Case studies. 4. Stocks--Prices--Europe, Central--Case studies. 5. Country risk--Europe, Central--Case studies. I. Title.
HC244.J36 2010
330.943--dc22

2010021267

hors série.

A CIP catalog record for this book is available from the British Library.

The Edwin Mellen Press
Box 450
Lewiston, New York
USA 14092-0450

The Edwin Mellen Press
Box 67
Queenston, Ontario
CANADA L0S 1L0

The Edwin Mellen Press, Ltd.
Lampeter, Ceredigion, Wales
UNITED KINGDOM SA48 8LT

Printed in the United States of America

To my wife, Denise

Contents

Figures

Figure

Tables

Table

Foreword

As European economies begin the slow path to recovery from the Great Recession of 2008-2009, the focus of economic policymakers has begun to shift away from the larger, more developed nations of the West and toward the smaller and still vulnerable "transition" economies of Central Europe. In these former Soviet satellites may still be found the greatest risks, but also the greatest opportunities in the aftermath of the financial turmoil of the last two years. Their continuing economic integration with the older members of the European Union, and their likely accession to the common currency, already adopted by Slovakia and Slovenia, open the door to increased foreign investment, leading ultimately to economic expansion and higher living standards.

However, the path to development for these transition economies is still fraught with challenges in the areas of economic transparency and political risk, factors which can encourage foreign investment if addressed successfully, but can also deter it if neglected. In this book, Dr. Edward M. Jankovic presents the results of his studies on how transparency and perceived political risk can influence the decisions of foreign investors. His analysis focuses on such indicators as country risk ratings, financial market variables, and expected investment returns. The study breaks new ground and contains important information for academic researchers. Even more significantly, however, it constitutes a valuable resource for potential investors and especially for policymakers in the transition countries who seek to advance the development of their economies, the improvement of their citizens' living standards, and their region's continuing commitment to economic stability and free market democracy.

This book is an outgrowth of Dr. Jankovic's research, in which I had the privilege of participating as an advisor and colleague. In this work, Dr. Jankovic employs a unique approach, combining quantitative and qualitative analysis with clear and easy-to-understand graphics that illustrate and reinforce his conclusions. He makes his point more than adequately with quantitative analysis alone, and then proceeds to pound skeptics into the ground with his qualitative analysis and charts. His uncomplicated but comprehensive explanation of his quantitative techniques and the reason for using them is rare, if not unique, for studies of this kind, and makes this book easy to understand by even the non-academic layperson. Just as I enjoyed working with Dr. Jankovic in his research, I am sure that readers will enjoy this work and will gain from it a more extensive awareness of the economic forces at work in Europe's most vibrant economies.

Pan G. Yatrakis, Ph.D.
Professor of Economics and Finance
H. Wayne Huizenga School of Business
Nova Southeastern University
Ft. Lauderdale, Florida

Preface

Transition economies are by definition changing, or in transition. And the financial variables that explain the dynamics of those economies are also in constant flux. So this book is the attempt to illustrate current relationships among the factors that matter to policymakers in these countries so they can create a more profitable environment, attract more investment, and create a more stable economy.

Beginning with the classic seminal literature, the setting of this volume covers all reference points for the applicable branches of theory – international pricing, risk, monetary convergence, capital market efficiency, and FDI. Recent background literature follows, then current literature on all relevant topics is examined and this paper's place in the field of international finance is shown.

This compilation is really a history of developing market finance and an examination of yield components in the focus countries of Central Europe. Current account and exchange rates are trade-related risk measures; CPI is an inflation gauge; stock markets are leading economic indicators, measuring expectations; the lending interest rate prices demand and supply of domestic funds; and FDI inflow is the product of these variables.

Methodology is an innovation in this study. First, Vector Autoregression and cointegration analysis support a majority of the proposed hypotheses. Then, technical analysis is used on the graphed data to gain insight into the variables and verify the statistical findings. Lastly and most notably, qualitative research and field studies are generated on three of the countries using a multiple source approach, including expert testimony to an expert interviewer. This work demonstrates that a mixed methods approach to research strengthens conclusions, admits a wider sphere of readers outside traditional research frameworks, and allows for inclusion of disciplines that often combine with international finance, such as politics, law, and international business.

Acknowledgments

To my friends in high places, and places everywhere, who contributed to the quality of this study by offering their experienced views, I am grateful.

Chapter I
Introduction

Background and Purpose

Reasons to explore relationships among country risk factors, securities prices, and investment returns in Central Europe include gaining insights into the viability of the region's capital markets, policy implications, and both economic and political stability. Interest rate markets particularly allow the measurement of sovereign risk attributable to political, liquidity, and market factors.

At this time, emerging markets in general, and those of Central Europe in particular, are interesting because of their degree of compatibility with developed markets (see Barr and Priestly 2004; Kocenda 2001; Kutan & Yigit, 2004, 2005). As the new accession countries continue their integration with the European Union (EU), the important question of funding arises – funding to support the many activities and programs in which the accession group must engage in order to meet the monetary, fiscal, social, political, and market standards of the EU. Bonds are a likely source of investment inflows for promising economies in transition. Debt markets allow different strata and categorizing, from local to national, project to general obligation, collateralized, single-government, or regional consortium. Development, indexed, and government-backed industrial bonds, plus defined maturities (useful for comparisons) continue the idea of flexibility and potential varied ratings for debt in this region.

Some background work in country risk applies to equity markets as well as interest rate markets, and at times, this information will be useful in analyses. Bonds in this emerging market category have statistical correlations with equities and other asset classes, which are also useful in comparisons. The caution is the relatively short time that data has been available. JP Morgan's Emerging Market Bond Index (EMBI), for example, dates back only to January 1991. Another problem is a tendency to categorize all emerging market debt as one category. For example, the Asian financial crisis in 1997 prompted a massive sell-off of all emerging market bonds, including those of South America and Central Europe.

Importance of Studying Emerging Markets Finance

Understanding country risk and how it affects global investment strategies is a key aspect of improving liquidity and transparency of emerging economies' financial markets. Improved markets provide arrays of new and diverse investments. This research is an effort to show the relationships among country risk ratings, financial variables, and expected returns in emerging markets of select countries in Central and Eastern Europe. Results and conclusions are useful guidelines for subject countries to create strategies and develop policies that will create a more profitable financial environment for economic growth.

At this time, the Central European economies in transition have many of the resources needed for development, such as educated labor forces, an entrepreneurial orientation among the people, and land. Yet, another key resource, capital, is in short supply in the region. An important concept in obtaining capital is to demonstrate economic and political stability. By improving transparency of the legal, banking, and capital markets sectors, these countries will be able to make real progress toward their objectives of free and democratic societies.

The value of this research effort is to examine whether relationships among country risk ratings, financial market variables, and expected returns in this region exist and can be useful in improving the capital markets systems and so attract more capital to the region. This area of research has been gaining attention in the last few years, and the policy derived from it is still being tested.

Contributions Expected From This Study

These new democracies are dealing not only with their own economies and politics, but also in many cases (all case studies in this book) address the option of becoming part of the larger economic and political organization of the European Union. Therefore, the contribution to the literature is direct and beneficial to those determining policy for the various countries' legal, banking, and capital markets mechanisms and their fit with larger economic and political groups. This volume adds to the credibility of previous researchers by showing that their findings also apply to current times and to the newly emerging capital markets, which have only been in operation for a short time.

This book also breaks new ground in its use of qualitative methodology, where a second distinct contribution from this study is expected. Using field/case studies based on interviews with experts in the field and Grounded Theory, comparisons with previous research and research in this study can be made and verified. The discussion of this methodology is provided in detail in Chapter III.

History and Development of Capital Markets

Preliminary Groundwork

By nature, capital market theory has deep roots. The practice of trading and banking is ancient, and as markets developed through different stages as demanded by the users in the marketplace, practices adapted to the environment. Especially after World War II, in the United States but also worldwide, capital needs have increased tremendously. The rebuilding of Japan and Germany required funding on a scale that was previously unseen. As Wall Street and Main Street developed to meet consumer and industry demand, latent markets such as warrants, options, and preferred stock took on renewed life.

During the 1950s and 1960s it sufficed that a few "deans" of early financial theory produced the base theories for nearly all the branches. After all, the branches sprang from the same root. And the financial environment had been fairly stable for a long time, now only increasing in volume and liquidity as the primary differentiator from pre-War activity. Markowitz (1952), Fama (1965), Houthakker (1965), Lintner (1965), and Sharpe (1964) began to explain the activities of markets, portfolios, stocks and yields in scientific terms. These men began the modern age of financial literature. They are discussed in detail in this paper in Chapters II and III.

The stability of the early and middle years of the twentieth century's financial setting gave way to the production and trade tussles of the 1960s, the volatility of markets due to oil price shocks in 1973 and 1978, and spawned more mechanisms for protecting and creating wealth. Demand and supply curve shifts occurred that were on the scale of Germany's post-WWI inflation, the worldwide depression of the 1930s, and the financing needs of the world's militaries to fight WWII.

The era of creative financing began. Lending to developing nations, oil and alternative energy exploration, and the massive explosion of consumer durable- and non-durable goods production around the world began to create a need for money in many forms to finance these activities. Mere working capital and even usual long-term capital methods of financing of a firm did not seem sufficient to keep up with expansion plans and the idea of competitiveness that was soon to become a buzzword in business circles. The idea of hedging, financial flexibility, and locking-in prices was ripe for implementation.

Commodity and option markets, syndicated loans, and variations in bond maturity, risk, creditworthiness, and yield curve components became more widely recognized as valid pieces of the financing puzzle that offered new dimensions to financing and investments.

Current Research

Evolution of financial theory, especially into the international arena, continued with Solnik (1974), Bakaert and Harvey (1995, 2003), Erb, Harvey and Viskonta (1996b, 2000), Claessens, Oks and Polastri (1998, 2000), Mody, Taylor,

Kim (2001), Brada & Kutan (2002), and Brada, Kutan & Yigit (2004) among others, and these are all detailed in Chapter II.

Markets that developed during the 1980s and 1990s and were treated in this generation of literature included over-the-counter and exchange-traded currency options, bond options, emerging market debt, index options for a variety of stock and bond indexes, and restructuring schedules of both corporate and sovereign debt, accompanied by options, preferences, and warrants on tranches and different currency denominations of the same issues.

Extensions of the Use of Capital Markets

Using conclusions from the research in this study, policy measures can be taken to attract more investment to the focus countries. The concepts of country risk presented here and the resulting effects on Foreign Direct Investment (FDI) to the region indicate that the markets are useful on several levels. Traders, brokers, and investors are the usual key players, yet monetary and fiscal authorities and foreign relations policymakers also can obtain valuable information from the markets.

As more net capital inflows occur into emerging economies, the more liquid and deep the markets become. Both financial flows, including trading portfolios, and FDI are mechanisms of investing in foreign markets. Mody, Taylor and Kim (2001) define three types of capital, or financial flows in their analysis: equity, bond, and syndicated loans. FDI can also be subcategorized, into greenfield investments and merger and acquisition projects.

Ben S. Bernanke, the new Chairman of the U.S. Federal Reserve Bank, discusses how capital flows to developing economies afford those countries ways to take advantage of investment opportunities while providing savers with mechanisms to earn better returns and reduce risk. Access to the international capital markets also allows countries to acquire foreign assets in boom times and use those assets in lean times, thereby having a buffer to adverse changes in domestic income and production (Bernanke 2005).

Gwartney and Lawson (2005) offer further support that free trade and economic freedom increase standards of living and assists with the integration of emerging economies into the global economy. Their annual Economic Freedom of the World Report tabulates data and shows relationships among size of government, legal structure, access to sound money, international exchange, and regulation for the countries of the world.

Bevan and Estrin (2004) and Janicki and Wunnova (2004) discuss local determinants of FDI into transition economies, and Deichmann (2001) considers distribution of FDI into the economies based on geographic, economic, and trade factors.

The Need for Further Research

Due to the continued development of this part of the world economically and its integration into the West, research in emerging market finance must be ongoing. As each nation grows, demands more money for financing its growth, and its markets expand, elasticities of both demand and supply for funds will change. Countries' credit ratings will change, and reasons for those changes will change. The entire financial and economic environment is dynamic, demanding at least as much attention as developed markets, and here with new models and new methods of analyses.

Another area of future research that would naturally stem from this study would be in the method of analysis and interpretation. Investigating this region and its transition economies through the Austrian School of Economics would provide new insights into the underlying economic engines that are fuelling the transitions. This class of economics studies the world through the concepts of logic, human action and choice, competition, and has its emphasis on entrepreneurship and the market process. For emerging markets, this kind of analysis seems to fit well, looking at the circumstances of Central Europe, for example, with a market economy model as the lens. The websites of The Foundation for Economic Education and the Ludwig von Mises Institute offer good starting points for this research.

Critical Definitions for this Study

Sovereign Yields and Interest Rates

As taught in universities, yields and interest rates can include a number of components: inflation, cost of money, and a number of risk premiums: default, political, currency, maturity, and market or portfolio risk. Erb, Harvey and Viskonta (1996b, 2000) described key sectors of risk – political, economic, and financial – that apply to global investment strategies in emerging economies. Country risk ratings consider all parts of the yield equation.

These analyses have shown which components within the yield correlate most closely with the yield itself and thus demand the most attention. The emphasis of internal components may vary from country to country, but not significantly. Certain risks, a real rate of return, and market expectations can also be considered pieces of a country's sovereign bond yield. In a yield, the market allocates a risk, return, and expectation of these at any one point in time. Geography, level of economic development of the country, and financial and economic risk are all taken into account when a buyer and seller agree to a trade. Bond yields for some of the focus countries have limited histories, and long-term lending rates are the proxy for bond yields in the analysis.

Qualitative Analysis

An evolving and increasingly useful method of analysis in several fields of study is qualitative analysis. Widely applied in the social sciences (criminal justice, health care, and anthropology), qualitative analysis includes the following aspects of methodology which are applied in this study: thematizing, designing, transcribing, and analyzing (Kvale 1996, 1988); coding, which is transforming raw data into standardized forms; Grounded Theory (Glasser & Strauss 1967; Strauss & Corbin 1998), which compares incidents in similar categories, integrates the categories, and creates theory from the data and groupings; and case studies (Creswell 1998), based on interviews with experts, which create in-depth data collection and analysis of one subject in order to apply the results and solutions to similar subjects. A discussion of the kinds of qualitative research employed in this study and the justification for their use are detailed in Chapter III on Methodology.

Financial charts fit the coding category quite well, and the macroeconomic and financial data discussed and analyzed in a qualitative way provide additional confirmation of the answers to the research questions in this study.

Thomas Shelling, the recent 2005 Nobel Prize winner in Economics, does not believe that only mathematical models in economics and finance research make that research more understandable. He is a proponent of giving practical meaning to his discourse, including Game Theory for which he won the Prize. His primary method of qualitative research is the use of analogies and thought experiments.[1]

Statement of the Problem

The research question in this project is whether certain relationships among country risk, investor expectations, and security prices exist, and if so, which have predictive ability to assist policymakers in attracting investment to the those countries.

Sample Research Questions

The major questions asked (by country) are as follows:

- Do changes in the stock market index affect FDI?
- Do changes in the Consumer Price Index affect FDI?
- Do changes in the Current Account affect FDI?
- Do changes in the long-term lending affect FDI?
- Do changes in the exchange rate affect FDI?

---

[1] *U.S. News & World Report*, October 24, 2005 and *The Wall Street Journal*, October 11, 2005.

Since country risk rating changes can be positive or negative, there may be a directional effect of the independent variable (e.g., CPI) on the dependent variable (FDI). Each country is analyzed using each predictive factor, and this is done with three analyses.

Summary

This introduction describes the purpose, importance, and expectations of studying emerging markets finance. The practical bottom line of this book is to assist policymakers in creating stable financial environments that would attract increased amounts of investment into these transition economies. The development of capital markets is described through the research of the last half-century, and the uses of capital markets in research and applications are enumerated. Two key definitions of terms and methodology (yields (or interest rates) and qualitative research) are highlighted in this chapter but elaborated on in Chapter III. That there have been no formal qualitative research studies in international finance is a gap in the research that this book also seeks to fill. The last section of the Literature Review, Chapter II, discusses this issue.

Chapter II
Review of the Literature

Overview

The literature is organized by category and time from the 1950s to the present, and illustrates the development of the discipline. Subcategories by function or analysis are identified for summary and clarification purposes. There is much integration of asset classes (equities and debt) since many factors that affect one market affect the other. The task of this research is to focus on factors that work primarily on debt in the region of Central Europe. Country risk, including political risk, and investor attitudes are changing dramatically, and this is a prime time for an investigation of relationships among country risk, interest rates, and investment returns. Monetary, fiscal, and political policies are also discussed as a natural extension and practical matter of converging accession economies with the Eurozone. Some works are reviewed primarily to point out this project's justification of the use of certain variables and certain country selections, as well as methodology.

Seminal Literature of International Pricing, Risk, and Capital Market Efficiency

In much of the seminal work of the early researchers, empirical work precedes the development of the theory. Fama's (1965) work, which is an outgrowth of his 1963 discourse, is a prime example. This paper presents both classes of research intertwined, allowing the reader to judge more easily which of the empirical results are most relevant from the viewpoint of the theory. Later, in both Chapters

II and III, the theory and empirical work are shown together throughout the literature as leading to the model used in this paper.

Early work on domestic security prices, risk, and diversification was done by Lintner (1965) on equilibrium valuations of individual risk assets. He showed that a certainty-equivalent dollar return adjusts an expected return for risk. Specifically, relationships among the expected dollar return, an adjustment for its risk, the market price of that security, and the risk-free interest rate are shown to be robust, even when investors' estimates of probability are different. Also shown is that diversification gains come from "averaging over" the independent components of the returns and risks of individual stocks. Further, the objective of diversification is to produce the best portfolio – the best combination of risk and expected return – and not a portfolio with the least possible risk. A last conclusion is that common stock will continue to be held because the general level of all stock prices will always be low enough to make expected rates of return high enough to be attractive in spite of independent risks and levels of general business conditions, and in spite of those investments offering riskless positive returns.

The behavior of a maximizing risk-adverse investor with such a security is normally distributed when there is a risk-free asset available. Cash and risky assets are contrasted and it is shown that a regression of the rate of return on each security provides a selection mechanism for buying securities.

Sharpe (1964) proposed a theory of market equilibrium under conditions of risk. This provided the start of a body of microeconomic theory dealing with risk. His idea described the investor as able to obtain higher rates of return by incurring additional risk along a capital market line. So a price of time, or pure interest rate, was contrasted with a price of risk, the reciprocal of the slope of the capital market line to the expected rate of return. An optimal investment policy for an individual was derived using a model of investment opportunity curves (indifference curves). The model allowed choices from a set of investment opportunities that would maximize an investor's utility.

A discussion of the optimal investment policy for the individual includes the investor's preference function, the investment opportunity curve, and the pure rate of interest. A section on equilibrium in the capital market brings out the theory that while not all investors will hold the same combination of assets, all such combinations must be perfectly correlated since they lie along a linear border in a region on a graph defined as a relationship between level of risk and a standard deviation of a set of risks. Sharpe's conclusions on the prices of capital assets are:

> Results are consistent with classical theory, or a capital market line when considering the market as a whole; and
> Investors will accept a lower expected return from securities that have low response to economic movements than they will accept from securities with higher responses to changes in economic conditions.

Markowitz (1952) ploughed early ground in portfolio theory. Both expected returns and the variance of returns for a one period investment were covered. He regarded risk as part of anticipated returns, and illustrated that expected return is desirable and variance of return is undesirable. His model is often called a "mean variance" model, and provides an algebraic base for the Capital Asset Pricing Model (CAPM).

Fama's (1965) work on the behavior of stock market prices supported, with empirical evidence, the random walk theory – that the market has no memory of price changes and that price changes are independent and identically distributed random variables. The applicability to emerging markets is to augment the argument that a new environment of post-Communist funding activity demands a fresh approach to qualifying and utilizing new available capital markets. Later, Fama (1970 and 1991) reviewed both the theoretical and empirical literature on the efficient capital markets model (that markets reflect all relevant information) in all three forms – weak, semi-strong, and strong. He concluded that, with few exceptions, the efficient markets model holds. In 1992, together with French, Fama evolved a cross-sectional study of expected stock returns based upon size and book-to-market equity. The variation in market returns was shown to have relationships with market betas, size, leverage, book-to-market and P/E ratios. When market beta was not related to size, market beta and average return were flat. This was an attempt to explain contradictions in Sharpe (1964), Lintner (1965), and Black (1972), where they promoted cross-sectional returns as related to market beta and expected market returns.

Recent Background Literature of International Pricing, Risk, and Capital Market Efficiency

Pricing

Fama and French (1992) find weakness in pricing with CAPM, specifically estimating a beta premium. Due to the statistical uncertainty (a large standard error) with the variation in expected return and the inability of the beta to explain it, the conclusion of the researchers is that the market portfolio is not efficient and CAPM is an empirical failure. Further, Fama and French (1998) find that these problems with CAPM pricing also exist in foreign markets and in emerging markets.

Fama and French (2004) prepare a three factor model used widely in empirical research when expected returns are considered. However, one school, the behaviorists (markets are not always rational) faults CAPM because it does not account for investor irrationality. Thus the three factor model contains a momentum effect that is left unexplained, especially as compared to a value effect.

Barberis and Thaler (2003) provide a comprehensive literature review of recent behavioral finance theory that helps to sort out the rationality versus irrationality aspects of investors meeting in the economy. A revealing conclusion in the series of papers is that irrationality can have a large and lasting effect on prices. Barberis, Huang, and Thaler (2006) bring the concept of investor beliefs or preferences into focus with a decision-making tool that evaluates a next action in the stock market. Their idea of "narrow framing" explains how evaluating a new trade in isolation may be a more important feature of decision-making than previously understood.

Both Bechev (2006) and Nguyen and Fontaine (2006) examine stock market efficiency in converging and segmented markets in developing economies. Further, Wooster (2007) raises the idea of behavior to the level of FDI by introducing the variable of choice of investments by foreign investors between acquisitions or new plant investments, depending on the stage of transition of the economy and the expectations of the investor.

Solnik (1974) provides the current base of analysis for the international pricing of risk by looking at world capital market structure. Working off the Sharpe (1964) and Markowitz (1952) market model, Solnik's great contribution is to expand the traditional Sharpe-Lintner CAPM into an International Asset Pricing Model (IAPM).

In determining the international market structure of asset prices, a simple world index model seemed unrealistic due to the importance of national factors. Solnik (1974) looks into several stochastic price processes to develop a multi-index specification taking into account both national and international factors. He also shows that a domestic capital asset pricing model for each country could be consistent with a single and perfect international market.

All capital markets, he states, should be perfect with free flow of capital among nations. Each country has a market for borrowing and lending, but these individual markets do not reflect the same rates since the risk free asset of one country becomes a pure exchange risk asset for a foreign investor. A way to cover this exchange rate risk is by a forward contract. That would be equivalent to defining a risk-free international rate on a covered basis. Likewise, an uncovered investment in the stock market contains both market and exchange risk for a foreign investor. The standard assumption in portfolio theory is that all investors hold the same expectations about exchange rate changes and the distribution of returns in their own nation's currency.

If the assumption is further narrowed to an investor consuming only his home country's goods, there is a national segmentation of the product market and only partial equilibrium. Remaining is the exchange risk hurdle: for all nationals of a country, exchange rate changes affect the return on a foreign asset in the same way.

Erb, Harvey and Viskonta (2000) relate country risk to pricing international sovereign bonds and this is discussed in detail in the section of this chapter titled "Market Segmentation, Risk, Credit and Investment Literature."

Solnik (1974) tests his idea of the international market structure with a single index market model, then refines the test with a nationalistic model that considered that all securities are affected by the international factor through their national index. He finally uses a Multinational Index Model that attempted to account for the events outside a national risk: international links of the firm, foreign subsidiaries, international competition, and import-export patterns. Variables in his Multinational Index Model include country risk factors that affect only one country and those which may affect the world as a whole: expected returns on a security in local currency, interest rates in the security's country, an expected return on the world index, and average world interest rate, and a measure of international systemic risk of the security.

Transition Economies and Market Capitalization

Claessens, Djankov, and Klingebiel (2000) provide projections on transition economies in the region, their market capitalization, and prospects for development based on macroeconomic and financial data.

Some of their conclusions are that domestic stock markets will be difficult to develop for many of the transitional economies. Obstacles to reaching critical economies of scale include weak laws and regulations, slow progress in privatization, limited numbers of institutional investors, and macroeconomic uncertainties.

While domestic markets remain undeveloped, the services of stock markets are still available. Several European markets, the USA, and Japan are all options available for transition economies. Even so, transition economies need to improve their financial sector infrastructure by creating stronger legal property rights for creditors and shareholders, providing better information, greater disclosure, having well-governed institutional investors, and supporting public and private institutions. This focus on institutional development plus legal reform rather than trying to develop costly stock markets will facilitate domestic corporations' access to global markets. (Details about the importance of institutional aspects of transitioning economies are discussed in the "Identification of Risk Categories..." section and the last section of this chapter.)

To explain market capitalization, Claessens et al (2000) use several tools to analyze their variables. Simple correlations identify market capitalization as positively correlated with single-digit inflation, size of institutional investor assets, and high shareholder protection. Regression analysis is used to control for other variables such as income and integration with other more developed countries. Their study shows low inflation, good shareholder protection, and size of institutional investors' assets are important in explaining market capitalization even after controlling for income or distance (integration) to other markets.

Market capitalization is also shown to be positively correlated with ratios of private credit to GDP in transition economies. With shallow banking systems in many transition economies, private credit registers less than ten percent of GDP (Claessens et al 2000). Since banking systems generally develop before stock markets, the economies in transition should focus on developing the basic financial infrastructure of investor protection, contract enforcement, and sound accounting standards for both equity and debt markets. The advantages of focusing on the institutional framework are confirmed in a growing literature stressing the importance of creditor rights in developing banking systems (LaPorta and others 1999; Levine, Laoyza, and Beck 2000). Their results show that weak creditor rights are an important reason for undeveloped banking systems in transition economies. Conversely, the better the quality of creditor rights, the more developed the banking system.

A policy conclusion of this literature is that transition economies should focus on improving and enforcing creditor rights to foster their banking system development. A further conclusion is that improved creditor rights is a most effective way to nurture the development of small and medium-size enterprises, which is a key source of economic growth.

Market Segmentation, Risk, and Investment

Sobol (1996) concludes that while some market participants might view the region of Central and Eastern Europe as a single entity, many seem to be distinguishing among the countries when making investment decisions. Her concern is how the imported capital is being used. If capital goes to finance current consumption, it fails to contribute to the productive capacity of the economy and so cannot promote long-term growth. But if it goes mainly to finance investment, there are few concerns about its long-term productivity. Also, while evidence of the uses of imported capital is mixed, the fact that private capital flows have continued to go the region despite political and economic changes is a market vote of confidence in these countries.

Erb, Harvey, and Viskanta (1996) develop hurdle rates for emerging country investments, which are useful for markets segmented by different expected returns depending on the national origin of the security. Returns are compared against market integration (a portfolio approach) or risk ratings (individual national securities). The beta has some ability in one study to discriminate between developed and emerging markets. Volatility as a function of time allows for a dynamic risk measure. In further separate works that same year, Erb, Harvey, Viskanta (1996) describe five different measure of country risk – political, financial, economic, and composite risk indexes plus country credit ratings. These risk measures are linked to expected returns using time series and cross sectional analyses. Lastly, connections between country risk and investment strategies are investigated and show that risk indexes are highly correlated with fundamental information like book-to-price ratios.

Further studies by these researchers discuss changes in cross-sectional variation and implications for asset allocation. In Erb, Harvey, and Viskonta (1999 and 2000), emerging market bonds are examined in detail through the emerging market crash and show that country risk measures are valuable in explaining expected returns and volatilities in these markets. Credit spreads are compared with country risk ratings. Erb, Harvey, and Viskonta (2000) break down risk into three categories: interest rate risk, currency risk, and sovereign or country risk. Country risk helps to explain the pricing of a bond due to its country of origin and the specific country risk factors that currently affect the country. Included in this pricing are results from country rating services like Moody's, Standard and Poor's, and Fitch International, which consider a country's political, economic, and social conditions and then create a composite report on stability and ability of the country to repay its debts. These researchers also consider distributional characteristics of emerging market bonds, the slope of the yield curves of the countries, sentiment, and portfolio context. They conclude that the markets are low-capitalization markets, a negative skewness exists which must be offset by higher expected returns, and the markets are highly volatile.

Market Integration and Capital Flows

Bekaert and Harvey (2002) describe how market integration affects expected returns. Analyzing correlations with the Morgan Stanley Capital International (MSCI) and International Finance Corporation (IFC) databases, it is demonstrated that as countries' industrial structures become more integrated with world industry, there is increased correlation with the world average and expected returns decrease. This association is measured by the beta relative to a world market return, obtained here from IFC and MSCI databases.

Also noted is that market integration is often gradual. Each nation in transition has particular circumstances that cause the barriers to integration to be overcome at different rates of speed. Bekaert (1995) uses three categories of barriers to emerging market investment: legal barriers, indirect barriers due to information asymmetry, and barriers of accounting standards and risks that define liquidity, political, economic policy, and currency risks. These barriers, which discourage foreign investment, are unlikely to come down at a single point in time.

Barr and Priestly (2004) use a conditional asset pricing model to conclude that only about one-quarter of the total expected excess return is related to local market risk, while the remainder is due to world bond market risk. Their variables include the spread between long-bond yields and stock dividend yields and the spread between long-term and short-term rates. Their results determine that world factors contribute 70 percent to domestic returns, and so world bond markets are not integrated as much as perhaps thought, considering an absence of cross-country investment barriers. Other conclusions are that governments therefore pay higher rates for funds than necessary, but that they may be willing to do so to avoid fiscal discipline that might be imposed by further integrated world bond markets.

As countries liberalize their capital markets, a ratio of "investable" market capitalization to "global" market capitalization is used as a proxy for the degree of integration. Bekaert and Harvey (2003) develop a model of market integration distinguishing between market liberalization and integration. This model adapts to changing circumstances of contagion, corporate finance, market microstructure, and stock selection in emerging markets. The volatility of capital flows, the impact of financial liberalization on country risk, and the performance of emerging market investments are explained with interesting results. For example, it is seen that capital flows to emerging markets as a group are less volatile than capital flows to developed countries as a group. The effects of the liberalization process on economic growth, real exchange rates, and income inequality are shown to have a positive average effect.

Fratzscher (2002) tests for integration of equity markets since the 1980s using a complex trivariate GARCH model. This class of model tests factors such as exchange rate volatility and monetary policy in explaining increased interdependence among Europe's financial markets. Both of these factors are important in countries that have joined the EU and are moving toward European Monetary Union (EMU). Other considerations about financial integration are that integration increases efficiency and competitiveness and has made individual markets increasingly interdependent, with fewer opportunities for investors to diversify within the Eurozone.

Dockery and Vergari (2001) use a Johansen (1995a) cointegration analysis and Engle and Granger's (1987) concept of including long-term constraints like vector auto-regression (VAR) to refine results, in this instance, to determine how well certain Eastern European capital markets are financially integrated with two major EU equity markets. Their conclusions provide support to the integrated market hypothesis, which implies long-term benefits to portfolio risk reduction using diversification.

Much background information on capital flows to Central and Eastern Europe and former Soviet satellite countries is in the work of Claesens, Oks, and Polastri (1998). Sustainability and vulnerability issues are discussed. Reform efforts and commitments to them are shown to be the most important determinant of private flows. The buildup of reserves also promotes private flows, reflecting improved perceptions of creditworthiness and better potential integration with the West. The authors discuss in detail the policy effects of large capital inflows to the Czech Republic, Poland, Estonia, Hungary, and Russia. These countries were among the earliest and fastest reformers of factors affecting their capital markets. An attempt at identifying the motivation of the sources of capital flows to these countries results in distinguishing global from country-specific factors.

The authors determine that factors that promote private capital flows are distinct from those that promote official flows. For private flows, creditworthiness resulting from structural reforms and strong macroeconomic fundamentals plus economic and financial opportunities (such as high interest rate differentials) are primary drivers. For official flows, political factors, the government's commitment to reforms, and the fiscal deficit matter most.

Subsets of private flow factors include both domestic and international interest rates and demand conditions. Domestic factors include: the degree of openness and transparency; banking sector stability and depth of financial markets; GDP growth and related ratios like propensity to save, debt, and monetary base to foreign reserves. Creditworthiness in the economies in transition often requires a restructuring of old Soviet debt for new and manageable repayment plans via a Paris or Brady debt relief program. Poland and Bulgaria exemplify this form of restructuring and have seen a resultant increase of private capital flows.

Official flows depend on different sets of factors. Official assistance to countries in the early stages of reform often takes the form of balance of payments considerations, budgetary support, and debt relief. As receipts from fiscal revenues fall, international financial institutions and certain country donors provide partial financing for these fiscal deficits.

Conclusions are that capital inflows increase when structural reform efforts such as liberalization, privatization, decentralization, stabilization, and institutional changes are sustained. FDI has helped improve productivity and access to markets, thereby fostering integration of transitional economies into the Western system.

Current Literature of International Pricing, Risk, and Capital Market Efficiency

The following two sections have the purpose of detailing factors affecting FDI and capital flows in emerging economies. Two of the variables in this discourse, FDI and investor expectations, which key off of sovereign risk ratings, find their definitions and descriptions covered in these and the sovereign credit ratings section which follows them.

Financial Sector Analysis and Capital Flows

Christian Thimann has edited (2002) a major compilation of European Central Bank data that describes the structure and functioning of the financial sectors of the twelve countries that have recently entered or are in the process of accession into the EU. Some conclusions are: that the banking sector is fundamental for development of the accession countries, as capital markets in most cases are not yet an alternative to banks; the level of financial intermediation in candidate countries is bound to rise considerably over the next years and enhance growth prospects; supervision is crucial because of the high degree of foreign investment.

Caviglia, Krause and Thimann (2002) show that to a large extent, the low level of financial intermediation is due to the limited ability of credit institutions to channel financial savings into investment. Foreign subsidiaries in the corporate sector of certain economies reduce firms' dealings with the domestic banking sector because many investments are financed by cross-border borrowing or FDI. At the small and medium-sized enterprise end of the scale, these firms are more dependent on the domestic banking sector but have the hurdles of asymmetric information with only a short credit history as a common feature.

Stock markets in accession countries to the EU are used infrequently as financing mechanisms. Capitalization of both stock and bond markets relative to GDP is a fraction of that in the Eurozone. Due to the relatively low levels of GDP in the transition countries, market capitalization in absolute terms is particularly low. Additionally, stock markets have a lesser role in financing in the accession countries than in the Eurozone due to their shorter histories, and because issues of privatization, legal and regulatory frameworks, governance and shareholder protection are less developed. Also, after the demise of the centrally planned economic systems, several countries experienced recession, periods of slow growth, and low investment. Caviglia et al (2002) point out that liquidity is low, with annual turnover of the entire group of accession countries' stock exchanges roughly equivalent to about ten days of turnover on the Deutsche Bourse.

Further background analysis of sovereign debt securities is available from Reininger, Schardax, and Summer (2002). A holding structure of publicly issued central government debt securities is detailed. The importance of the financial system is its role in allocating resources by channeling funds from households to businesses, by providing risk-sharing opportunities for households and firms, and by minimizing transaction and information costs.

Buch, Kokta, and Piazolo (2002) describe patterns of FDI between the Southern European and Central European countries. Lower labor costs, increased institutional and political stability, and the prospect of the twelve more advanced countries of Central and Eastern Europe joining the EU seem likely to redirect FDI from the region of Southern Europe. Net FDI flows into Spain and Portugal became negative in the late 1990s. Using bilateral trade and GDP per capita data (cross sectional data for 18 years from Germany and comparing expected with actual data), the authors conclude that the Southern European countries have come quite close to expectations in FDI stocks. The value of this study to the current discourse is that FDI to Central Europe is increasing on its own merits and is providing increased liquidity and market depth as time goes on.

Buch and Lusinyan (2001) assess the experience of the transition economies of Central Europe with liberalizing short-term capital flows, quantify the possible effects of EU enlargement, and analyze factors affecting the share of short-term capital flows. Their study shows how domestic policies affect the structure of capital flows, and concludes that as the accession states join the EU there would likely be a decline in their share of short-term securities issued. As the governments increase their borrowing needs, short-term debt totals should decrease and long-term borrowing should increase. This would provide more liquidity in the long end of the government debt markets.

Further, these authors point out that the transition economies now integrating into the EU are doing so under the same conditions that current EU members face. This is in contrast to previous rounds of enlargement (Greece in 1981, Spain and Portugal in 1986), which took place prior to the establishment of the Single Market and the introduction of a common currency. The discourse on the literature is a reinforcement of the importance of identifying relationships between country risk, yields, and expectations.

Mody, Taylor, and Kim (2001) discuss the importance of capital flows to emerging markets and the effects of those flows on market volatility due to the potential reversibility of those flows. The authors conclude what policies the countries may need to implement to offset adverse effects of large influxes of capital. The paper treats three aspects of capital flows: equities, bonds, and syndicated loans. A fundamental-based analysis includes a detailing of how capital flows can be driven by internal, country-specific factors or external, world market factors. The distinction of country-specific factors that "pull" in funds to the country is made with global factors that "push" funds toward any particular emerging market. Risks that exist in the domestic set of factors are compiled from such variables as consumer prices, industrial production, domestic short-term interest rates, the short-term debt to reserves ratio, credit ratings, and the domestic stock market. Three of these are variables used in this discourse.

Yildirim and Philippatos (2007) examine the banking sector in transition countries in the region and find that one-third of banks' profits are lost to inefficiency. The amount of competition and GDP growth generally increase efficiency but market concentration detracts from it. Foreign banks are more cost efficient while domestic banks are more profit efficient. This sets the stage for possible knowledge transfers that would improve banking practices and provide better service to the developing markets.

Goldberg (2007) emphasizes the importance of the relationship between FDI and financial sector growth. The growth in financial sector FDI draws attention to foreign ownership of host country banks, and that lessons from foreign ownership of industrial firms and primary resources apply to financial sector situations. Investments into financial sectors of emerging economies strengthen institutional development and foster overall economic growth.

Transition and Foreign Direct Investment (FDI)

Brada, Kutan and Yigit (2004) discuss the effects of political instability on FDI inflows to Central Europe and the Balkans. They address the methodological questions of explaining transition as a volatile process and separate the effects of economic factors, transition, and political instability on FDI to these economies. They further distinguish between external sources of political risk such as war or border clashes, trade embargos, economic sanctions, and war or conflict in neighboring states, and domestic political instability like strikes, riots, and civil unrest. Their conclusions are that the Balkan economies saw a shortfall in FDI compared to Central European transition economies, and the shortfall is attributable to regional political instabilities.

Kaminski (2001) looks at FDI to the transitional economies from a geographic point of view and a closeness of policy to EU members by the transitioning nations. Those emerging economies that liberalized quickly and started toward reforms that harmonized with EU standards were the largest beneficiaries of FDI inflows. Physical proximity, i.e., contingent borders, to EU states counted for some increased inflows to those contingent countries with only two exceptions.

Deichmann (2001) also looked at the distribution of FDI through the lens of various local factors: transportation networks, population (representing market size), value of investments, likelihood of nationalization, and market growth represented by change in GDP. His work supports that of Kaminski (2001) in the areas of proximity to EU markets and political stability.

Bevan and Estrin (2004) consider unit labor costs, market size, and proximity the most important influences in attracting FDI flows to the transition economies. They have also shown that announcements on EU accession have an impact on FDI for future member countries. Other findings include that FDI flows to the transition economies are not affected significantly by market evaluations of country-specific risk, possibly because that risk is included in other variables. For example, exchange rate risk could be included in unit labor costs, or the distance variable could account for difficulty in assessing an unfamiliar environment or culture.

Janicki and Wunnava (2004) counter Bevan and Estrin (2004) and declare that host country risk is indeed a key to increased FDI inflows. They do this by including an exchange rate variable, which is their proxy for market stability and represents the risk environment through a risk rating. Their model shows that trade is the key determinant to investment, using openness to trade, labor costs, country risk, and market size, similar to Bevan and Estrin (2004). Krkoska (2004) shows that the growth rate of transition economies is significantly influenced by an increase in FDI inflows, especially when the flows increase at a gradual pace instead of in volatile waves, in or out.

Eichengreen and Choudhry (2005) offer transition economies advice on ways to deal with FDI and capital inflows. They stress that the current account (CA) is a factor financed by capital inflows. And interest rates in the region are higher than in advanced economies and therefore also attract capital inflows. They advise the recipient countries to keep sound fiscal management and caution that sterilizing inflows can become expensive and lead to another fiscal problem. They note that the emerging markets of Europe have run larger CA deficits and relied on foreign financing for a larger share of their investment than have the emerging economies of Asia. This is a warning to those countries (until they adopt the euro) that their currencies are vulnerable to capital flow interruptions. Gourinches and Rey (2005) make an US-based analysis for relationships between current accounts and exchange rates.

Tille and Wincoop (2007) touch the area of portfolio choice in examining determinants of international capital flows. Their dynamic stochastic general equilibrium model identifies factors that result from time-varying expected returns and risks, concluding that these comprise characteristics of sources of international capital flows.

Monetary Policy, Inflation Targeting, and Market Convergence

This next section serves as a basis for the current project's use of the variables CPI and interest rates, which also supports Mody et al (2001) and their emphasis on these factors. This body of literature is distinct from much of the rest of this paper, but the few reviews here demonstrate that there is a focus on inflation as a key variable in transition economies, as was introduced in the section titled "Financial Sector Analysis and Capital Flows."

Bernanke (2005) discusses links of monetary policy and capital flows using the "trilemma" facing a country's policy regime: a choice of free capital mobility across borders, fixed exchange rates, or independent monetary policy. He develops the argument that transition countries should let their exchange rate float, and make low, stable inflation the focus of monetary policy. Targeted inflation as the emphasis of the system makes sense because the general price level is more directly linked to economic welfare than is the exchange rate, and domestic price stability improves the operation of markets and reduces the costs of administering the system.

Mishkin (2000) looked at inflation targeting as a useful guide to monetary policy in many, but not all emerging economies. Inflation targeting comprises five main components with all variables desired to be sustainable over the medium-term:

- A public announcement of medium-term targets for inflation,
- An institutional commitment to price stability as a prime goal of monetary policy to which other goals are subordinated,
- A "total information" approach in which many variables are used for setting policy, not just monetary aggregates,
- Increased transparency by communicating with the public and markets about all aspects of the plans and objectives of the monetary authorities, and lastly,
- Increased accountability of the central bank for its inflation objectives.

Advantages of this medium-term strategy are that it allows a focus on domestic issues and can respond to shocks in the domestic economy in contrast to exchange rate pegs. It also has the advantage of using all information to determine the best settings for the instruments of monetary policy and does not depend on a stable relationship between money and inflation. Also, inflation targeting is understood by the public and is highly transparent. Politically, inflation targeting keeps the focus on the central bank's ability to control inflation and deflects attention from the central bank's lack of ability to reduce unemployment, increase competitiveness, or raise productivity.

Mishkin (2000) offers Chile and Brazil as successful examples of countries that have used inflation targeting. Chile's inflation fell from twenty to three percent over a ten-year period. Many aspects of inflation targeting were used: phasing in the plan gradually, switching from projections to "hard" targets, and switching from target ranges to point targets as inflation moved toward, then under ten percent. Chile also kept the currency strong until the economy went into recession (the first recession in fifteen years) in 1998.

Brazil, in contrast with Chile, showed that a full-fledged program could be put in place quickly (in 1999) after its currency crisis. The effect was rapidly successful in getting and keeping inflation under ten percent. Within four months a policy was implemented like those in industrialized countries, and an "Inflation Report" was published with an inflation forecast. Brazil's deeply rooted fiscal problems remain.

Bernanke and Mishkin (1997) presented inflation targeting as a policy framework where transparency, coherence, and flexibility are advantages. They discuss this strategy in practice, using many countries as examples and stress the increased communications with the public about the plans and objectives of monetary policy makers. Their survey of the use of inflation targeting brings out that the CPI was the target series definition in all but one country.

Kutan and Yigit (2002) investigate economic convergence of transitional economies both within their own group and to the EU Relaxing assumptions of homogeneity in convergence rates from previous studies by Kocenda (2001), and using a longer, more stable period (after 1993), the conclusions are that first round candidate countries have made significant progress in monetary policy convergence relative to the EU. Second round candidates need more preparation, including choosing an optimal exchange rate policy.

Brada and Kutan (2002) study linkages of German monetary policy with those of recent EU members. They show that clear linkages exist in the cases of certain Balkan countries (Slovenia and Croatia) and the Mediterranean country candidates. Other Balkan candidates and Turkey have no ability to follow Bundesbank policy. In those countries where the ability to follow policies of the Bundesbank does not exist, there is a need for strengthening the financial sectors of those countries, for macroeconomic stabilization, and for time to pass until their policies can tie in to the European Central Bank before they can be considered for serious EU membership.

Orlowski (2003) examines the impact of various monetary policies on the ability of accession countries to lower inflation and exchange rate risk premiums as they converge with the Eurozone. He proposes a monetary policy setting of flexible targeting of inflation risk premiums that would help manage those risks. A model of inflation and exchange rate risk premiums is developed and the trends in these risk premiums in Hungary, Czech Republic, and Poland are tested. By controlling these risks, confidence in the economies can begin to increase and a case for improving capital market liquidity is possible.

Orlowski (2005) later refines a flexible approach to direct inflation targeting which should expedite economic transition and monetary convergence to the Eurozone for accession countries. The model examines the connection between inflation and certain monetary variables in the countries of Hungary, Czech Republic, and Poland. The reaction, or elasticity, of the Consumer Price Index is measured against expectations, nominal exchange rate movements, the Eurozone inflation rate as a whole, and production changes. Conclusions are that monetary convergence starts with flexible inflation targeting and has the end result of monetary harmonization with the larger framework of the Eurozone.

Bruha and Podpiera (2007) discuss a general equilibrium model of unequally developed countries. The model highlights convergence of quality investments and real exchange rate appreciation seen in transition economies. Price and nominal exchange rate factors valuable to policymakers in Central Europe are the focus. Lewis (2007) analyzes the hurdle countries confront when attempting to hit both an inflation and exchange rate target during convergence. Conditions under inflation-targeting and fixed exchange rate systems are compared and it is shown that the convergence environment changes under these different criteria.

Identification of Risk Categories and Their Importance to This Work

There are primarily three categories of risk applicable to this work – political risk, economic risk, and financial risk. This discussion will lead into the next section, which details issues of sovereign risk and credit ratings of countries, i.e., determining the rate of interest on sovereign bonds for these economies in transition.

Harvey's (2004) clear, valuable, and visual paper on political, financial, and economic risk sets the stage for a good part of this discourse's format. His descriptive statistics are not precisely those of this project's, but the examples and medium are close to the intent. Harvey (2004) uses the International Country Risk Guide (ICRG) for his country risk ratings and analyzes the components that comprise the Guide.

The ICRG is also tailored to emerging markets rather than developed markets, consistent with developed markets being fully integrated into world capital markets. Harvey (2004) also shows there is a strong correlation between country risk and expected returns using implied cost of capital. He verifies through constructed portfolios of varying degrees of risk that the information in the country risk measures of ICRG are useful for predicting and trading equities in emerging markets.

Wade (2005) discusses political risk analysis in transition economies. His work on identifying stability factors starts with a study of the country's current and past governments. Those factors include: government transition after elections; demographics; nongovernmental organizations (NGOs) and their part in governing and make-up of the social fabric; internal social, ethnic, and religious conditions; trade; and unemployment. This case study method of analysis using a multidisciplinary approach captures many aspects of the political and economic environment that contribute to a complete picture for potential investors.

Wade (2005) concludes that, based on his criteria:

- Poland has benefited from its proximity to Western and Eastern Europe, although frequent government changes keep it from moving into a low-risk climate;
- Hungary is the success story of the past decade due to its fiscal restraint and overall implementation of sound monetary policy;
- Czech Republic, Slovakia, and Slovenia have lowered their risk profiles greatly and improved their economies over the past decade;
- The Baltics are among the fastest growing economies in Europe;
- Romania, Bulgaria, and Croatia would benefit greatly from the stability of membership in the EU.

Sovereign Credit Ratings

Reinhart (2002) looks at linkages among currency crises, defaults, and sovereign credit ratings using a "crisis and signals" approach through matrix analysis. She finds that the large majority of defaults are associated with currency crises, but the converse is not true. Less than half of currency crises are linked to default. However, the fact that downgrades in credit ratings usually follow currency crises suggests that currency instability increases the risk of default.

Brook, Faff, Hillier and Hillier (2004) emphasize a stock market impact of sovereign rating changes versus the majority of the literature which emphasized individual stock impacts of rating changes. They use an event study methodology to detect abnormal returns (ARs) resulting from an upgrade or downgrade announcement and conclude that only sovereign downgrades convey information to the market; i.e., the event day shows significant negative impact. Upgrades over the sample show little evidence of ARs.

Steiner and Heinke (2001) look at daily excess German Eurobond returns associated with announcements of watchlisting and rating changes by Standard and Poor's and Moody's. They observe significant bond price reactions for announcements of downgrades and negative watchlistings while upgrades and positive watchlistings do not cause announcement effects. Price reaction is stronger after downgrades into speculative grade. Issuer nationality determines the intensity of the price reactions and ARs. Lowest price reactions are observed on bank bonds (where transparency is highest – due to regulatory requirements); government bonds show stronger reaction, and corporate bonds show the strongest price reaction

Kaminsky and Schmukler (2002) find the effects of rating and outlook changes are stronger during crises, in nontransparent economies, and affect neighboring countries. Therefore, changes in sovereign debt ratings and outlooks have cross-country contagion. Kaminsky and Schmukler (2002) fill a gap in the literature about changes of ratings of assets in one country and a spillover effect into others, and whether changes in ratings of one type of securities affect other asset markets.

The model in Lemmen and Goodhart (1999) permitted the authors to isolate the market's perception of government default risk. The factors that determine a government's willingness and ability to pay its debts include: a government's tax raising ability, the ability to control spending, a government's debt management policies, the degree of federal support from the EU, the capacity of the political system to produce sound budgetary operations, and the government's socioeconomic environment. The three variables the authors devised offer a better explanation of government default than previously available. Those three are the tax raising ability, a lagged inflation measure for socioeconomic success, and the variability of inflation when governments do not take into consideration the political consequences of increased tax rates.

Cantor and Packer (1995, 1996) offer broad explanations and confirmation about methodology used by credit rating agencies to determine creditworthiness.

Sovereign ratings are accorded a good deal of attention because sovereigns are some of the largest issuers on the international capital markets and also because the ratings of sovereigns affects the ratings of a large number of other borrowers of the same nationality. The authors investigate in depth the effect of rating announcements on market yields by their own occurrence, and whether they dispel any systematic relationship between ratings and deficits. The 1996 study also determines that ratings announcements have immediate effects on market pricing.

Reisen and Maltzan (1998) focus on significant effects on dollar-denominated bond yield spreads when rating agencies downgrade or put on alert a sovereign. The sample is comprised of ratings of sovereign foreign currency debt between 1987 and 1996. The benchmark is the ten-year US Treasury bond since 70 % of government bonds observed also were of ten-year maturities. Shorter maturities introduce differences in yield spreads related to the yield curve, but in this study, the shorter maturities applied only for 1992-95 when the US yield curve was relatively stable. Regularly traded bonds were found in 26 countries of the 60 countries in the sample rated by Standard and Poor's or Moody's. For every rating observation, the most regularly traded (most liquid) bond was used for the analysis. Historical volatility was the second risk measure used for the spreads.

Berk and Knot (1999) discuss the phenomena of declining international bond yield spreads and the effects of long-term interest rates, globalization of financial activities, and exchange rates on those spreads. Their study is thusly connected to Solnik (1974). Their focus on long-term rates and a PPP-based measure of exchanges rate expectation permits an assessment of the uncovered interest rate parity (UIP). They then hypothesized that increases in international capital mobility will validate the UIP due to interest rate arbitrage increases, particularly by the use of the swap market.

Bernoth, von Hagen, and Schuknecht (2003) examine yield spreads across EU countries between 1991 and 2002. They conclude that investors are risk averse and yields are determined by default risk premia and the risk aversion of investors toward credit risk. The implication is that credit markets do monitor fiscal performance and that imposes fiscal discipline on governments. These researchers divide the yields into credit and liquidity components after eliminating foreign exchange risks. A further conclusion is that the formation of the EU had important effects on bond and spread pricing of the members' sovereign issues. Benefits of membership in a larger federal union thus include lower liquidity risk premiums and increased financial market integration.

Hauner, Jonas, and Kumar (2007) investigate the example of the new EU member states joining the supranational entity of the EU and the effects of the accession on the credibility of their sovereign credit. Since the EU has higher policy credibility, the new members find that joining gives them higher credibility based on foreign currency spreads, sovereign ratings, and local currency yields.

Kim and Wu (2006) look at the other side of the issue and start with the ratings themselves, and then determine the effects of the ratings on international capital flows to the country and on the development of financial intermediaries. Fitch Ratings (2006) provides special emerging market analysis for sovereigns and covers multiple sectors, including macroeconomic accounts, banking and capital flows.

A study by Depken, LaFountain, and Butters (2006) shows the impact of corruption on sovereign ratings, with the result that a one standard deviation decrease in corruption improves sovereign credit ratings by nearly one category.

Other Political, Financial, and Economic Aspects of FDI

Even in a financial project like this discourse, a complete picture of factors responsible for growth can only truly be seen in broad perspective. Bekaert and Harvey (2002) list agency issues, legal environment, and the role of political science in finance. Politics plays a much more prominent role in emerging markets than in developed markets.

Roland (2002) presents an analysis of the political economy of reforms and makes an investigation of reforms in transition economies. He relates duration of governments to economic performance. He also identifies the literature of reform as broken into two broad categories: normative and positive. Normative literature focuses on decision-making problems of reformers with political constraints. A package of reforms would be presented to the voters, and usually, it becomes an all or nothing situation.

Positive political economy of reforms analyzes the interaction of interest groups. Here, the emphasis is on understanding the evolution of the balance of power across countries and across time.

Roland's (2002) conclusions are that in creating institutions of democracy, governance, new social norms and values, openness, and contracts, the political aspects of the process cannot be ignored by economists when analyzing transition economies. The institutional perspective of economics needs to consider the legal, social, and political environment of contracting. Further, institutions evolve, and successful ones continue the progress of economic and democratic growth. If momentum is lost, inefficient institutions can result, with a consequence of lack of growth.

Zapal and Schneider (2006) show that political costs of cutting expenditures from the transition economies' budgets vary, depending on where the countries are located. The Baltic nations seem to be holding their reform policies and are seeing strong economic growth due to responsible fiscal work. The Central European countries other than Slovenia and Slovakia have become lax in their reforms and find it politically expedient to postpone deficit reductions.

Qualitative Aspect of the Literature

There has not been any formal application of qualitative research and analysis to the field of international finance. While several researchers, including Wade (2005), Roland (2002), Kyrkilis and Pantelidi (2006) and others look at factors like political risk, and social and legal issues, there are no formal "traditions of inquiry" as used in the discipline of qualitative research. Kyrkilis and Pantelidi (2006) begin to identify determinants of FDI inflows from a qualitative point of view that is revisited in this work in Chapter V.

This type of structured framework, which is described in Chapter III of this discourse, is a singular and rigorous approach to research and analysis used in many fields of the social sciences. There are more than twenty citations and references throughout this discourse and especially in Chapter III about the origin, use, and methodology of qualitative analysis. By using a formal approach in qualitative analysis, this study is breaking new ground in international finance and capital market research.

Chapter III
Methodology

Overview

The primary approach to analysis in this discourse is qualitative. This study incorporates several distinct methods of analysis on a complex relational problem, namely, visual data and collection, expert testimony and focused interviews, case study development, and traditional statistical analyses.

The visual section employs numerous charts of macrofinancial and macroeconomic data as a basis for discovering variables. Identification, convergence, and/or divergence of the dependent variables are uncovered as the research proceeds.

Interviews with experts are used in two sections of this work – one to validate the concept of country risk, its measure, and its relationship to other variables in the study, and the second to obtain a broad-brush case study picture of thee focus countries so that results and applications can be applied to the rest of the group.

The case study method, based on those interviews with experts, analyzes a situation from several sources to form a complete picture of the situation. The objective of this method is to be able to use the results from one situation to solve a problem in another situation with a similar nature.

Traditional statistical analyses include regression, correlation, and cointegration analyses, which are used to compare data and validate certain models uncovered by the qualitative analyses. These methods have been used nearly exclusively in the research and analysis of international financial topics.

The rest of this chapter is explained through the flow chart diagram (Figure 3.1). This display of the entire plan and process of the discourse serves as a location indicator of where in the work we are. In this chapter, the description of methodology, the focus of the discussion comes from the boxes on the diagram. Concepts from the boxes are discussed relative to the methodology.

Research Design and Development of the Methodology

This methodology begins with deriving a hypothesis that matches the issue of transparency and liquidity in emerging countries' financial markets with the theoretical literature described in the literature review. From the hypothesis, preliminary variables likely to contribute to the model are derived. These variables include country risk factors, exchange rates, macroeconomic and financial indicators, political and commercial ratings, foreign investment levels, banking regulations, and legal system assessments.

Selecting the Countries

Selecting the countries for this study has certain implications. One is that the more advanced economies are ready to integrate into the EU. Another is that the focus countries are at different stages of economic, financial, and political readiness, and while some fit well as measured by certain standards, other indicators do not show such fit. So conclusions drawn from this study help to confirm or deny previous research from a wide range of studies.

Countries that have gained entry to the EU in this study are Hungary, Czech Republic, Slovakia, Slovenia, Poland, and Lithuania. Also included in this project is Croatia, which is on the waiting list for EU membership. Reasons for these selections include: geographical diversification, varying size of the economies, and how far advanced the economies are in complying with EU standards on issues like national budgets and fiscal ratios, monetary policy, banking and finance sectors, transportation and industry infrastructure, privatization, and strength of legal institutions.

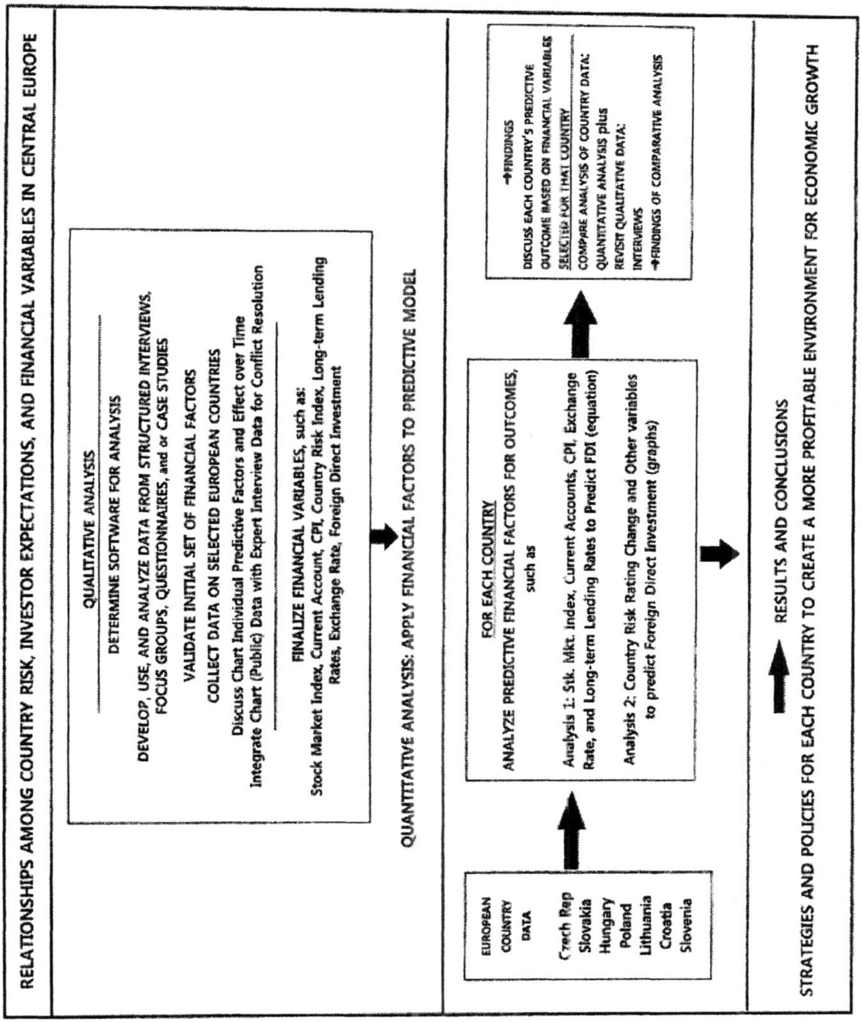

Figure 3.1 – Relationships Among Country Risk, Investor Expections, and Financial Variables in Central Europe

The total number of countries that had been considered for selection in this study included: the Baltics – Lithuania, Latvia, and Estonia; Balkan countries of Slovenia, Croatia, Macedonia, Albania, and Bulgaria; Romania; Turkey; Czech and Slovak Republics; Poland; Hungary; Ukraine; Russia; Belarus.

This array of countries includes some who have met nearly all EU standards, some who are in the middle with further reforms still to be accomplished, and others who have major hurdles to overcome and are more than a few years away from membership qualification. Those with reform levels or economies too distant from possible EU membership, or those too corrupt politically, or, in the case of Russia, not a candidate even though the economy is indeed in transition, are excluded.

Selecting the Variable Factors for Economic Growth

Certain macrofinancial sectors of economies have predictive abilities (Bernoth, Von Hagen, and Schuknecht 2003) and this study seeks to determine their and other variables' predictive ability for this group of focus countries. Some countries like Croatia are not so far out of line economically and this kind of analysis identifies the hurdle to membership in this case as political.

The variables used in this study have been selected for several reasons. One reason is that these variables and data are readily available for the focus countries. Also, other researchers have used these variables and this allows readers to compare this study with others. These variables also consider the macrofinancial sectors of the countries that lead to a composite country risk rating for the research purposes stated.

One analysis in this study considers the relationships among a country's stock market index, its current account, its consumer price index (CPI), its exchange rate, and its long-term interest rate and their predictive effects on foreign direct investment (FDI). A second analysis shows the relationship between country risk rating changes and FDI. Since attracting more FDI into an emerging economy is one key to growth, this analysis can be most useful to policymakers. All these variables are defined in detail in the section of this chapter titled "Definitions of the Data and Variables" on page 59.

Graphical (Chart) Analysis

The method for these visual analyses of macrofinancial factors is graphical representation of the factors, then a determination of their convergence or divergence over time with the expected outcomes. This method is a simple visual depiction of the variables. If CPI of Hungary moves lower and in an opposite direction than the country risk rating, we conclude that less inflation results in a better rating. If the stock market index of Slovenia coincides with a positive change in the country rating, the conclusion is that increased stock market prices (a confidence barometer in many financial circles) results in an improved country risk rating.

Convergence and divergence of trends and indicators is now a well-established method of analysis in the investment world (Appel 2005)[1]. It is also a simple and clear visual method of contrasting or confirming trends.

Details of the Visual, Technical, or Chart Analysis Method

Although the "masters" of classic, fundamental security analysis, Graham and Dodd (1958), did not believe charting played a valid part in analysis at their time, they did allow that the growing influence of charts and their use was reason enough to pay at least some attention to this method.

Fama (1991) held that the Efficient Market Hypothesis (EMH), even in its "weaker and economically more sensible version," does not allow anyone to profit from historical market data such as price and volume information. This key researcher's take on technical analysis regarding *forecasting* did not close the door on the use of charts for *analysis*, and EMH today does have a place in the accepted common wisdom.

Edwards and Magee (1966) found charts differently – as invaluable patterns that repeat themselves and offer useful insight into market analysis. They defined

---

[1] Appel's Moving Average Convergence Divergence indicator has been widely used in trading and investment research since 1973.

technical analysis as the study of the action of the market itself as opposed to the study of the goods in which the market deals. It is a science of recording, usually in graphic form, a history of trading, then deducing from that picture of history, a probable future trend.

A Principal Concept of Chart Analysis

Charles H. Dow, inventor of the Dow Theory, did not consider his theory as a device for forecasting the stock market, or even as a guide for investing, but as a barometer of general business trends (Edwards & Magee 1966). This original intent makes charts and chart analysis nearly an exact fit with this study: general trends of prices and economic numbers that would indicate whether risk is increasing or decreasing, here, at an overall country level.

Current Authorities in Technical Analysis

Pring (1985) defines a technical approach to investment as essentially a reflection of the idea that the stock market moves in trends, which are determined by the changing attitudes of investors to a variety of economic, monetary, political, and psychological forces. Identifying a change in a trend is the art of technical analysis.

Murphy (1986) mentions three premises on which the technical approach is based: one, market action discounts everything; two, prices move in trends; and three, history repeats itself. Understanding and accepting these premises is the key to making sense of technical analysis.

That all information of a market or security is reflected in its price activity is Murphy's (1986) first premise. All supply and demand information (fundamental economic, political, and financial news) is by nature included in the data that comprises a price range or a series of an economic indicator for any time period. This is because all market participants or analysts incorporate the fundamental information into their trading or reports, and they create the price range by trading or by reporting their forecasts.

The second premise is a corollary to the premise of Newton's first law of motion: that a trend in motion is more likely to continue than to reverse. In other words, the trend continues until it reverses.

The third premise is based on human psychology, which tends not to change. So there exists the axiom that the key to understanding the future lies in a study of the past.

Lastly, Murphy (1986) shows that technical analysis is flexible and adaptable to any market, time frame, and medium. It is useful for economic forecasting as well as individual securities or futures or for portfolio management.

Charts in this study are primarily time series depictions of the variables in the study. These allow a presentation of CPI or a country's stock market to be seen visually on a page over a period of ten to fifteen years. Changes in direction (contraction or expansion) of the economic activity of an economy are visible and can be compared or contrasted with other variables to determine convergence or divergence and then to identify the variable that leads, lags, or coincides with the test variable. That will form a conclusion that a predictive variable has been discovered. The use of charts in this discourse is for analysis and not for forecasting. The chart pictures are an auxiliary means of making clear points in this discussion.

Statistical Analysis

Vector Autoregression (VAR) and Cointegration analyses of the securities and sovereign countries' variables provide the comparison of data and testing of the model. Early in the analysis, regression helps determine strength and validity of the variables. If variances in an error term are not constant or appear randomly, given the explanatory variables, the condition is defined as heteroskedasticity. The ARCH class of models (Autoregressive Conditionally Heteroskedastic Models) was introduced by Engle (1982) to handle conditional heteroskedasticity and has been used extensively in financial econometrics to account for the unpredictability of returns. The GARCH Model (Generalized Autoregressive Conditionally Heteroskedastic Model) is an extension of Engle's (1982) original model and handles high-frequency data efficiently. ARCH and GARCH models would be a natural research extension of this discourse if portfolio risk was to be investigated. These models could also be used to explain collinearity or multicollinearity between or among variables.

The models that were applied to this paper's data frequencies and observations were VAR and cointegration. Engle and Granger (1987) devised a vector of time series data connecting moving averages, autoregressions, and error correcting systems. This is employed and the application explained in more detail in Chapter IV as it is used. Lutkepohl (2005) adopts Engle and Granger (1987) to include impulse response analysis, which is able to measure FDI inflows and outflows in transition economies.

FDI is depicted as a function of a country's current account balance (CA), its exchange rate (XR), its inflation rate as measured by consumer prices (CPI), its stock market index (SM), and its long-term lending rate (LR). Then the relationship between country risk and FDI is examined separately and visually. This is done for each country (j) in the study and for each time period (t) to create a series of data for analysis. The equation for the statistical assessment of factors affecting FDI becomes

$$FDI(t,j) = f(\, CA(t,j), CPI(t,j), SM(t,j), XR(t,j), LR(t,j)\,)$$

and the relationship between country risk, FDI, and each other variable is shown graphically

$$FDI(t,j) = f(\, CR(t,j)\,)$$

where CR represents country risk.

Houthakker (1965) shows the value of regressions comparisons within countries and comparisons among countries and then examining the differences between these two effects. Differences within countries are mostly short term while differences among countries are mostly long run effects. The differences are highly significant both statistically and economically.

Qualitative Analysis

Recently, qualitative analysis has gained value in confirming or denying conclusions drawn by other methods of research. In international finance, it is only just breaking into the discipline. Research in international finance has been largely involved with numbers that regress, auto regress, correlate, or compare using processes like ANOVA (a test of variance), MANOVA (a technique allowing comparisons of groups within groups), and the ARCH class of models for statistical analysis. (But note that Fama's (1964) work can be considered Grounded Theory – he gathered his data from the field and created his theory from it.)

And three primary researchers in transition economies and emerging markets who focus on Central and Eastern Europe, Brada, Kutan, and Yigit (2004), Bekaert and Harvey (2003), and Harvey (2004), while using mathematical models as part of their analysis, rely heavily on charts to display their variables and show many of their relationships. So this model of analysis (charts and deductions from them) has been moving into this area of research for clarity and comparison, notably in these three papers where the data being examined is political risk and stability and the separation of them from economic or financial factors.

Defining Qualitative Research and Analysis

Qualitative research focuses on participant views and writing about the process using expressive and persuasive language (Creswell 1998). Researchers generally spend a great deal of time in the field gathering data and work toward reaching audiences receptive to qualitative approaches. Qualitative research is complex due to the holistic process of data collection and analysis, such as interviewing, then analyzing both word and picture data, then coding observations and forming categories or themes before creating a model or theory for testing. Qualitative research, as opposed to quantitative, does not employ hypotheses as a tool of analysis.

Traditions of Inquiry

The entire approach is framed in a "tradition of inquiry." The prominent five traditions of inquiry are Ethnology, Biography, Phenomenology, Grounded Theory, and Case Study. Qualitative research has the capacity to incorporate quantitative analysis or compare results with it, as in developing a Grounded Theory or exploring a representative case. This discourse uses the Field or Case Study method ("field" and "case" are interchangeable terms throughout this discourse) and Grounded Theory to determine if results can be verified with the results of the statistical analysis also employed.

Grounded Theory (GT) (Glaser and Strauss 1967; Strauss and Corbin 1998) has four basic stages – comparing incidents applicable to each category, integrating categories, delimiting the theory, and writing theory. GT is a method of organizing, arranging, and grouping, like the investment community has done for decades with price charts. Then a constant comparison method of analysis is used based on patterns and repetitive levels of trading, or in the case of economic data, trends of strengthening or declining indicators, which then provide guides for policymakers.

GT generates theory from the data itself. It uses comparative analysis to determine differences, which build into a theory. Then the theory can be tested with other comparison groups. It is a rolling cointegration concept, or a running theoretical discussion (Glasser and Strauss 1967). Not a lot of cases are necessary to use GT with validity. One case could be used to generalize conceptual categories, and a few more cases used to confirm the indication. "The researcher's job is not to provide a perfect description of an area, but to develop a theory that accounts for much of the relevant behavior" (Glasser and Strauss 1967).

Charts are a form of coding, i.e., creating graphics from raw data. The charts contain both manifest and latent content (Berg 1998). The outward or manifest picture forms the basis for this study's section of the latent information provided by technical analysis.

A field study, which here is an in-depth analysis of three countries based on interviews with experts and including other sources, points toward the likelihood of extrapolating the results to other countries in this study

Elaboration on the Importance of Field or Case Study Analysis

Case study, in qualitative research, is the study of a "bounded system" with the focus being a case or an issue illustrated by the case (Stake 1995). A qualitative case study provides an in-depth investigation of this "system" based on a diverse array of data collection materials, and the researcher positions this system or case within a larger context or setting.

Field studies can incorporate information on legal, political, and social aspects of market integration and development that standard statistics cannot. For a detailed look at this concept in practice see the "Identification of Risk Categories" (especially Wade 2005) and the "Other Political, Financial, and Economic Aspects of FDI" sections of Chapter II.

Recent suggestions of the value of case study work has come from the Wall Street Journal, reporting that Austria is being studied as a case model for Germany in Germany's attempt to restructure many areas of its economy.[1] Over the past decade, Chile has been held up as an economic transition model for many other South American countries and emerging economies. The use of flat tax rates in emerging economies has been so successful that this tax system is now being used as a model for application in developed countries to cure budget deficit woes.[2]

The World Association for Case Method Research and Application (WACRA), an interdisciplinary organization comprised of professors, researchers, policy-makers, professionals and business executives promotes studying and applying the Case Method in research, teaching, planning and training. WACRA identifies quality attributes in case method research and application, and has developed standards for scholarship and research excellence in case study work.

---

[1] *The Wall Street Journal*, October 13, 2005, p. A 12.

[2] *The Wall Street Journal*, October 7, 2005, p. A 16 and August 15, 2005, p. A 12.

Characteristics of a Good Qualitative Research Study

- Employ rigorous data collection procedures, e.g., time in the field
- Frame the study within the assumptions and manners of the qualitative approach to research
- Use a tradition of inquiry
- Start with a single focus or problem, not causal relationships of variables or comparisons of groups (these may evolve later)
- Use detailed methods and rigorous approach to data collection and analysis and report writing
- Write persuasively
- Analyze using levels of abstraction, moving from the particular to the general, in order to develop themes (Creswell 1998).

Qualitative research also accounts for causality. Qualitative studies, meta analysis, and program theory work better than large-scale studies because each approach takes into account more of the total social complexity of a situation by framing the study in a more precise, although different, way. Meta analysis uses individual studies, each of which occur in separate circumstances of rich variation (our country case studies), which makes generalization possible (Cook 1993). Maxwell (1996) concludes that qualitative studies create a picture of social interaction, of people and events with other causal factors in context. This limits causal possibilities and alternatives.

His research relates to the seminal work on causation done by Mackie (1974), which states there are not only gaps in our knowledge of events, but there are gaps that we do not even know we do not know. There are always things for which we cannot account. The application in this work is the case studies of the countries that are used as models for the rest of the region and lets us see more completely which variable is cause and which is effect.

Reasons for Qualitative Analysis

One reason for doing a qualitative study in international finance is to reach new audiences who would be receptive to this approach. Researchers, writers, or those outside the discipline may find this manner of research useful and understandable to their framework. Someone familiar with this methodology from another discipline may be able to transfer that method to a new discipline and benefit from it.

It is appropriate to use the techniques employed here. GT and other methods of qualitative analysis have been used extensively in the social sciences, of which economics is one. And finance is a division of economics. International finance and especially emerging market finance is evolving rapidly. Research in this area has spurred advancement and adoption of old models, and the development of new models to deal with the new relationships arising from this field (Bekaert and Harvey 2003).

The effort to confirm or deny the research done in this study's quantitative section will add substantial dimension to the study. Doing in-depth studies of Slovenia and The Czech and Slovak Republics by qualitative methods adds to the literature and validates three countries' conclusions. Predictive value of these determinations for other countries is discussed.

Qualitative Analysis Finds Underlying Problems

As in the example of adoption of law to harmonize requirements for EU membership (Maiden and Williams 2001), too much too fast has become a blockage to its own progress. Here, quality of legislation has suffered and amendments in the bankruptcy area alone total 110 in eight years. This continued revision due to speed creates uncertainty in the legal environment among clients, lawyers, and judges. This, in turn, hinders project and structured finance, and security interests (Maiden and Williams 2001).

Developing deeper and more liquid capital markets simply takes time, and after the lucrative initial public offerings (IPOs) are done, it is not often as interesting or profitable for a banking firm to sit down, start, and maintain a trading desk, and make a market in the security for the long term. That is, a domestic or regional market reaching the investor-friendly level of Bonn, London, Frankfurt, or Paris, may take years or decades.

So there is no reason *not* to view the Czech Republic, e.g., with its ten million people, as a profitable market that will grow as the economy grows, and as integration with the rest of the EU, both old and new members, harmonizes (Maiden and Williams 2001). A conclusion could be that a profitable approach in these new emerging markets is a long-term approach.

Further Reasons for Qualitative Analysis

These markets contain interest from several disciplines that combine investment and capital markets with political science, law, international economics and aspects of international business, such as FDI, market integration, and cost of capital (Bekaert and Harvey 2002).

Standard databases used in much of emerging markets research are fairly short in history and understandably limited to financial and economic data. This is due to a lack of reliable information available about the formerly centrally planned economies of the Central European region, which has only been collected in understandable and computable categories since the fall of Communism. Examples are: International Finance Corporation's (IFC) database is from 1976 and Morgan Stanley's Capital Index (MSCI) is from 1986. The year 1990 marks the beginning of much of the emerging markets' tracking of comparable research statistics. That year began the large wave of capital market liberalizations and research advances of recent years (Bekaert and Harvey 2002).

Using qualitative research can add depth to a study and its analysis that can pre-date the market liberalizations of fifteen years ago. By building a theory "from the ground up" where data is available, or by studying one case with great intensity and attempting new applications, gaps can be filled, perspective added, and additional understanding gained.

Verification of the Data and the Analysis in Qualitative Research

As with any study, the question will be asked, "How can the reader know the study is accurate, believable, and true?" Qualitative research, with its formal traditions of inquiry, maintains standards such as guidelines for publication and reciprocity of trust between researcher and the event or people being researched. Verification is a process occurring throughout the data collection, analysis, and report writing. There is a dependability and confirmability established through an auditing of the research process.

Eisner (1991) uses credibility guides such as structural corroboration, consensual validation, and referential adequacy. Structural corroboration is the use of multiple types of data to support or contradict the results. Consensual validation seeks the opinions of competent others to assess that the interpretation and evaluation of the situation are correct. In this discourse's expert interviews, several evaluation questions regarding both the process and the content are asked of the experts after the initial interviews are completed. Referential adequacy uses criticism to illuminate the subject and increase understanding with depth and perception.

Creswell's (1998) approach to verification considers the following:

- Verification is made due to the extreme amount of time spent in the field, due to detailed, thick description of the situation, and due to the closeness of the researcher to the participants in the study.
- Using the term "verification" in place of "validation" is particular to qualitative research and establishes qualitative research as a legitimate approach to research in its own right.
- Using the terms "trustworthiness" and "authenticity" creates general concepts in establishing the credibility of a study.
- Procedural implications verify a study and the researcher can assess these implications.

In GT, after obtaining the data and writing the theory, the researcher references the literature to give supplemental validation for the accuracy of the findings or to show differences from the published literature. Strauss and Corbin (1990) identify criteria to judge a GT study. Questions such as the following guide the general research process:

- On what grounds was the sample selected?
- What major categories emerged?
- What events or actions helped to identify some of the categories?
- What guided data collection and was it representative of the categories?
- What were some of the hypotheses pertaining to the relationships among categories and how were they tested?
- Were there incidences when the hypotheses did not hold up against what was actually found?

In field studies, extensive verification is required and Stake (1995) devotes great emphasis to the triangulation, or convergence, of information. When assertions are made, or when key interpretations are offered, or when "dubious and contested description" is involved, extra effort must be made toward confirmation. To do this, he recommends using multiple data sources to identify themes and to check the final account with select informants or participants, known as member checking.

Stake (1995) provides a list of twenty criteria for assessing a good case study report:

- Is the report easy to read?
- Does it fit together, each sentence contributing to the whole?
- Does the report have a conceptual structure?
- Are its issues developed in a serious and scholarly way?
- Is the case adequately defined?
- Is there a sense of story to the presentation?
- Is the reader provided some vicarious experience?
- Have quotations been used effectively?

- Are headings, figures, artifacts used effectively?
- Was it edited well, then again with a last-minute polish?
- Has the writer made sound assertions, neither over- nor under-interpreting?
- Has adequate attention been paid to contexts?
- Were sufficient raw data presented?
- Were data sources well chosen and sufficient in number?
- Do observations and interpretations appear to have been triangulated?
- Is the role and point of view of the researcher nicely apparent?
- Is the nature of the intended audience apparent?
- Is empathy shown for all sides?
- Are personal intentions examined?
- Does it appear that individuals were put at risk?

Data and Data Collection Methodology

Some former Soviet satellite countries have been better at compiling and displaying national accounts information, financial history data, and macroeconomic data than others. Letting outside agencies in to measure and determine creditworthiness is new to these former Communist countries and not all have progressed at the same rate of openness and improvement in exterior relations. So data transparency has been sporadic in some countries, more complete in others, and ratings changes themselves more reliable and meaningful over the last five years versus the early 1990s, when the transition to market economies began.

Data for the Graphs, Credit Ratings, and FDI

The graphs in this study are derived largely from data obtained from the Economist Intelligence Unit's WorldData, the IMF, and central banks. Due to the above reasons regarding completeness and quality of data, some graphs may be slightly different as to start and end periods in the various categories of analysis. Due to reporting differences and time for compilation, lags of up to three quarters are sometimes seen. Some countries had not started compiling data on certain accounts until after beginning the transition to market economies. Other sources for this data are from among the countries' government websites.

Credit ratings changes and histories are taken primarily from FitchRatings Ltd. Emerging Portfolio.com Fund Research fills in some gaps for certain countries. Standard & Poor's, Moody's, Fitch, and International Country Risk Guide (ICRG) were the four major country risk rating agencies investigated, and it is found that when one agency changes a country's risk rating, within a quarter or two, the other agencies frequently update their ratings of that same country. The entire investment world is familiar with each of these agencies. Allowed here is that a change in any of the ratings of either the currency, the Eurobond, or the sovereign debt would be equal-value prompts for a look at the variables.

A credit rating change or moving a country to a watch list for a possible change is considered having the same effect for the time window viewed. The difference is noted on the charts. Due to data frequency, here quarterly intervals, the change in money market rates, current account, consumer price index (CPI), lending rates, stock market index, or exchange rates is noted from the time of the announcement to the next quarter. Although a rating may not change, even when a country is placed on a watchlist, this is also observed for purposes here since it is an alert that a rating change may soon occur.

Data collection from these secondary sources (readily available and commonly used in the academic literature) such as brokerages and banks, provides actual price and yield histories. The World Bank, IMF, and central banks of Hungary, Czech Republic and Poland provide the macroeconomic factors in the collection stage. Long-term lending rates are primarily taken from IMF Balance of payments.

FDI data comes primarily from IMF databases, but also from OECD International Direct Investment Statistics Yearbook and various central banks with supplements from the World Bank Development Report & other World Bank and IMF publications.

Qualitative Aspects of Data and Data Collection

Qualitative research is a distinctive dimension in the methodology used in both data collection and analysis here. Several aspects of it are used:

- Coding, as in content analysis, which in this study consists of charts for the economic data depictions
- Kvale's (1996; 1988) seven stages for the complete interview process adapted to the chart section of this study – thematizing, designing, transcribing, and analyzing
- Interviews with experts in the field
- Description, identifying themes, and making assertions based on the data

Data itself may come from varied sources, such as documents, interviews, archival records, observations, audio-visual material, and reports.

Interviews with Experts

Interviews with experts for this study contribute in two ways to the data: as primary sources of experience in answering the research questions, and, in some cases, as focal gathering points for data from other primary sources in the case study countries. In other words, some interviewees have positions that allow them to act as gatekeepers to the focus countries and bring several opinions together, reporting them separately from their own interviews.

Depending on the availability and physical location of interviewees, interviews are done by telephone, by email, in person, by postal mail, or by audio-visual technology. Recording of the data is accomplished primarily by note taking.

Regarding the interview structure, the questioning begins with an overarching question on the discourse topic, followed by subquestions. Central guiding questions regarding the research hypotheses and the environment of the country's business and financial risk are used to elicit the rich data that forms the narrative of each case study. These are open-ended, evolving, and non-directional, allowing the development of themes to characterize the cases. Each interview shows the ties that country risk and investor expectations have with political, economic, legal, and social issues besides the interviewees' own personal experiences. Sample questions and the questionnaire used as starting points in each interview are in Appendix A.

Experts are selected from among the following: Janko Kralj of Maribor, Slovenia, a retired business executive and professor emeritus of international business and management; Hans Klein of Massachusetts and formerly of Czechoslovakia, an officer of WACRA who has designed and organized many conferences and seminars in and about Central Europe and around the world; Dusan Valachovic, former Director of Research and Science Education for the Ministry of Czechoslovakia; Dmitri Vasiliev, Chairman of the Board of the Investors Protection Association in Moscow; Martin Butora, former Ambassador of the Slovak Republic to the United States; Dana Linnett of the U.S. State Department and political/military analyst; Dr. Helena Hessel, Director of Sovereign Ratings at Standard and Poor's Corporation; Dr. Oleg Kuznetsov, Head of Public Law at Chita State Technical University in Chita, Russia. Other experts are used depending on availability and applicability to the research.

Software in Qualitative Analysis

For qualitative studies using large databases (500 pages or more) of field notes, more than twenty or thirty interviews, or multiple types of information, certain computer programs can offer an advantage (Creswell 1998). This software assists researchers by providing a system to store and organize files, search for themes, cross-reference themes (as ANOVA and MANOVA do in statistics), diagram, and create visual templates for overviews.

This discourse does not use software because there are only a few interviews and the data is manageable by hand with simple tables. The value of software systems would be evident in creating a plan for future research that include case studies of more countries in the region and the desire to manipulate the data and compare them.

Definitions of the Data and Variables

In the charting and statistical sections of analysis, each country is looked upon as an individual case and analyzed on its own merits. There is no cross-country comparison work in the statistical study, which would require creating indexes starting at base periods or levels for similarity purposes.

The current account balance is the trade balance plus net services plus net income plus net current transfers. The number is quarterly and is shown on the chart as a change in its scale from the previous quarter. Gourinches and Rey (2005) present a US-based discussion of the relationship between exchange rates and current accounts.

Exchange rates are in local currency measured against the U.S. Dollar and are daily quotes at the end of the quarterly periods. Stock market indexes are the actual value indexes like the Dow Jones Industrial Average or the Standard and Poor's 500 Stock Index, and, in the focus countries, are quotes at the end of the quarterly periods. Markets are good at predictions, partly because markets are excellent collectors of information, especially compared with more centralized means of gathering intelligence. So the variable for investor expectations in this study is the stock market variable. Rocha and Garcia (2005), in discussing the term structure of sovereign rate spreads, note that although real exchange rates do not directly represent a country's solvency, they do have the advantage of being a daily market variable that quickly reflects changes of opinion about a country's financial status through the trading of its currency.

Long-term interest rates are the bank lending rate to companies or corporations for capital projects, usually lasting more than five years.

CPI is a usual end-user economic price indicator and measure of inflation. Von Hagen and Hofmann (2004) related this measure of inflation to several macroeconomic variables and aggregate demand in the Euro area. It is a quarterly number and for each country is marked on a scale having a base index starting after a semblance of economic stability was attained after the fall of Communism.

Research Questions and Hypotheses

Overview

The transition economies in this analysis have distinct macrofinancial and macroeconomic variables that allow certain relationships to be verified. For each focus country, indicators are available that measure inflation, trade, investor expectations, sovereign yields, and country risk. The data measuring FDI is also readily available.

In the first method of analysis, the quantitative analysis, the comparisons and variables for each country's CA, SM, LR, CPI, XR and FDI inflows are made using VAR and Johansen Cointegration Analyses. The results of each of these analyses show support or lack of it to the hypotheses.

The second analysis is the chart comparison of each country's variables to its FDI, plus the country risk rating change variable. This separate step of introducing country risk rating changes is key to the completeness of this work. Country risk comprises categories such as political, economic, social, and legal conditions. These categories further consider business and financial risk, interest rate and currency risk, inflation, and trade, all building to a total country risk rating. The combination of variables and comparisons shows all aspects of relationships among country risk, investor expectations, and long-term interest rates as described in the intentions of this discourse. The charts display three variables at a time: FDI, country risk rating change, and each of the other variables, one country at a time, for clarity and precision, plotted against each other. Each picture, or chart, allows the relationship to be seen and measured for positive or negative correlation. Conclusions are drawn about which variables are predictors of FDI.

Results of the chart work are then integrated with the results of the third analysis, expert interviews, for conflict resolution. Next, the statistical analysis is incorporated into the model and gives support or shows differences from the previous analyses.

Details of Hypotheses Construction

The stock market is a leading indicator of investor sentiment due to its liquid nature and the transferability of funds. Therefore, the stock market index of a country is a proxy for investor confidence and expectations, and would be expected to show correlation with country risk. Although in small economies it could be argued that there are liquidity and volatility issues and hurdles, this study is differentiating portfolio or financial flows from investment in physical assets like mergers and acquisitions or Greenfield projects, which FDI represents. So while some stock markets are more liquid than others, stocks and financial assets are the most liquid investments available in the focus countries.

The measure of inflation used for each country, CPI is plotted against the FDI. A reason to measure this relationship is because inflation has been a hurdle to stability in many transition countries' economies.

The long-term lending rate reflects the demand and supply of funds over a time frame that attempts to form a trend apart from the short-term market volatility (see the discussion in Chapter IV on cointegration). This interest rate is a measure of corporate credit risk as the marketplace views it, and is in contrast to a country risk rating, which, as noted above, is an overall estimate of business conditions along with the general economic, political, legal, and social environment. The long-term lending rate is also plotted against the country risk rating for each country to determine the intensity of correlation between the two variables, and to determine how much of the rate is responsible for overall country risk.

The current account indicates some degree of openness and some degree of political freedom if exports are fairly diverse in nature. After determining how the financial and economic variables relate to country risk, country risk itself is examined as a predictor of FDI.

Hungary (h)

Data and measures for Hungary (h) are fluid and continuous for the period examined. Its stock market index, The Budapest Stock Exchange Index (SM), its current account (CA), or trade balance, its CPI, its exchange rate (XR), and its long-term lending rate (LR) are each measured against its FDI. The five hypotheses for Hungary are as follows:

- H1h Do changes in the Budapest Stock Index affect FDI in Hungary?
- H2h Do changes in the Hungarian current account balance affect FDI in Hungary?
- H3h Do changes in the Hungarian CPI affect FDI in Hungary?
- H4h Do changes in the Hungarian long-term lending rate affect FDI in Hungary?
- H5h Do changes in the Hungarian exchange rate affect FDI in Hungary?

Poland (p)

Data for the variables used in the analysis of Poland (p) is readily available. The Warsaw Stock Exchange Index publishes its data reliably, as do other organizations for current account data, CPI, long-term lending rates, exchange rates, and FDI numbers.

The hypotheses for Poland are:

- H1p Do changes in the Warsaw Stock Exchange Index affect FDI in Poland?
- H2p Do changes in the Polish current account balance affect FDI in Poland?
- H3p Do changes in the Polish CPI affect FDI in Poland?
- H4p Do changes in the Polish long-term lending rate affect FDI in Poland?
- H5p Do changes in the Polish exchange rate affect FDI in Poland?

Czech Republic (cz)

Data for the Czech Republic is accessible for the Prague Stock Exchange Index, current account, CPI, long-term lending rates, country risk, exchange rates, and FDI. The hypotheses for Czech Republic are:

- H1cz Do changes in the Prague Stock Exchange affect FDI in Czech Republic?
- H2cz Do changes in the Czech current account balance affect FDI in Czech Republic?
- H3cz Do changes in the Czech CPI affect FDI in Czech Republic?
- H4cz Do changes in the Czech long-term lending rates affect FDI in Czech Republic?
- H5cz Do changes in the Czech exchange rate affect FDI in Czech Republic?

Lithuania (li)

This Baltic country is the study's representation of the most northeast geographic location. The same organizations and central banks provide reliable data to create the hypotheses for Lithuania (li):

- H1li Do changes in the Lithuanian Stock Market Index affect FDI in Lithuania?
- H2li Do changes in the Lithuanian current account balance affect FDI in Lithuania?
- H3li Do changes in the Lithuanian CPI affect FDI in Lithuania?
- H4li Do changes in the Lithuanian long-term lending rate affect FDI in Lithuania?
- H5li Do changes in the Lithuanian exchange rate affect FDI in Lithuania?

Croatia (c)

Croatia (c) is the only country in this study that has not won entry to the EU. It is in the next wave of applicants and has all data available for the analyses here. The hypotheses for Croatia are:

- H1c Do changes in the Croatian Stock Market Index affect FDI in Croatia?
- H2c Do changes in the Croatian current account balance affect FDI in Croatia?
- H3c Do changes in the Croatian CPI affect FDI in Croatia?

- H4c Do changes in the Croatian long-term lending rate affect FDI in Croatia?
- H5c Do changes in the Croatian exchange rate affect FDI in Croatia?

Slovenia (s)

Slovenia borders Austria and Italy to its north and has been grouped with Western Europe in many ways for most of the last century. Historically, Slovenia was part of the more developed Austrian half of the Austro-Hungarian Empire, and has retained many similarities to Western culture and attitudes. This is in contrast to Slovakia, Croatia, and Bosnia, which were part of the less developed Hungarian half of the Empire. Data accessibility for Slovenia is not a problem. The hypotheses for Slovenia (s) are:

- H1s Do changes in the Ljubljana Stock Exchange Index affect FDI in Slovenia?
- H2s Do changes in the Slovenian current account balance affect FDI in Slovenia?
- H3s Do changes in the Slovenian CPI affect FDI in Slovenia?
- H4s Do changes in the Slovenian long-term lending rate affect FDI in Slovenia?
- H5s Do changes in the Slovenian exchange rate affect FDI in Slovenia?

Slovakia (sl)

Data for Slovakia is obtained from the Bratislava Stock Exchange and other sources for current account information, CPI, long-term lending rates, exchange rates, and FDI statistics. Slovakia's economy is less developed than that of the Czech Republic or Poland, and in the conclusions, it is highlighted which other focus countries might provide a guide for Slovakia to follow. The hypotheses for Slovakia are:

- H1sl Do changes in the Bratislava Stock Exchange Index affect FDI in Slovakia?

- H2sl Do changes in the Slovak current account balance affect FDI in Slovakia?
- H3sl Do changes in the Slovak CPI affect FDI in Slovakia?
- H4sl Do changes in the Slovak long-term lending rate affect FDI in Slovakia?
- H5sl Do changes in the Slovak exchange rate affect FDI in Slovakia?

Summary of Methodology

The reasons and research methods regarding this discourse have been presented in detail in this chapter. The formal hypotheses are also listed by focus country, expressing the relationships that are tested. In the Table 3.1 (on the following page), all aspects of the methodology of the research design, data collection, and processes of analysis are summarized. Because of the mixed mode (qualitative and quantitative) method of research design and the number of countries and data collection sources under investigation, this summary section to methodology is presented.

Several traditions of inquiry in the qualitative field are explained, including the case or field study method, Grounded Theory, and the value of interviews with experts. There is also a chart, or technical analysis section used to describe the country risk rating change with all other variables visually, and a statistical methodology section used for comparisons and validations.

Qualitative research in this discourse is comprised primarily of field studies of the focus countries. Interviews with experts on the topics of country and business risk and international finance are used to build a database for the studies. The list of potential experts interviewed begins on page 58 and is summarized in Table 3.1.

Table 3.1 – Summary of Methodologies

<table>
<tr><th>Qualitative Analysis</th><th>Quantitative Analysis</th></tr>
<tr><td>Uncovering and defining variables, theories, model</td><td>Proving theory, defining hypotheses</td></tr>
<tr><td>Develop, organize, analyze data</td><td>Database determination for variables in emerging markets country risk, inflation, Security prices, FDI,...</td></tr>
<tr><td>Interview design and protocol</td><td></td></tr>
<tr><td>Focus meetings</td><td rowspan="7">Collection of data for focus countries' quantitative analyses
Slovenia
Czech Republic
Slovakia
Lithuania
Hungary
Poland
Croatia</td></tr>
<tr><td>Structured and open-ended questionnaires</td></tr>
<tr><td>Reports from credit rating agencies, commercial companies</td></tr>
<tr><td>Reports from banks, organizations, governments</td></tr>
<tr><td>Expert interviews (See Chapter III, p. 57)</td></tr>
<tr><td>2-4 interviews for each focus country</td></tr>
<tr><td>Telephone, email, in person</td></tr>
<tr><td>3-5 countries selected from the following:
Slovenia
Czech Republic
Slovakia
Lithuania
Hungary
Poland</td><td>Finalization of variables from: quantitative analysis; statistical analysis; regression, multiple regressions ARCH; modeling; cointegration; Vector auto-regression; country comparative analyses as appropriate</td></tr>
<tr><td>Sources representing multiple perspectives: foreign, USA, banks, embassies, agencies, universities, organizations, economists, politicians, businessmen, academics</td><td></td></tr>
</table>

Qualitative Analysis	Quantitative Analysis
Tentative list of experts for interviews: Dr. Janko Kralj, ret prof, Slovenia Dr. Hans Klein, Pres, WACRA Dusan Valachovic, fmr Dir Research, Ministry of Czechoslovakia Dimitri Vasiliev, Chr., Investor, Protection Assoc., Moscow Martin Butora, fmr Ambassador of Slovakia Dana Linnett, US State Department Dr. Helena Hessel, Dir Sovereign Rating, S&P Dr. Oleg Kuznetov, Chita St. Tech Univ Dr. Dusan Zbasnik, Prof Economics, Univ of Maribor & Gov, Bank of Slovenia Pavel Preml, ret Party Sec, Slovenian Christian Socialists & ret engineer Miecyzlaw Kurdziel, businessman, Poland Vladimir Lavrac, Ljubljana Dr. Tina Zumer, Bank of Slovenia	
Documentation of observations, literature search	
Software use, as appropriate	
Finalize financial factors, variables	

The purpose of using mixed methodologies in this work is to strengthen the case for hypotheses testing and reaching conclusions on those hypotheses. Sage Publications, a leading resource in qualitative research analysis and methodology, is the publisher of a new journal called Journal of Mixed Methods Research. This is a new, quarterly international journal that aims to publish empirical, methodological, and theoretical articles about mixed methods research (www.sagepub.com/journal). The timing of this discourse, then, coincides with other researchers' interests in combining qualitative and quantitative research methods.

Qualitative research is more intricate than straight statistical work because the research must still be validated and verified. The time spent in the field, the use of multiple sources and types of data, and a continuous process of evaluation throughout the research campaign all contribute to a triangulation or convergence of information on the topic. The quantitative research can be used as confirming data for the qualitative conclusions.

Specific to this discourse is the careful selection of experts, documents, and reports that identify relationships among country risk, investor expectations, and securities prices to allow the hypotheses to be tested. Two methodologists, one qualitative and one quantitative, have been consulted to assure that all standards of research are met or exceeded.

Interestingly, the author of this project is a qualified expert in the field of technical analysis. He spent a successful career on Wall Street functioning as an analyst and broker, using charts and technical analysis as a basis for doing business in the commodity industry around the world. This work is an example of how expert testimony can be combined with case study work or other qualitative methodology in validating a research approach.

After discussion with several methodology experts, Table 3.1 is presented to address their input for this mixed methods approach. In an effort to show that the methodology used is beyond satisficing, this project use three cases for the analysis, exceeding the recommended one case.

This chapter explains the entire project at each level of analysis, and uses experts like Creswell, Yin, and Strauss to summarize and show application of the combined methodologies to a discipline that does not normally use this approach. This allows readers and researchers outside the field of international finance or quantitative analysis to be able to investigate this discipline in a more familiar framework.

Chapter IV

Analysis and Presentation of Findings

Overview

The presentation of the research and data now divides into three parts: First, the quantitative section displays the relationships of the variables current account (CA), consumer price index (CPI), the exchange rate (XR), the long-term lending rate (LR), and the stock market (SM) to the dependent variable of foreign direct investment (FDI). The Johansen Cointegration Test and Vector Autoregression (VAR) analyses are used to show support or disprove the hypotheses.

Second, the chart section incorporates the variable of country risk into the analysis and visually shows the relationship of it to the other variables. Because country risk is a primary focus of this study, it has been given this separate and distinct step in the examination and display of variables. This chart section connects naturally from the statistical analysis in three ways. First, the data for both comes from the same numbers. Next, the introduction of the country risk variable with the rest of the variables is made. Finally, there is a common link in both VAR and the graphs called long-range persistence, or infinite memory patterns. This link is explained completely a few pages following.

Third, the qualitative section brings together the current data from field studies on relationships between country risk and FDI gathered from expert interviews, specialized industry reports, and primary written and archival sources. This qualitative work describes differences of country risk across focus countries and is the culmination and combination of the three analyses. It is presented in descriptive form adopted from qualitative research methodology that is commonly used in several disciplines and now originally applied in this international finance study.

Conclusions are drawn in each section about the data in that section, as well as possible implications, weaknesses, and reasons for using particular methodology and sources. Outcomes are detailed by methodology and also by country. A larger, more comprehensive determination is then made about the results of the analyses related to each other and to the current environment existing in the focus countries.

Comments on the significance of the results for the field and the usefulness to policymakers are left until Chapter V, as are suggestions for future research, evaluations of this work, and this study's value to the fields of knowledge in both the area of international finance and in the application of qualitative methodology to this area.

Statistical Results – Descriptive Statistics

Vector Autoregression (VAR) – Explanation

Vector autoregression (VAR) analysis is a model that regresses all variables in an analysis against themselves to discover what effects each variable has on all others. VAR helps find the best lag to explain the effects of the independent variables on the dependent. Sims (1980) advanced the use of VAR models for large simultaneous equation models, but those did not often account for the dynamic structure in time series using quarterly or monthly frequencies. Lutkepohl (2005) explained that *Structural* VAR models were thus developed to identify impulse or lag responses to data.

Engle (1982) was the pioneer of the model that explained how variations in past periods affect variations in current periods. He showed that large fluctuations are often followed by further large changes, and that small changes tend to be followed by further small changes. Volatility varies over time. And the variance of the random error in a certain time period systematically depends on previously realized random errors. This condition is termed autoregressive conditional heteroskedasticity, and the acronym is commonly termed ARCH.

The search in the VAR analysis is to find the best lag, or how many periods following an event, for the effect of one variable to be felt on another. Throughout the analysis here, four lags were run (except in the case of Lithuania, where the number of observations in the available data did not permit an effective VAR analysis with more than three lags) to see what effects on current periods might occur due to changes in data in periods from up to a year ago. Understanding that every lag takes away an order of freedom, the analysis did not use more than four lags. But four lags are reasonable due to the nature of the macrofinancial variables and the time it takes to observe the impact of them. Four lags are also the convention in current academic literature.

In this VAR analysis, all variables were regressed against each other. The variables, except FDI, explained themselves well (with an exceptionally high R2 – often at the .98 or .99 level). FDI showed a looser fit or connection to all the independent variables. In a way, this is logical. FDI, CA, and XR are the true "international" pieces of the analysis, so other factors, especially external factors, may have influences on these three variables.

Vector Autoregession (VAR) – Results

Throughout the tables in all statistics sections, the following terms are used:

CA – current account
XR – exchange rate
SM – stock market
Log CPI – consumer price index
LR – long-term lending rate
FDI – foreign direct investment
inc – inconclusive

Vector Autoregression Estimates

Table 4.1 – Croatia

Change in FDI affected by:	Lag	Coefficient	T Statistic	Diagnostic Tests
Change in prev. periods FDI	4	-0.452	-1.44	R2 = .688 AIC = 14.09 SC = 15.21 Log likelihood = -214.56
Change in CA	inc	inc	inc	
Change in XR	inc	inc	inc	
Change in SM	1 2	1.245 1.226	1.72 1.58	
Change in log CPI	inc	inc	inc	
Change in LR	inc	inc	inc	

The VAR analysis of Croatia did not reveal much insight into the variables' effects on FDI. The SM had a mild effect on FDI with both a one and a two period lag but is too slight for conclusions. FDI itself is more volatile, perhaps due to the fact that the effect from one quarter to the next has more impact on the smaller sized economy than on larger ones. One of the hypotheses for Croatia has some support.

Table 4.2 – Czech Republic

Change in FDI affected by:	Lag	Coefficient	T Statistic	Diagnostic Tests
Change in prev periods FDI	1	-0.521	-2.07	- R2 = .399 AIC = 16.68 SC = 17.74 Log likelihood = -308.60
Change in CA	3 4	-1.18 -1.2721	-2.03 -1.81	
Change in XR	1 2 3 4	-176.000 154.735 215.191 222.285	-1.42 1.11 1.45 1.49	
Change in SM	1	6.936	1.77	
Change in log CPI	inc	inc	inc	
Change in LR	3	1050.456	2.11	

FDI in Czech Republic is very robust, having a strong effect on itself with a one period lag. It is rather stable, with a rise in one quarter correcting by a smaller amount in the next. When the CA improves, there is a pronounced positive effect on FDI three periods following, and a less significant but also strong effect in the fourth period following CA improvement. Krkoska (2001) discusses the relationship of CA deficits and the need to cover them with FDI inflows.

There is also a mild positive effect on FDI resulting from a strengthening of the XR in each of the previous periods but without any clear conclusions. The LR has a strong effect on FDI with a three period lag. Depending on how long money takes to move through the pipeline to project initiation and the capital intensity of the project, this may also relate to some of the XR and CA effects.

The SM variable has a noticeable effect on FDI with one lag, possibly indicating substantial co-financing from this source. Krkoska (2001) also discusses links between FDI and other sources of financing. The hypotheses for CA, SM, and LR are supported with this analysis, and there is some support for the hypothesis with variable XR.

Table 4.3 – Hungary

Change in FDI affected by:	**Lag**	**Coefficient**	**T Statistic**	**Diagnostic Tests**
Change in prev periods FDI	1	0.424	1.34	- R2 = 0.510 AIC = 15.51 SC = 16.56 Log likelihood = -293.01
Change in CA	inc	inc	inc	
Change in XR	3 4	21.03 -30.09	1.55 -1.81	
Change in SM	inc	inc	inc	
Change in log CPI	inc	inc	inc	
Change in LR	inc	inc	inc	

The one significant result from this analysis shows a strong XR effect on FDI from four periods previous and a mild effect from three periods previous, concluding that XR is a primary driver of FDI in Hungary. Weak relationships between FDI and the other variables lead to insignificant and inconclusive results. The hypothesis for XR is supported for Hungary.

Table 4.4 – Lithuania

Change in FDI affected by:	Lag	Coefficient	T Statistic	Diagnostic Tests
Change in prev periods FDI	1	1.418	4.03	R2 = 0.953 - R2 = 0.745 AIC = 10.90 SC = 11.84 Log likelihood = -106.34
Change in CA	1 2	1.130 -2.555	3.58 -5.42	
Change in XR	3	-1086.102	-2.98	
Change in SM	3	-3.086	-2.02	
Change in log CPI	2 3	-22351.89 -25736.93	-4.17 3.30	
Change in LR	1 2	-287.307 261.50	-3.56 2.31	

Lithuania's analysis is one of the most robust. All hypotheses are supported for Lithuania. Only three lags were run due to a less number of observations than the other focus countries. Low SC and AIC tests indicate that fewer extraneous factors are influencing the variables in this country's analysis. The adjusted R2 is very robust, as is R2, indicating that the variables in Lithuania's analysis explain FDI very well.

There is a very strong CA effect on FDI from a lag of both one and two periods. The XR increasing three periods ago increases FDI by nearly a multiple of three.

The SM effect is strong from three periods ago, which could signify Greenfield effects on FDI. In a strong economy, the conclusion could be that three periods are enough to see fruition of foreign investment. Nearly all stock markets contain a great deal of investor expectations in their movements and are considered leading economic indicators.

There are strong inflation effects on FDI, with FDI reacting favorably to decreases in log CPI from two and three periods previous. Also in the interest rate sector, as LR decreases in the previous period, FDI increases. This effect is also seen with a two period lag.

Table 4.5 – Poland

Change in FDI affected by:	Lag	Coefficient	T Statistic	Diagnostic Tests
Change in prev periods FDI	2 3	-0.579 -0.530	-2.46 -1.98	-
Change in CA	3	0.348	1.62	R2 = 0.430
Change in XR	3	-652.121	-1.54	AIC = 14.00
Change in SM	2	0.597	1.45	SC = 15.05
Change in log CPI	inc	inc	inc	Log likelihood = -262.05
Change in LR	4	117.816	2.10	

Poland has a corrective effect on its FDI with a two period lag, giving stability to the overall trend of those inflows. The three period lag also is noticeable, continuing the effect and reinforcing interest in FDI inflows.

The CA has a sharp effect on FDI, with an increase in CA three periods ago increasing current FDI inflows.

A mild XR effect shows that as the Zloty appreciates three periods ago, there is a positive effect on current FDI. Also, a higher LR with a four period lag increases FDI in the current period. This could imply that portfolio transfers occur first, and are then either used as Greenfield investments or put into the stock market. SM shows a mild effect on FDI with a two period lag, offering some support of that path of the flow of funds.

Table 4. 6 – Slovakia

Change in FDI affected by:	Lag	Coefficient	T Statistic	Diagnostic Tests
Change in prev periods FDI	1 2	0.479 -0.642	1.53 -2.135	- R2 = 0.105 AIC = 16.58 SC = 17.63 Log likelihood = -306.57
Change in CA	inc	inc	inc	
Change in XR	3	216.621	1.433	
Change in SM	inc	inc	inc	
Change in log CPI	inc	inc	inc	
Change in LR	inc	inc	inc	

Overall robustness of Slovakia's VAR analysis is low. The low adjusted R2 indicates diffusion in the ability of the independent variables in explaining FDI. A strong corrective effect of a two period lag on FDI is clear, and there is a mild corrective effect from the one period lag. There is a mild effect with a three period lag on the XR. FDI, therefore, has a stable accumulation trend, while an appreciation in the dollar decreases FDI three periods following. The hypothesis for XR has some support for Slovakia.

Table 4.7 – Slovenia

Change in FDI affected by:	Lag	Coefficient	T Statistic	Diagnostic Tests
Change in prev periods FDI	inc	inc	inc	- R2 = 0.20 AIC = 12.84 SC = 13.88 Log likelihood = -238.21
Change in CA	1	0.607	1.32	
Change in XR	inc	inc	inc	
Change in SM	4	-0.262	-1.45	
Change in log CPI	inc	inc	inc	
Change in LR	inc	inc	inc	

There is generally low robustness for Slovenia's VAR analysis. FDI is mildly affected by a change in CA one period previous. A change in SM levels also mildly affects FDI, but with a four period lag. The low adjusted R2 indicates that

FDI is therefore likely driven by external and not domestic factors. Some support exists for the CA and SM hypotheses for Slovenia.

Cointegration Analysis – Explanation

Cointegration is a method of regression that reveals long-term relationships among variables that would be hidden by short-term movements. It is similar to the communications problem of separating the message from the medium of transmission, or to the economic problem of differentiating between a random movement and a correction back to equilibrium. In this section of the book, cointegration allows regression analysis on non-stationary variables (variables that are stochastically trending) with statistically valid results.

In econometrics, means of time series of data like those in this study are not useful or significant as a measure. They do not show anything of value statistically. Waiting a time period or two or three for prices or indexes to revert to the mean nearly always does nothing for the analysis. This property is "non-stationarity," and the variable is said to be "non-stationary." (Rubin 2004)

In contrast, a variable that is stationary might be the time series of the difference of the original variables from one observation to the next. This difference from one quarter or month to the next may have wide variation from the mean, and a quarter or month later, the difference returns to the mean. This return to the mean would identify the series as stationary.

Non-stationary time series are integrated. The cause of the integration results from random influences on the variables. Random walk is the simplest integrated process and is said to be integrated of order one because if it is differenced one, it becomes stationary. If a variable can be made stationary by differencing it d times, it is said to be integrated of order d. When a combination of two integrated time series results in a stationary time series, the data is cointegrated. Two series that are cointegrated may be individually non-stationary but will not move very far apart over time. Multivariate cointegration analysis permits regression modeling that eliminates simultaneity bias. This bias can result when causality runs not only from independent to dependent variable, but when it runs from dependent to independent variable. Simultaneity bias would invalidate results, and cointegration solves this bias problem by breaking the model into a matrix of equations where the dependence of each variable on the others can be measured statistically.

Economic price series are often non-stationary (i.e., trended) and so automatically correlated, and it is important to see that a high correlation does not itself signify a causal relationship (Engle and Granger 1987). This is to say that the variables in the analysis do not necessarily cause FDI to move or react, but they may move with FDI, and cointegration allows us to see how much they move together just because of correlation. Cointegration analysis separates and identifies long-run or systematic equilibrium relationships among variables, and also distinguishes short-term changes in values from the stochastic trend. For variables integrated of order one, this divides the components into stationary and non-stationary categories. This analysis improves traditional linear regression, which is invalid when applied to non-stationary variables.

If the levels of variables contain their history and their differences show short-term changes, the multivariate cointegration vector autoregression model is the key to splitting the movement of each variable into long-run and short-run effects and allowing statistical analysis to be done on each (Rubin 2004).

Moving further into the concept of persistence or long memory leads to the model used here and the interconnection of the three parts of this chapter.

Financial data often displays generally trending patterns called long-range persistence or long memory due to the presence of non-stationary components in the series (Gourieroux and Jasiak 2001). Empirical evidence of several series of data in this study would suggest that prices or indexes of consumer prices, interest rates, stock markets, and perhaps even national current account balances would display common non-stationary patterns in the long-run. The Royal Swedish Academy of Sciences (2003) describes concepts to which cointegration analysis can be usefully applied. By modeling stationary returns, information on long-term movements of prices and indexes are lost. But as noted previously, Engle and Granger (1987) devised the cointegration process to account for both long-term and short-term volatility and the long-term persistence of trending data series. This modeling of both log prices and their differences is called the error correction model.

What Engle (1982) succeeded in doing was separating the random error of a model's forecasting error into the volatility part of the random error due to previous periods' changes and fluctuations and a "rest of" part of random error.

An error correction model holds that a proportion of disequilibrium from one period is corrected in the next period (Engle and Granger 1987). So a change in foreign direct investment, e.g., during one period might depend upon the degree of excess in consumer prices in the previous period. By rearranging terms in a multivariate system, any set of lags can be tested to permit gradual adjustment, or best fit, toward a new equilibrium (Engle and Granger 1987). Engle and Granger's (1987) error model differs here from other applications in that the definition of a multivariate application does not rely on the exclusion of a subset of the variables. The Granger Representative Theorem (Granger 1983) and Granger (1981) proved that error correction models could represent cointegrated series. In summary, normal examples of error correction methods are determined from the reaction of one variable, the dependent variable, to shocks of another variable, the independent variable. And although the model used may show causal orderings and weak and strong relationships, all variables are treated as equally influential on each other within the cointegration analysis (Engle and Granger 1987).

Johansen (1988, 1991, 1995) took cointegration to a next level by deriving sequential tests for determining the number of cointegrating vectors. He also derived a maximum likelihood estimator using reduced rank regression. This is regarded as a second-generation approach to cointegration, building on maximum likelihood estimation instead of relying partly on least squares. We therefore use cointegration analysis to determine if our variables in this study are in equilibrium in the long run, and if they are, to determine if they are independently so or if they are cointegrated. The Trace Rank Test is used as it is the most popular, producing more robust results.

The section of this chapter focusing on graphic representation of the variables is the visual detection of cointegration among the variables plus the introduction of the country risk variable. Long- and short-run price and index movements illustrate the differences of variation, or volatility in the time series.

The long and infinite memory patterns frequently observed in financial data in this work are demonstrated both with statistical models and visual representations. Long-term memory patterns are evidenced as chart depictions. Technical analysis identifies convergence or divergence of variables. Finally the concept of ARCH modeling of nonlinear conditions shows how state of the art methodology accommodates the variation of risk in financial markets modeling.

Cointegration Analysis – Results of the Johansen Cointegration Trace Rank Test

Table 4.8 – FDI as Cointegrated with Current Account, XR, Stock Market, CPI, LR

Country	No. of Cointegration Equations	Trace Statistic	McKinnon .05 Critical Value	Prob.
Croatia	1	127.24	95.75	.0001
Czech Rep	1	118.27	95.75	.0006
	2	77.01	69.82	.0119
	3	48.00	47.86	.0484
Hungary	1	125.07	95.75	.0001
	2	75.67	69.82	.0158
Lithuania	1	183.31	95.75	.0000
	2	111.01	69.82	.0000
	3	66.78	47.86	.0003
	4	34.60	29.80	.0130
Poland	1	119.80	95.75	.0004
	2	77.76	69.82	.0101
	3	48.32	47.86	.0452
Slovakia	1	122.64	117.71	.0234
Slovenia	1	143.16	95.75	.0000
	2	82.24	69.82	.0037
	3	52.36	42.86	.0178

All variables have been tested for stationarity using the ADF (Augmented Dickey-Fuller) Test (Dickey and Fuller 1979, 1981) and the majority are non-stationary at their levels, thus suitable for cointegration testing, but not for least squares time series regression analysis.

The cointegration equation for each country is described with the standard error in parentheses below the coefficient. Results are discussed for each country.

Croatia

$$FDI = -.969CA + 156.34\ XR - .163425\ SM + 853.1487\ logCPI + 45.393\ LR$$

(0.08497) (88.254) (.28173) (1353.61) (52.8146)

> Results: FDI cointegrated with CA is very significant; with the exchange rate, mildly significant; and with other variables, insignificant. Two of the five hypotheses are supported for Croatia, the third smallest economy in this paper's focus group and the country least ready to access to the European Union. The high level of FDI cointegration with CA is also explained by Krkoska (2001), who concludes that foreign capital flows are needed to cover large CA deficits in general and also to bolster underdeveloped financial sectors. The small capitalization of Croatia's SM may explain why there is no significant relationship developed yet with FDI.

Czech Republic

$$FDI = +3.44CA - 516.84\ XR - .153863\ SM + 7411.640\ logCPI - 586.712\ LR$$

(0.76339) (97.201) (2.043) (4794 10) (183.016)

> Results: FDI cointegrated with CA is strongest; with the exchange rate, logCPI, and the lending rate fairly significant; with the stock market, insignificant. Here, four of our five hypotheses are supported by cointegration analysis. This second largest economy in the study has had its FDI flows affected by merger and acquisition activity on an international level, which Brada, Kutan and Yigit (2004) showed affected Czech Republic's SM. In this study, this relationship did not materialize, likely because Brada, Kutan and Yigit (2004) did not use cointegration as an adjustment for the short-term effects of merger and acquisition on the overall stock market.

Hungary

$$FDI = +0.178CA + 5.08\ XR + .207936\ SM + 6073.288\ logCPI + 83.542\ LR$$
$$(0.2070) \quad (2.702) \quad (0.0328) \quad (5164.36) \quad (57.992)$$

Results: FDI cointegrated with exchange rate, stock market and lending rate very significantly; with logCPI significantly; with current account, insignificantly. Therefore, four out of the five hypotheses have support in this third largest economy in the focus group. Hungary has been an active and early policy reformer, generally aligned with Western trade and policies, so the trends of cointegration have had somewhat of a more established beginning. The relationships among the variables of XR, SM, and LR and FDI have had time to develop along the thoughts of Merlevede and Schoors (2004) and along the lines of infinite memory or random walk theory, described in this and the literature review sections.

Lithuania

$$FDI = +1.3035CA - 1254.21\ XR - 2.3159\ SM + 21237.84\ logCPI + 179.560\ LR$$
$$(0.2480) \quad (73.224) \quad (0.3250) \quad (1930.03) \quad (12.497)$$

Results: With only 24 observations, there is a high degree of cointegration. FDI cointegrated with all variables very significantly. All hypotheses are supported in this analysis of the country with the smallest economy in this study. This Baltic nation has Scandinavia as its largest concentration of foreign investors and commercial partners (Merlevede and Schoors (2006). With that geographic particular as a stabilizing economic and trade factor, Lithuania is actively working toward reform. Further, Brada, Kutan and Yigit (2004) suggest that Lithuania's transition policies of reform improve the possibilities of realizing more FDI.

Poland

$$FDI = +0.4379CA + 601.7\ XR + 0.6140\ SM + 3742.08\ logCPI - 11.947\ LR$$
$$(0.1262) \quad (141.83) \quad (0.1551) \quad (2131.47) \quad (15.304)$$

Results: FDI is cointegrated with all variables except LR very significantly. Poland is the largest economy in this study, and with all variables but LR offering insight into FDI levels, a more open and outward-looking economic atmosphere in Poland can be inferred. Other outside variables such as the legal system, monetary and fiscal policy, and private sector institutions and organizations can be expected to benefit from (and contribute to) the general trend of increased market-oriented policies. Merlevede and Schoors (2004) discuss reform, FDI, and growth as benefiting from a gradual process of policy changes and lessening the volatility of FDI flows.

Slovakia

FDI=+0.3778CA + 122.48XR + 2.5866SM – 28808.98 logCPI – 99.643LR +504.92ttrend

(0.2018) (27.403) (1.8386) (6246.41) (32.851) (110.045)

Results: A time trend variable was used in this equation because otherwise there were no cointegration results. Thus this is a deterministic vector versus all other equations, which are stochastic.

Using the time trend variable, FDI cointegrated with all variables except logCPI very significantly. LogCPI was insignificant. Therefore, all hypotheses except the inflation hypothesis are supported, and this medium-sized transition economy's sources of FDI respond to changes in the variables described in theory.

Slovenia

FDI = +6.0946CA – 8.78 XR – 0.5259 SM + 3143.576 logCPI -59.61 LR

(0.6843) (3.59) (0.161) (1436.41) (14.27)

Results: FDI cointegrated with all variables very significantly, especially so with current account. All hypotheses are thus supported with cointegration analysis. Slovenia's open economy, its small size, and its aggressive pursuit of FDI may all be factors in explaining the high degree of cointegration here. Supporting theory could be inferred from Obstfeld and Rogoff (2005), where relationships between trade and finance among regions were shown using a CA balancing model. Further work by Gourinches and Rey (2005) shows that valuation effects caused by XRs explained CA changes in the United States and may have application to other economies.

Statistics Summary

Common drivers, those variables that affect FDI in all or a group of countries, are useful to identify for policymakers and for possible application to other countries that may want to emphasize proven methods of attracting FDI.

One common driver to all focus countries in the cointegration analysis is the exchange rate (XR), with a strong effect on all except Croatia where the effect is mild. So fostering factors to strengthen a currency increases FDI while a weaker currency tends to discourage FDI inflows. FDI and other financial flows contribute to higher growth (Schadler et al 2006), the policy objective in attracting FDI.

Current account (CA) is another common driver of FDI, with a strong effect in all countries except Hungary. This supports the research of Schadler et al (2006), which shows that CA improvements do affect FDI and other financial flows, with a direct effect on economic growth. SM had a strong effect on five of the seven focus countries, the exceptions being Croatia and Czech. The last common driver of FDI with a strong effect is LR, having the effect on all except Croatia and Poland.

The VAR analysis does not result in such defined clusters of results. Of the variables, SM and XR effects were evident in five of the seven countries, supporting the cointegration work and identifying the importance of these variables in attracting FDI.

FDI, Country Risk Rating Changes

Graphical (Chart) Results

As can be sensed in both the literature and the methodology of technical analysis, the chart picture and its analysis is the bridge between quantitative and qualitative analysis, yet this exposition also falls into each of these categories in their own domain. The data that supplies the raw material for the statistical section of this work also provides the data for the charts, so this is a quantitative setting. The analysis of these graphical depictions tends to be more interpretive, or of the qualitative realm, depending on the researcher's experience in their use. As mentioned, this researcher has great familiarity with this discipline, having had an accomplished career using and imparting technical analysis around the world.

In each of these charts for each country, the variable of country risk is introduced. Along the bottom of each chart are the country risk rating change indications. These signify, as the legend explains, a change in the risk rating itself or a change in the outlook, which often precedes an actual rating change.

Besides the country risk variable, FDI is plotted against each other financial variable in the analysis. So on each chart for a country, two variables are the same (FDI and the risk ratings) and one is different so the visual analysis can be made clearly. There are a total of thirty-five charts, and those that showed support of the hypotheses or a defined conclusion about the variables are in this section. The others are included in Appendix D without comments.

Within each country's chart analysis are intertwined results from the statistical analysis that coincide or contradict the visual deductions. This shows how the two methods work together to form stronger conclusions.

The legends used on each chart for risk rating changes are noted below:

△ Indicates a positive risk rating change

▽ Indicates a negative risk rating change

□ Indicates outlook changed to positive

○ Indicates outlook changed to negative

Positive or negative risk rating changes are self-explanatory. An outlook change means that conditions in the country have shifted but do not yet justify an actual rating change. The effect is nearly always the same in the markets and variables, especially if the change is unexpected.

Following are the charts with analysis and comments:

Croatia

Figure 4.1 – Croatia Stock Market vs FDI

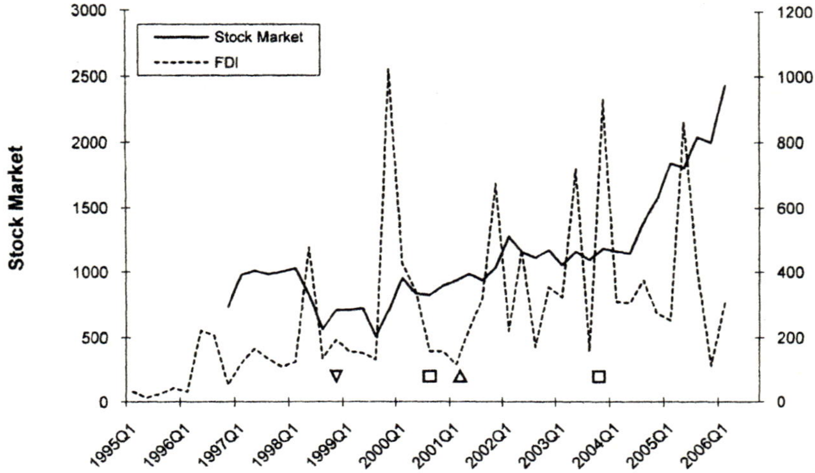

The Stock Market (SM) variable experiences a clear effect from a risk ratings change, with a two period lag in most cases. The change in outlook in 2003Q4 is followed by a radically steep move in SM two periods following. The risk ratings change has a quick effect on FDI, confirming the VAR analysis. Both SM and FDI, while broadly moving higher together, show no correlation or cointegration, confirming the cointegration analysis of insignificant cointegration.

Figure 4.2 – Croatia Current Account vs FDI

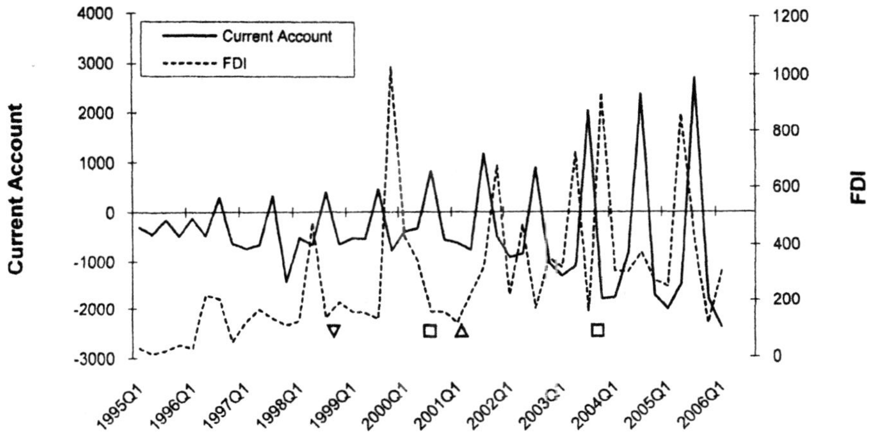

CA does not react in any discernable pattern to changes in country risk ratings changes, but FDI is positively affected by changes in those ratings changes. CA moves very clearly in step with FDI, confirming the cointegration analysis.

Figure 4.3 – Croatia Lending Rate vs FDI

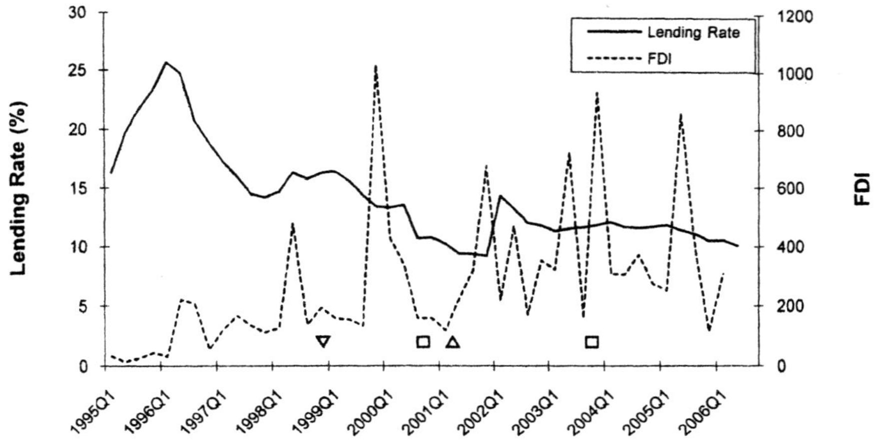

The lending rate (LR) moves lower in a generally downward path, but risk rating changes do not seem to affect it. The trend continues lower in 1999 when the risk rating is changed to negative, continues lower when the outlook is changed to positive, and jumps higher two periods following a change to positive. The downtrend resumes in the next period. FDI is more responsive to the risk rating changes, changing directly with the risk rating changes. Convergence of the FDI and LR variables in recent years could indicate a more stable financial environment is occurring.

Figure 4.4 – Croatia Exchange Rate vs FDI

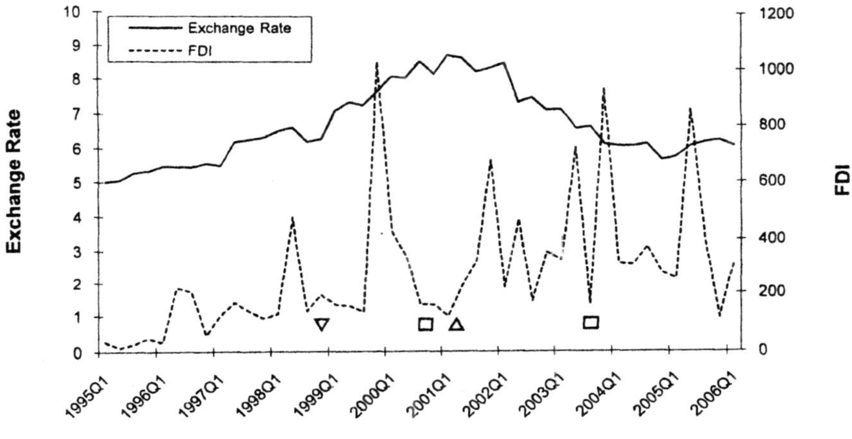

Overall, changes in country risk ratings have an inverse effect on Croatia's XR. The one negative change continued the weakening trend of the currency, while both positive outlook changes and the positive rating change itself coincide with a strengthening currency. The relationship between FDI and XR is different in each half of the ten-year period – in the early years, the trends move together, but after 2002, they converge, and show a generally inverse relationship. This picture supports the cointegration analysis that shows mild significance of the variables' cointegration.

Czech Republic

Figure 4.5 – Czech Republic Stock Market vs FDI

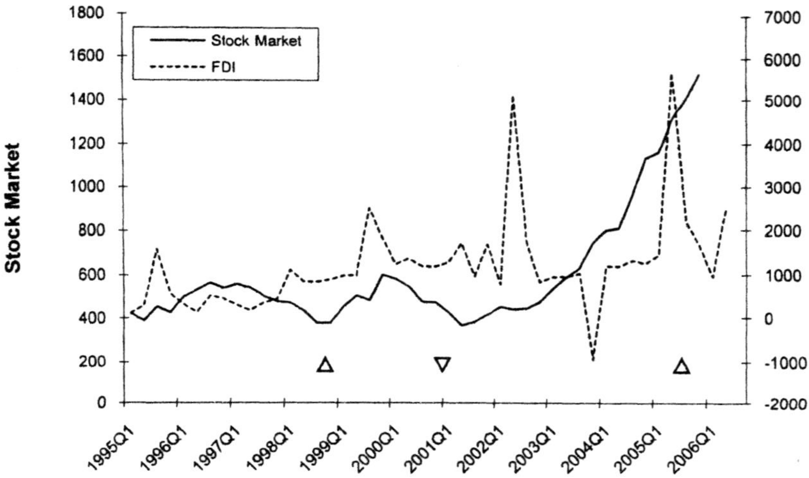

Risk rating changes have immediate and direct effects on SM movement, both negative and positive. Positive risk rating changes do seem to affect FDI flows quickly, while the one negative change in 2001Q1 only seemed to dampen or delay the pop higher four periods later, which then retreated to the original level. FDI is much more volatile than SM, but with two exceptions – 2003Q4 and 2005Q3 – these two variables seem to move together in the same direction. This lends some support to the VAR analysis.

Figure 4.6 – Czech Republic Current Account vs FDI

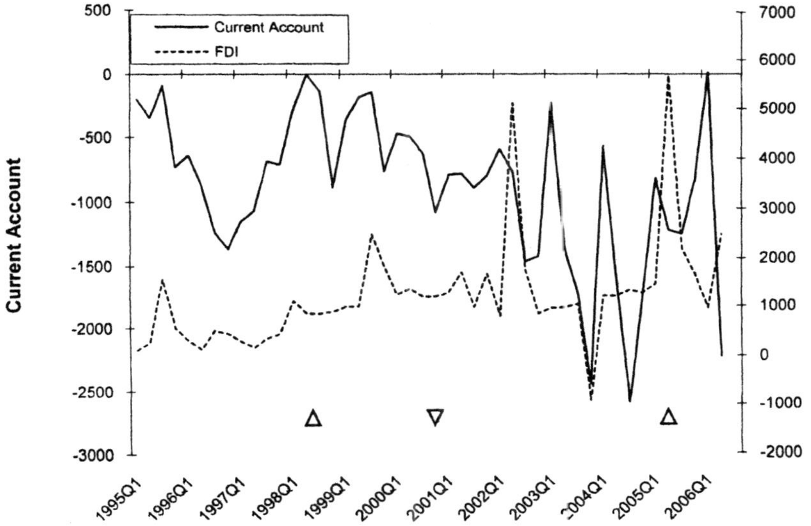

Country risk rating changes only have a predictable effect on CA two out of three times, not useful or reliable information. CA does track closely the same moves as FDI, though, with two or three exceptions over the eleven-year period. This confirms both the VAR and Cointegration analyses.

Figure 4.7 – Czech Republic Lending Rate vs FDI

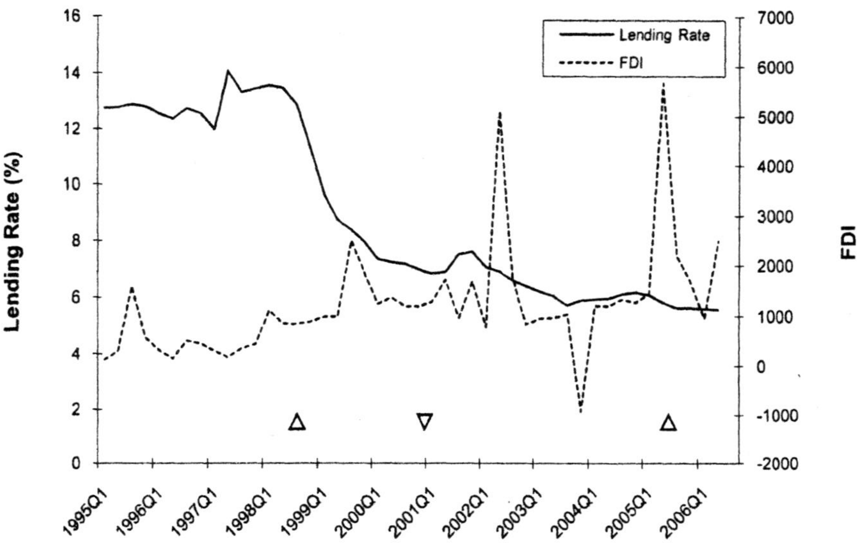

LR is affected by all three credit risk rating changes, but seemingly with less of a lag visually than the VAR analysis shows. The opposite movement of the variables supports the statistical results of the cointegration analysis.

Hungary

Figure 4.8 – Hungary Stock Market vs FDI

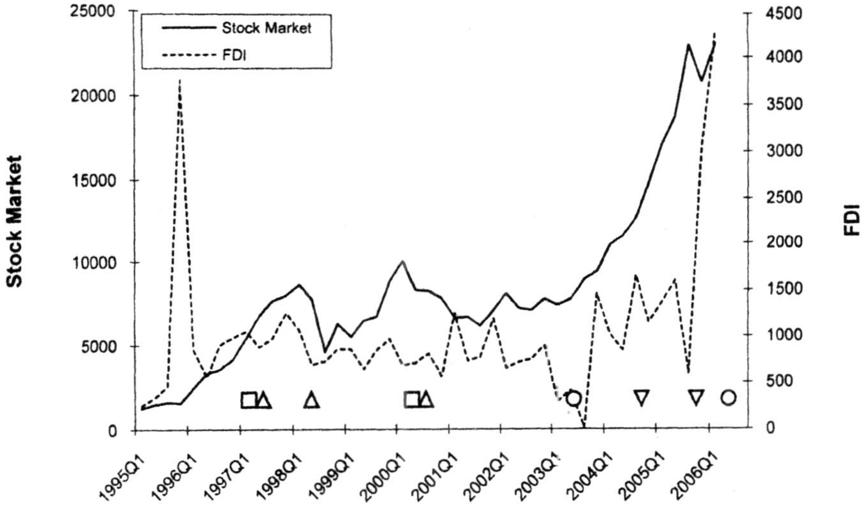

Positive risk rating changes affect the SM variable negatively two out of three times, and one of these with a one period lag. Negative changes or outlook changes affect SM positively. This chart picture also adds support to the cointegration results where SM and FDI are significantly cointegrated. There is no pattern to changes in FDI compared to risk rating changes.

Figure 4.9 – Hungary Current Account vs FDI

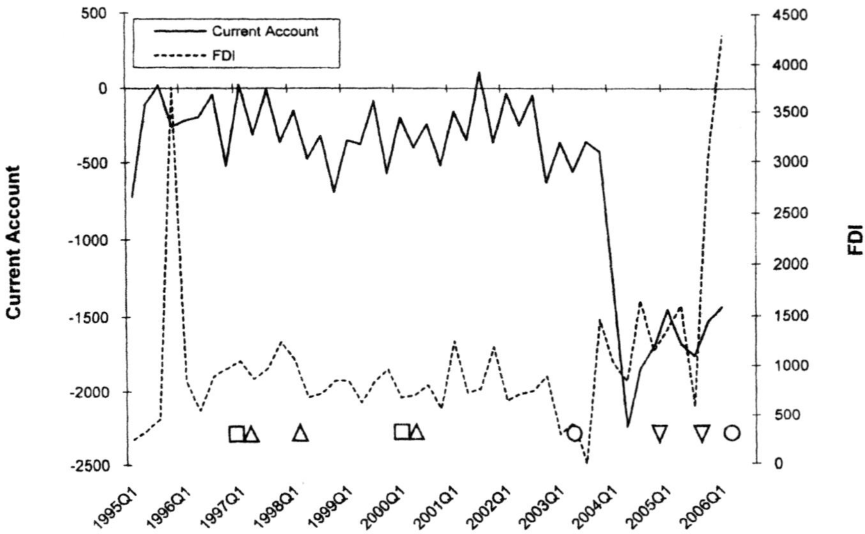

Country risk rating changes have an opposite effect on CA, all very short term. Positive changes cause an increase in CA while negative changes cause improvement. Positive changes affect FDI directly, but also for very short time periods, i.e., the effects do not seem to be lasting. There is no discernable relationship between FDI and CA.

Figure 4.10 – Hungary Lending Rate vs FDI

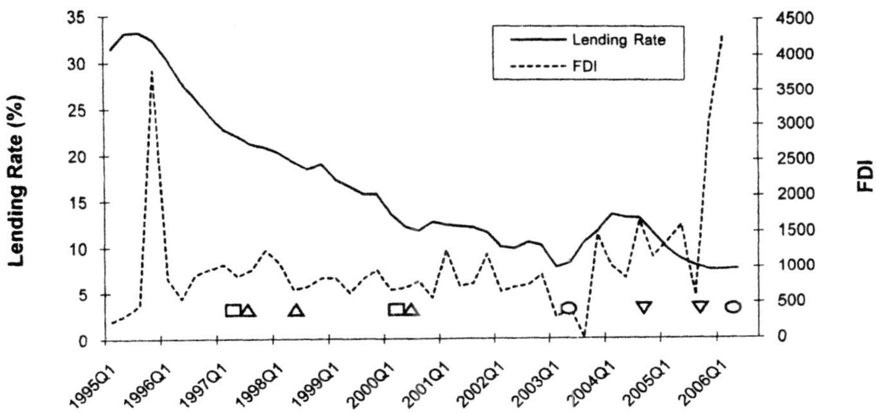

Country risk rating changes have a long-term effect on LR, the exception being in 2004Q3 when the actual change resulted in a "buy the rumor, sell the fact" event. The change of outlook to negative kept the theme, with a move higher in LR. But when the rating actually was changed to negative, LR continued falling for another four periods. With a further negative rating change, LR turned higher. The overall trends of the LR and FDI variables are generally inversely related, supporting the cointegration analysis.

Lithuania

Figure 4.11 – Lithuania Stock Market vs FDI

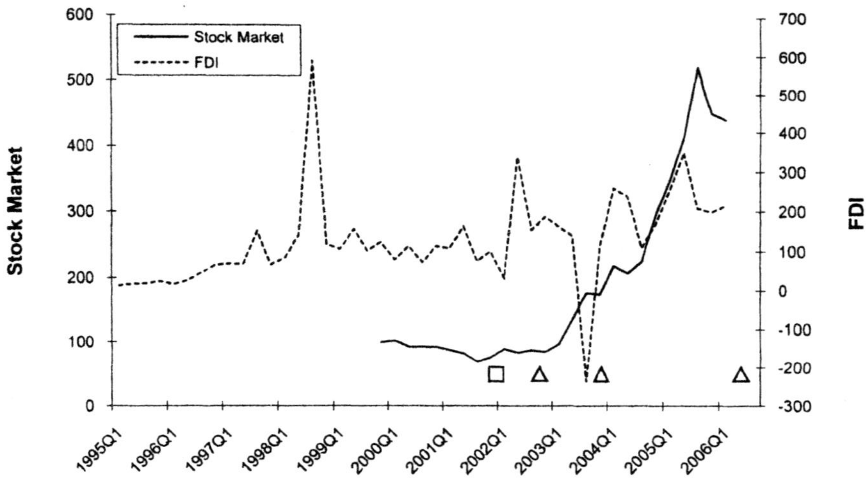

There is less stock market data available for Lithuania than other countries. The three positive changes, one an outlook change and the others actual changes, all resulted in SM moving higher immediately or with one lag. FDI moves positively with the positive rating change only two of three times, an unreliable indicator. The visual co-movements of the variables are not as clear as the cointegration analysis describes.

Figure 4.12 – Lithuania Current Account vs FDI

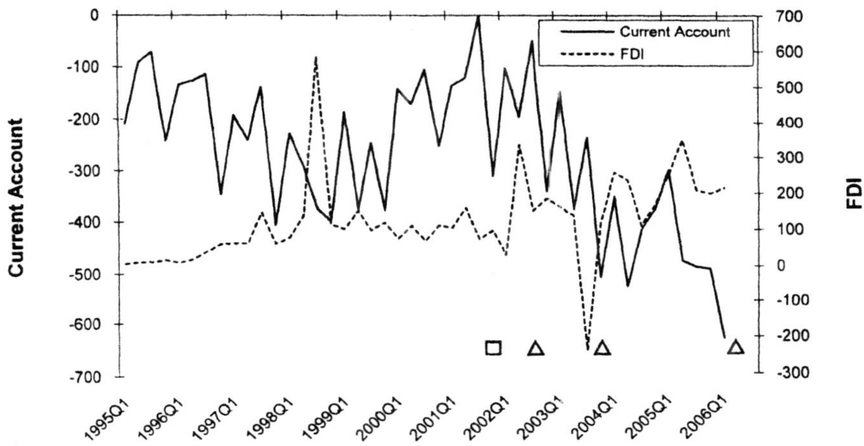

Positive outlook or actual changes in credit risk rating have a positive effect on CA and FDI. The CA effect on FDI is as clear visually as in the VAR results, lending good support to that statistical work. And the co-movement of these variables also illustrates support for the cointegration analysis. The coinciding of all three analyses signifies strong and verified conclusions about Lithuania.

Figure 4.13 – Lithuania Lending Rate vs FDI

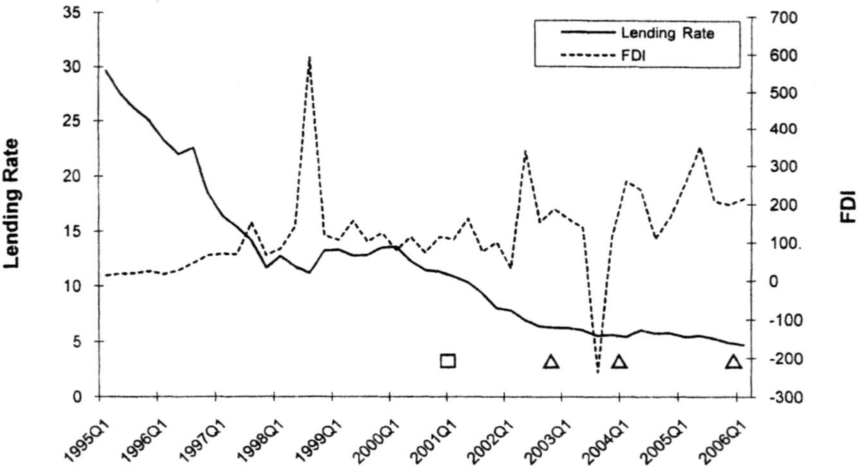

The three positive rating changes are followed immediately by a short-term rise in FDI. The overall trend shows LR decreasing as FDI increases, implying more funding taking place from sources outside the country. The trends verify both the VAR and Cointegration Analyses with high definition.

Figure 4.14 – Lithuania Exchange Rate vs FDI

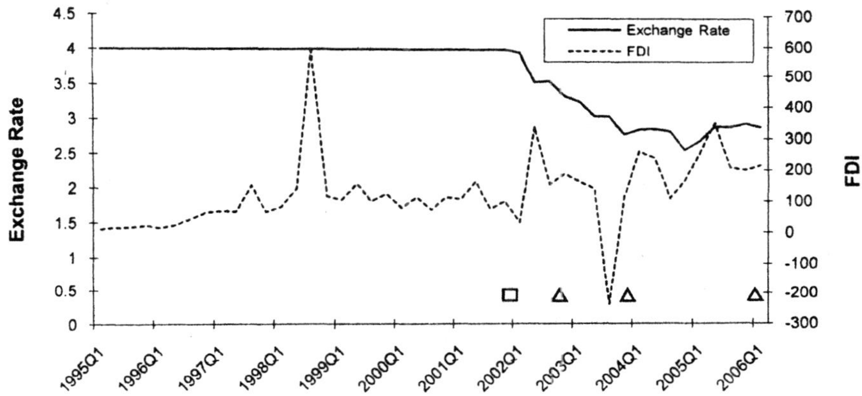

Positive country risk rating changes have a clear strengthening effect on XR in Lithuania. These same positive ratings changes also have clear short-term positive effects on FDI. The relationship between FDI and XR converges in recent years, indicating a more stable financial environment is developing between the variables and adding support to both the VAR and cointegration analyses.

Poland

Figure 4.15 – Poland StockMarket vs FDI

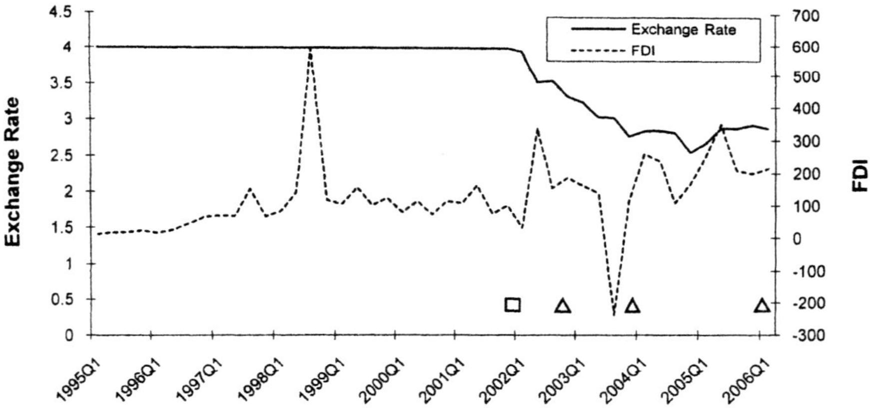

The first two risk rating changes are positive, one in outlook, one actual. Each is followed by strong moves higher in SM, lasting at least a year. But a negative change in ratings five years later (a new era of economic development) also is followed by a continuing rise in SM. The relationships between country risk rating changes and SM are therefore not conclusive. Country risk rating does seem to have an immediate and direct effect on FDI in the three events in this chart picture.

Relationships between FDI and SM appear strongly inversely related in the short-term but with an overall long-term pattern of moving together. This supports the cointegration work from the statistics section.

Figure 4.16 – Poland Current Account vs FDI

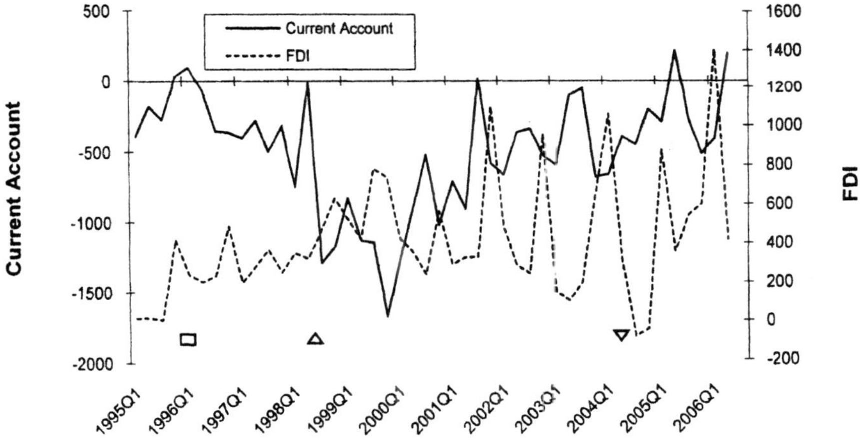

Country risk rating changes do not show consistent effects on CA, but they do affect FDI levels directly for one to two periods following the change in outlook or actual change. The CA and FDI visual relationship confirms the VAR analysis of CA leading increases in FDI by three periods.

Figure 4.17 – Poland Lending Rate vs FDI

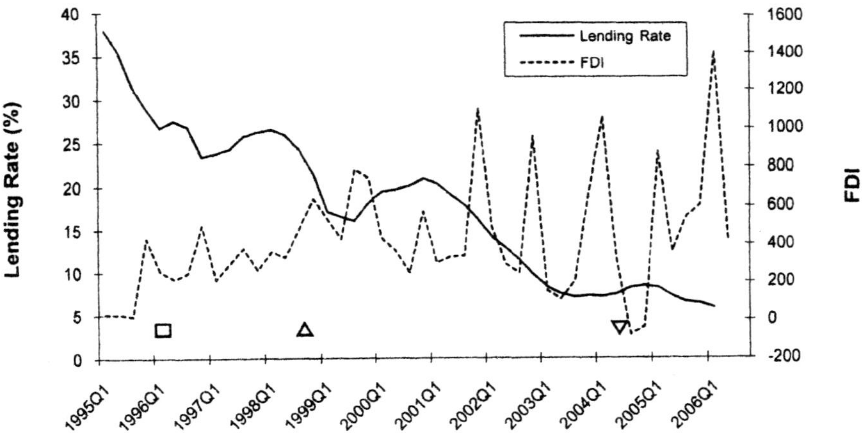

Country risk rating changes or changes in outlook have clear direct effects on LR in Poland for at least two periods following the change. There are immediate and short-term direct effects on FDI from the same changes.

The short-term relationship between LR and FDI supports the VAR work, which describes a direct effect. Long-term, however, these variables are moving inversely to each other, supporting the lack of cointegration found in that analysis.

Figure 4.18 – Poland Exchange Rate vs FDI

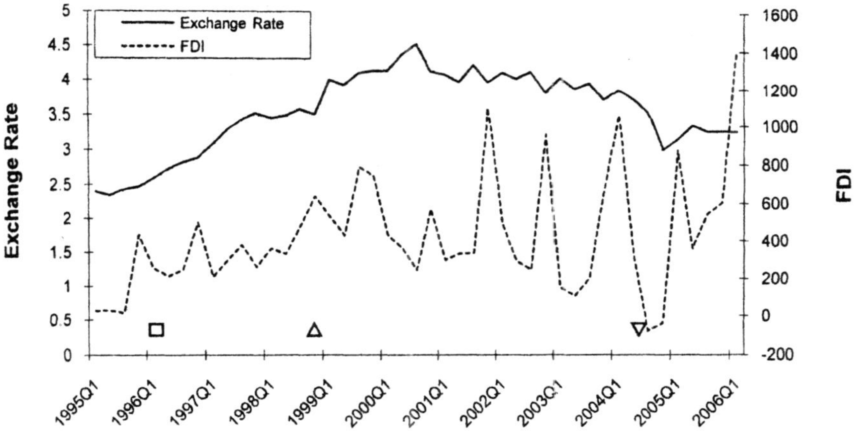

Country risk rating changes show a direct short-term relationship with XR in Poland. The one positive outlook change and one positive rating change occurred during a weakening trend of the currency, and the one negative change occurred during a strengthening trend. The overall chart picture supports the VAR conclusion that an appreciation in the currency increases FDI with a three-period lag. The cointegration analysis is also supported by the trends, generally moving together, although FDI is much more volatile.

Slovakia

Figure 4.19 – Slovakia Stock Market vs FDI

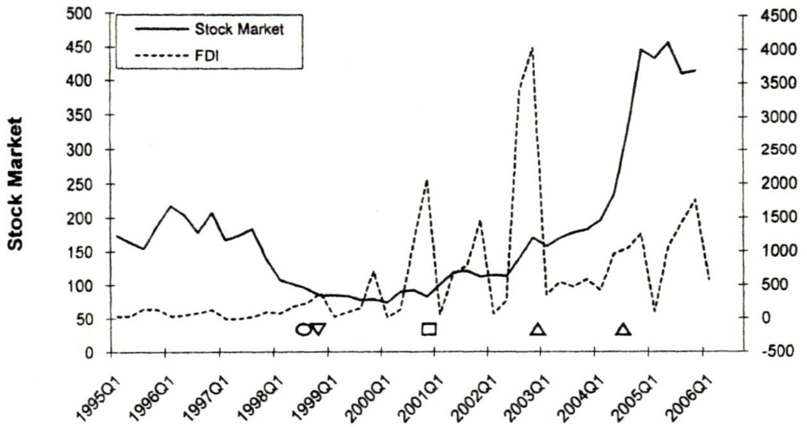

Country risk rating changes in Slovakia have a direct effect on SM there. The VAR analysis is not very robust, and introducing the variable of country risk offers new insights into SM from this chart picture. Country risk ratings have a quick or one period lag direct effect on FDI.

The FDI/SM relationship can be broken into short-term and long-term effects. Short-term SM moves track FDI movements very closely, although they are not as volatile. Long-term movements are inverse in the first six years of the picture, but seem to begin moving in the same general direction in 2001. Again, FDI flows are much more volatile than SM movements.

Figure 4.20 – Slovakia Current Account vs FDI

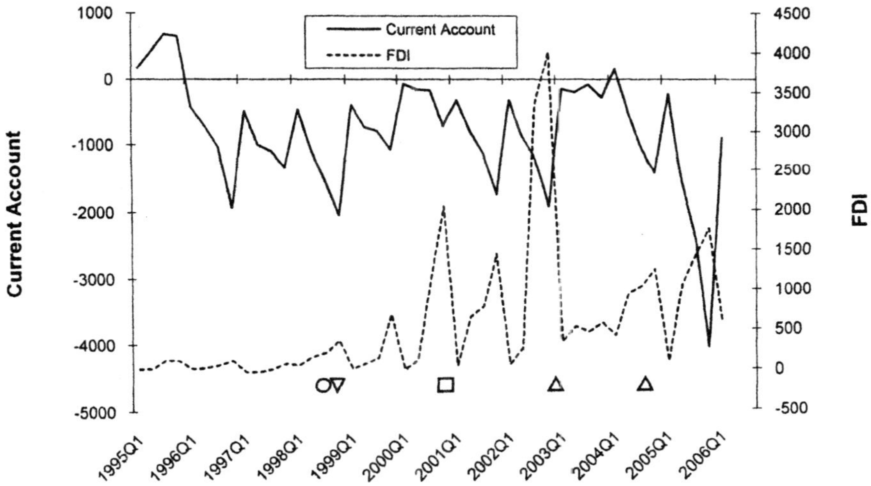

Risk rating changes give direct results for Slovakia's CA variable four of the five times the event took place. A negative change or outlook narrows the CA deficit, while a positive change widens it, albeit by a small amount in the 2003Q2 event. The last rating change, an additional positive change, has a two-period lag before the steep widening move occurred. The risk rating change effect on FDI is direct and immediate in the period following. The FDI/CA relationship is nearly exactly inverse in the short-term, implying foreigners are financing trade-related investment.

Figure 4.21 – Slovakia Lending Rate vs FDI

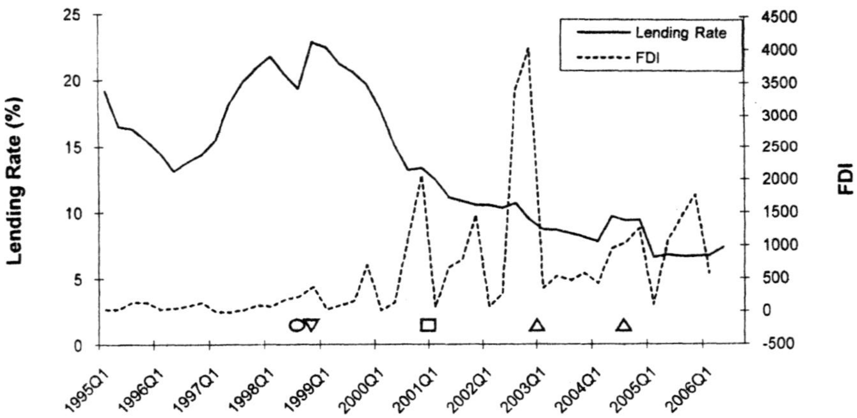

A negative rating or outlook here has a very short-term inverse effect on LR. Conversely, a positive rating or outlook change seem to continue the downtrend in LR, last seen in 2004Q3, with a sharp move lower. Due to the overall clear seven-year downtrend, it is likely inconclusive that positive risk rating changes are alone responsible for the lower LR.

Risk rating changes have immediate direct effects on FDI, some only short-term and some more sustained. No conclusive pattern is discerned between FDI and LR, although the variables converge in recent years, signifying more stability to the relationship than in early years of the analysis.

Figure 4.22 – Slovakia Exchange Rate vs FDI

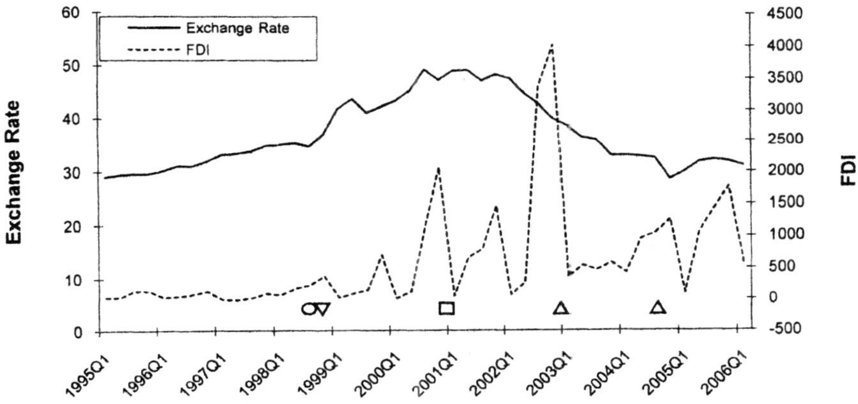

Country risk rating changes have an inverse effect on XR in Slovakia and a very short-term direct effect on FDI. The relationship between FDI and XR is similar to patterns in a few other countries in this analysis: in the early years of the time period examined, the trends move together, but in recent years, there is a convergence of the trends. Again, by itself, this indicates a more stable relationship between the variables. There is support here for both the VAR and cointegration analyses.

Slovenia

Figure 4.23 – Slovenia Stock Market vs FDI

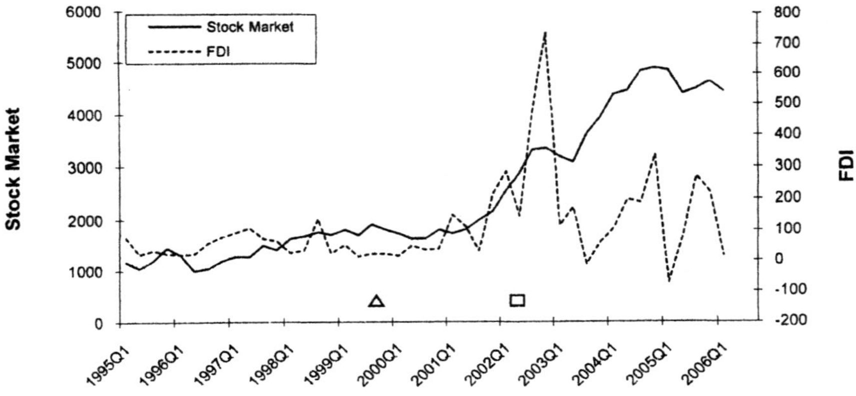

After the two country risk rating changes for Slovenia, the SM variable seems to flatten out or decline, signaling possible regrouping or consolidation before continuing its move upward. There are no conclusions about FDI and country risk rating changes.

The relationship between SM and FDI looks clearly correlated, even when the variables widened apart in the chart picture. This supports the high level of cointegration found in the cointegration analysis.

Figure 4.24 – Slovenia Current Account vs FDI

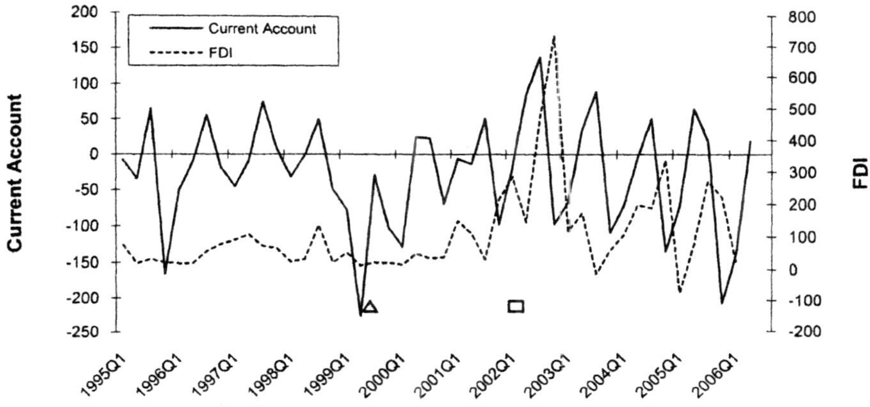

The positive change and positive outlook both are made just before CA peaks, and CA then increases its deficit in the following periods. The effect on FDI is also rather inconclusive in this chart. The relationship between FDI and CA is much tighter in the last four years than previously, and that picture lends support to the cointegration analysis from the statistical section.

Figure 4.25 – Slovenia Exchange Rate vs FDI

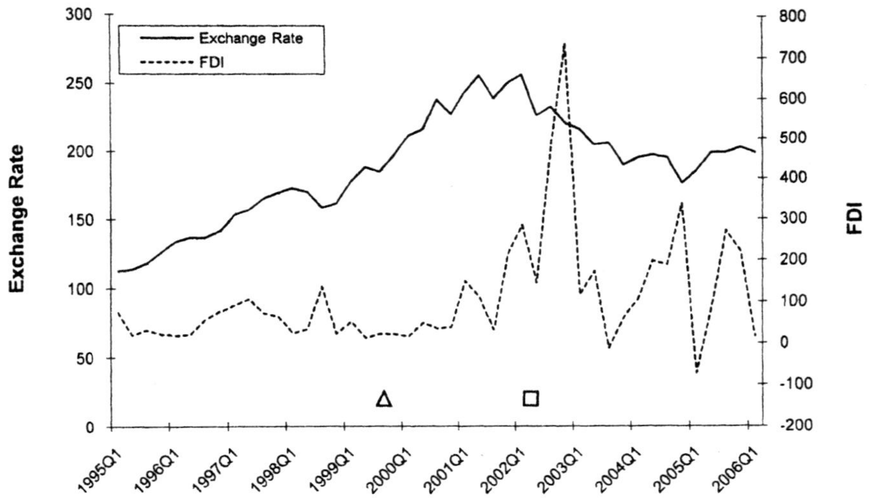

Country risk rating change effects on both FDI and XR are inconclusive. But the chart picture of the trends of the variables shows clear divergence and convergence throughout the time period examined, indicating an inverse relationship and supporting the cointegration results for XR.

Charts Summary

Many chart pictures in this section provide support for the statistical analyses. This is especially notable in Lithuania's three analyses. This strengthens the conclusions about the relationships among the variables and adds credibility to the use of technical analysis in this kind of discipline, both major objectives of this book.

Interestingly, the common variable that was inconclusive in each country's chart analysis was CPI. In the cases of Hungary and Poland, CPI has trended downward, while in all other countries the inflation trend has moved higher. In all cases, there are no perceptible visual relationships using this variable. One reason may be that CPI is not affected by country risk ratings changes.

Chart pictures display relationships that in some cases are easier to identify than they are with statistical analyses. Changes in trends, convergence and divergence, and points in time are easy to see on a chart. Statistics provide precise insight while charts offer an overview at a glance. Applying both methods to the same problem is a way of introducing the subject of international capital markets to a wider audience who may be receptive to the visual methodology. The field studies that follow are a third dimension of this study that should add further depth to the work and breadth to analysis.

Qualitative Results – Field/Case Studies

Explanation – Points Covered

The primary points covered and the structure of the case in each country field study are listed below and then explained in some detail.

- The context, or setting of the case, with general background, time, and place
- The issue and purpose of the case with an explication of the problem
- Information gained and a thorough description of the process observed and sources of data
- Personal assertions and any naturalistic generalizations that changed due to input from sources
- Closing notes, lessons of the study, and conclusions

Qualitative studies are narrative and organized within a contextual framework, and the case studies in this section reflect a broad and "flavorful" view of the conditions and factors in the focus countries. Each country study opens with a general economic, political, and social picture of the current environment. Historic information that adds perspective is described. Things that cannot be gleaned from statistics alone, and that would add value or depth to the country analysis, should be found in a qualitative study. The story of the European Union (EU) and candidates for accession to it is the context and background to this study's investigation of the links among country risk, FDI, and financial factors. The entire idea of the field studies here is explanatory, using inductive reasoning.

The design of the mixed methods research (qualitative and quantitative) used for the book as a whole is a multilevel model of triangulation design (Creswell and Clark 2007). This is shown in Table 3.1 – Summary of Methodologies. The purpose of this dual approach is to compare and contrast the results of the statistical study with the qualitative findings of the field study data and expand understanding from one method to another. As displayed in the model, the three segments of the research (statistical, graphical, and qualitative) are brought together to validate the results of the other segments.

A great deal of time was spent in the field in order to verify the trustworthiness and authenticity of the data. The closeness of the researcher to those interviewed also helps to authenticate the information. Every effort is made to bring the field information to a point of convergence where it can be coordinated or seen to be accurate due to the multiple source approach.

For these field studies, sources include the use of written and audiovisual documents, reports from banks and brokerages, data from international credit rating agencies, written and oral interviews, and information from national and international governmental and private agencies. Sources of interviewees are identified by title or office and not by personal name to allow the sources more freedom in their responses. This is especially productive when interviewing government ministers and former officials. Interviewing these certain elites has given valuable and unique information and an overall view to the analysis. The questionnaire itself builds from qualifying the respondent as an expert to uncovering information useful to the study to evaluating the questions and respondents themselves. Each interview is actually a conversation with an old friend, now for a particular purpose. This is due to the personal connection of the researcher with each person interviewed. Consensual validation is also employed, using the opinions of competent others. All questions are non-contrived (no particular answer is sought) and open-ended to allow minimal interference in the flow of ideas and responses to the interviewer. The interviewer's experience spans thirty years at different levels and purposes of interviewing, giving him expert status in this function.

A discussion of important elements and issues is made for each country, then personal assertions and in-depth aspects are brought out. The final conclusions are presented and verified with multiple sources and evaluation questions of the participants.

The number of case studies also helps verify the results of the other data. Three case countries are used, allowing independent differences in results by country but common conclusions from the overall studies themselves. Three cases also strike a balance between not diluting the overall analysis while avoiding the single case possibility of being vulnerable to a narrow analysis. This number of cases permits a more powerful outside generalization of the findings than would be possible from one case alone.

Altogether, the field studies comprise a written documentary of the quality made by historians, archaeologists, or economists for their own general and specialized audiences. These focus countries are analyzed as closely for this purpose as a corporation or organization would investigate the prospect of an overseas venture.

The particular countries in the field studies are chosen purposely, not randomly. The researcher has had personal experience with these countries, and information of the kind needed is readily available for each country. All countries in the study have a clear bounded system of time and place. The time boundary for all begins shortly after the break up of the former Soviet Union and the achievement of independence by the focus countries. The economic and geographic boundaries are defined by nearness to Western Europe and by the level of integration into the EU, which is seen by foreign investors as an indication of stability.

Table 4.9 – Summary Table of Qualitative Field Study Terminology

Explanatory
Contextual Framework
Inductive Reasoning
Field Study
Minimal Interference
Non-contrived
Purposeful Sampling
Data Collection Instruments – Questionnaires, Interviews, Documents, Govt. & Private Reports, Observations

Slovenia

Context

Slovenia has borders with Italy, Austria, Hungary, and Croatia. Whether as an independent nation, a Former Yugoslav Republic (FYR), part of the Kingdom of Serbs, Croats, and Slovenes, or part of the Austrian part of the Habsburg Empire, Slovenia has been Western-oriented and cosmopolitan due to its strategic geographic location and commercial position between the open Adriatic and the Julian Alps. This "Slavic Switzerland" (Feig 2006) is a natural hub at the crossroads of European trade routes. It is a small, clean, and successful nation of about two million highly educated people. Its location has also kept it safe from the strife and destruction of war. Croatia was its buffer zone during the recent breakup of Yugoslavia and the ensuing war with Bosnia-Herzegovina and Serbia. In summary of its atmosphere and feeling, Slovenia has old world grace and beauty with all the standing of a nation transitioning to modern statehood and democracy.

Slovenia's economy is small but well diversified, and the political environment is stable. A change of governments from center left to center right in 2004 has formally changed priorities to increasing privatization and FDI inflows and reducing the already low deficit (about 1.8 percent of GDP) using more fiscal restraint. The major export markets are Germany (22 percent), Italy (13 percent), Croatia (9 percent), and Austria (8 percent), with FYRs comprising about 17 percent of total foreign demand from Slovenia. Concentrations of imports to Slovenia come from Germany (20 percent), Italy (19 percent), Austria (13 percent), and France (8 percent). Large FDI inflows come from Austria (28 percent), Switzerland (17 percent), Netherlands (11 percent), and France (8 percent) (EIU and IMF 2006).

Slovenia is a full member of the European Union (EU) and European Monetary Union (EMU), adopting the Euro at the start of 2007, complete with their own Slovenian Euro coinage. For the small economy, greatly dependent on trade, adopting the Euro is expected to augment growth since using the Euro can serve as a lessening of pricing competition within the EU. Slovenia assumes the presidency of the EU in 2008. The status of the focus countries relative to the EU, EMS, NATO, and other supranational organizations is noted because of the stability that those memberships imply and not because of any favor, promotion, or endorsement of them by the research.

Purpose and Methods of Study

The purpose of this field study is to describe and explain the relationships between country or business risk in Slovenia and FDI inflows using multiple sources. An overall investment picture of Slovenia is created. The process of transition to a market economy has progressed fairly easily and without major hurdles. Slovenia is investor friendly yet seems to be gaining FDI only slowly. Trade unions have opposed the flat tax proposals, and certain large government privatizations have been postponed, bogged down in special interest groups' searches for options to privatizations. These issues are discussed by several of the sources. Other sources touch upon legal, social, and political factors.

The richness of this case is derived from the variety of source types and viewpoints. It is also notable that each source, depending on expertise, emphasizes different aspects of country risk and themes for policy consideration. Issues particular to Slovenia and those about the region in general are compared and contrasted. So the distinctions from each source can be more clearly described, each interview is related in its own paragraphs with a summary and comparison section inserted at the end of the case. (This format is common to each of the field studies.)

Description of the Information Obtained and Sources

This first perspective comes from a member of the governing board of the central bank of Slovenia who is also a professor at the University of Maribor and has been associated with high-level economic and political activities for many years in Slovenia. Country risk has significantly decreased over the past decade, as reflected in Dun and Bradstreet (D&B) ratings and in Fitch ratings of commercial banks. In the Balkan region the entire situation has improved after peace was reached in Bosnia-Herzegovina, but country risk for the region is considerably higher that that for Slovenia alone.

Key themes regarding country and business risk and their effects on FDI in Slovenia over the past decade are: taxation of profits and tax incentives for FDI; level of wages, which lag behind productivity; social benefits, level of personal taxes and contributions; market size as one of the determinants to attract FDI.

Slovenia is a safe country for foreign investors. Its membership in the EU requires public, commercial, and civil law to be harmonized with the EU legal system. Slovenia is also a member of NATO. And Slovenia has adopted the Euro as its currency, eliminating exchange rate and monetary risk.

Relative to other countries in this study's focus group, all except Croatia are members of the EU. That fact in itself gives much reliability to member countries. In this sense, Slovenia is not unique, since Hungary and Czech Republic, for example, also have sound economies. D&B rates Slovenia as the leading country of the Central European region, yet Hungary and Czech Republic have bigger local markets (consumers, labor force, and faster privatization of state owned enterprises).

Following are factors that make Slovenia friendly and inviting to FDI. Slovenia is a parliamentary democracy, member of NATO, EU, IMF, and the UN. So there is no political risk, although there are natural tensions between business owners and unions. Leading political parties are oriented toward entrepreneurship and seek to stimulate both private domestic and foreign investment. Economic characteristics include a relatively high GDP per capita, good infrastructure, skilled labor, good education system and health care, low taxes on profits, and a good geopolitical location. Further, Slovenes understand the languages and cultures of other Balkan nations and with their history and character can act as a bridge or conduit to enter other Balkan markets. Slovenes, on average, also speak English, German, and Italian, rounding out a highly valued package for conducting business and offering quality employees to companies.

Internally, Slovenia has a need to get access to new markets, create new employment opportunities, and increase federal budget income. All these factors make Slovenia friendly as a host country for FDI.

The aspects of Slovenia that may be vulnerable to changes in investor confidence are changes in the tax system (which changes relatively frequently already). There are changing taxation rules on capital gains, interest, and dividends, and discussions of introducing a uniform VAT for all products and services. (This is not likely to be approved.) There are also discussions about changes in personal income taxes.

While FDI is stagnant at the moment, country and business risk is low and the country is well integrated with the EU. Outward investment of Slovenian firms is increasing as the natural part of their internationalization process.

The next set of data comes from a senior US-based commercial banker who has responsibilities for relationships with MNCs operating in South Central Europe. Major themes of the past decade regarding country risk in Slovenia and its effects on FDI include a very low level of FDI, especially compared to its peers in Central Europe. This is due to a protective economy that favors local companies. Also, the tax burden is among the highest among new EU member states, although gradual reduction to 20 percent is expected by 2010. Wages are highest among new EU member states, generating the highest labor costs among its peers. Privatization of major industries (oil/gas, electrical, financial sector) has been only partially conducted with very limited involvement of foreign companies. Large-scale privatization and institutional reforms are still a challenge. A last major theme noted is that FDI outflows totaled USD 55 million during 2006, with more than half of that going to FYR countries where Slovenian companies play an important role.

Riskiness to foreign investors is low. Slovenia is the most advanced country among new EU member states. It has solid growth and low inflation. It is the first among new EU members to fulfill Maastricht criteria and introduce the Euro, effective January 1, 2007. Favorable factors unique to Slovenia are the political and economic stability, good quality workforce, well-developed infrastructure, and low level of corruption. Negative points for foreign investors are the protectionist economy, high level of state involvement in the economy, high taxes, and high labor costs.

Factors that make Slovenia vulnerable to changes in investor confidence include an inward looking political culture, relationships with neighbors (especially Croatia), the high taxes and labor costs, and a lack of political will to tackle international issues and domestic challenges like institutional reforms, large scale privatizations, and pension reform.

Other concepts to consider about country risk, business risk, and the importance of FDI to Slovenia are the improving competitiveness and economic growth the country shows, the need to reform public administration, the need for tax reform, and the need to enhance labor market flexibility.

The following responses are from the director of a financial sector development project focusing on Bosnia-Herzegovina and Central and Southeastern Europe, which is partially funded by the US Agency for International Development.

Major themes about country risk in Slovenia and effects on FDI include the level of state ownership in the economy; Slovenia's GDP compared to old EU member states like Greece, Portugal, and Spain, as well as the eleven other new member states; the relatively small size of the country and economy; the proximity to and familiarity with other Balkan countries and markets.

Political riskiness to foreign investors is regarded as low, and with the adoption of the Euro on January 1, 2007, currency risk is nonexistent. Unique to Slovenia is this low risk and the proximity to and familiarity with other Balkan countries and markets. Possible negative factors are the relatively small size of the country and its economy, and the relatively high wage levels.

Other concepts to consider about country risk, business risk, and the importance of FDI to Slovenia are that Slovenia is a small country in which everyone knows everyone. It is smaller than many of its neighbors that would seem to be competitors for FDI. These factors should be considered when conducting due diligence about the attractiveness of Slovenia versus its peers.

This respondent conducts a survey about companies' disclosures in the English language on corporate governance, environmental policy and social policy. The latest survey is the ninth annual one for Slovenia. In Slovenia, the ten companies surveyed all have an English language website. 94 percent of CEE companies have an English language website. Nine Slovenian companies have disclosure of a corporate governance code in their annual report (PFS Program 2007). This information puts Slovenia high on the list regarding transparency issues.

The next set of answers is from a retired engineer and former secretary of a minor political party. His overall attitude is that if too much FDI comes into Slovenia, Slovenia will lose control over its own economy and become subject to outside influence. There is a fear of losing a national identity. Yet he sees FDI as a solution for many Slovenian companies to grow, especially large infrastructure projects like power plants on the Drava River. Risk is low for foreign investors due to Slovenia's integration into the EU. Existing infrastructure is good and expanding, the workforce is highly educated, and the small towns across the country provide a steady and well-diversified economic base of mining, textiles, banking, and agriculture. Electrical equipment and engine manufacturing industries are large exporters who would welcome FDI to grow and expand.

The biggest business risk to Slovenia is the possibility of weakening Western economies and a slowing of demand that would affect Slovenia's export markets. Slovenia needs to develop policies that attract FDI and lessen its vulnerability to external economic conditions, yet maintain majority control over its assets. From the grassroots level, Slovenia has a strong desire to harmonize with Western economies and welcomes knowledge transfers and FDI.

The next and last interview reflects the ideas of the director of sovereign ratings at a major international credit ratings agency. Overall themes of country and business risk and their effects on FDI in Slovenia are: attractive in terms of location, infrastructure, overall political and business risk, but unattractive in terms of high cost compared to other new EU members, a very small internal market, and generally slow progress in privatization compared to other CEE countries with low levels of FDI.

Therefore, risks are relatively low on all levels – political, social, and regulatory – but there are not too many opportunities due to the reasons named above. Although FDI/GDP at the end of 2004 was less than 20 percent in Slovenia versus 50 percent in Czech Republic and Hungary, indicating opportunity for increased FDI, the slow rate of privatization in Slovenia is the main reason this ratio will likely not increase soon. Nor would an investor favor Slovenia over Croatia, Czech Republic, or Hungary, with similar political, business, and governance risks. Corruption risk is lowest in Slovenia but wages are highest.

One recent shift worth noting is that while traditional FDI flows have been export and efficiency driven, newer FDI flows are becoming market seeking. In Poland, for example, FDI to retail industries has been an important source of productivity growth, resulting in lower prices and higher consumption. Therefore, other services like health, education, and transportation that have traditionally been provided by domestic firms could become more open to FDI in the decade to come.

Personal Assertions and Changes in Naturalistic Generalizations

From a history of self-contained villages to a country of villages going global. This seems to be the overarching theme of Slovenia's emergence into the EU and the world arena. Especially over the past fifteen years, the calm, self confident, cosmopolitan atmosphere of Ljubljana and Slovenia as a whole has evolved toward a more intense effort to preserve its identity yet incorporate itself into a larger political and economic whole.

The Slovenian economy is export oriented (exports comprise nearly 60 percent of GDP (EIU 2006)), so Slovenes know how to deal with outsiders. Alpine conservatism keeps politics stable and predictable. The recent president, Milan Kucan, held the office for ten years, until 2003, and Janez Drnovsek had been prime minister for ten years and then became president. Voters prefer the familiar and the known. From the author's personal knowledge of Slovenia and from family letters and telephone calls from there (including a cousin who is now mayor of Ljubljana), there is an attitude of interest in the world, as long as not too much has to change in the old neighborhood. This is deeply rooted in the character of the Slovene. Progress is welcome, as long as it can be managed and integrated into the current system. As another central bank governor mentions, by giving up control of monetary policy to Frankfurt, vulnerability to disequilibrium increases.

Although Slovenia is in good shape economically, socially, and politically coming into the EU and EMU, there is always a degree of distrust, even fear, of foreign control over any aspect of life. The prime minister himself reflects this in a way when he says that Slovenia will indeed move forward with privatization in banking, telecommunications, and energy, but does not believe Slovenia will be successful by selling everything. If the process [of privatization] stops at this point, he adds, no harm has been done, and the companies will continue to do well (Financial Times 2007).

It is a goal of Slovenia during its tenure of the presidency of the EU to keep the enlargement idea active for the rest of the Balkans. The prime minister mentions in several interviews and press releases that this a first political priority. And with the rest of the Balkans as a major export market for Slovenia and that territory politically fragile, it is a worthy goal for the entire EU to consider.

Closing Notes, Conclusions, and Lessons

A summary of all sources would include the following conclusions: country risk is low to nonexistent; Slovenia is a safe investment for foreigners but the small economy does not allow many opportunities; taxes are high; education and other social services are above average; the workforce is highly skilled and can serve as a bridge to the rest of the Balkans; the geopolitical location is excellent; current FDI is low; there is a protective economy and an inward looking political culture. Most notably, Slovenia is advanced by nearly all standards. With circumstances as they are, it would be profitable for foreign investors to await the right timing to enter Slovenia, especially with the advancing concept of FDI flows becoming market seeking, as FDI begins to replace services that traditionally have been provided by domestic firms.

A summary question for this field study is: Have there been any naturalistic generalizations that have changed due to the input of information since the setting and context of this case? The answer to this question is no, there are no surprises or startling revelations about Slovenia that have surfaced during the study. The statistics point to CA as a common effect on FDI from both studies, yet the cointegration analysis shows all variables highly cointegrated with FDI. This also is a conclusion of a well-diversified and strong economy. Perhaps the researcher is all too familiar with the country and region. But the composite of the research does reinforce all that the statistics and chart sections revealed about this focus country. Or perhaps the whole story is just as predictable as is the country.

Slovakia

Context

Slovakia's people have their roots in the Danube River Basin. The Slavic peoples who settled there in the sixth and seventh centuries B.C.E. were the first to enjoy the Tatra Mountains – really, rolling hills that provide a good setting for small farms and grazing pastures. Traditionally, the Slovak people have been relegated to the peasant class and to agricultural pursuits. Under the Austro-Hungarian Empire, Slovakia was administered by the Hungarian authorities, while the Czech region fell under the Austrian authorities. This kept Slovakia in the poorer and less advanced realm while the Czechs enjoyed a more industrialized nature and an air of importance due to closer contact with Western powers and political circles.

After WWI, the Slovaks joined the Czechs and Ruthenia to form Czechoslovakia and continued their peaceful lifestyle of farming and folklore until WWII, after which Czechoslovakia became a Communist nation under the Soviet Union. The contrast was startling. Before 1938, Czechoslovakia was the eleventh richest country in the world. After that, under German then Soviet control and a nationalized economy, the country became the poorest in Central Europe (Gabb 1992). Under Communism, a modest amount of industrialization occurred. Yet after the fall of Communism in 1989, the emergence of a free Czechoslovakia, and the peaceful separation of the Slovak and Czech Republics in 1993, many cultural traditions are still in place, and a large section of the elderly population is still rural and dependent on agriculture.

Slovakia joined NATO and the EU in 2004. As are the other new EU member states, Slovakia is en route to fuller and more promising roles in the region and in the EU. But Slovakia has a unique national character, comprised of its language, customs, laws, and conventions, and is influenced from centuries past by its Czech, Hungarian, and Austrian rulers, and its deep traditions of physical education, fraternal organizations, and love of freedom. There is a strong sense of history in the current social, political, and economic activity of Slovakia. It is again a new nation, but with so many ancestral ties to folk and farming ways.

The fraternal influence has likely been a basis for much of Slovakia's nationalistic stance. What began centuries ago as neighborly, fraternal, and social organizations for many aspects of life – social and athletic recreating, political groupings, and economic care and benevolent societies – made freedom a priority of the nation and region. However, at times, the system has been used to attempt to twist the country's path into more of a socialist orientation in a modern political sense. After independence in 1993, and as reforms toward a market economy continued, the strain of the sacrifices and long-term objectives have given way to some backsliding. From 1997, Prime Minister Miklos Dzurinda led Slovakia out of isolationism into the EU and NATO, helped attract large amounts of FDI, generated rapid economic growth, and reduced unemployment. In 2006, weary of the discipline of reforms, voters backed the populist promises of Robert Fico, the current prime minister, who has called for reversals in privatization and flat tax rates, and whose social policies seem more xenophobic, increasing fears of minority hostilities and divisions among ethnic Hungarians and gypsies (Schwammenthal 2006).

At this time in particular but also in the composite of its whole contextual history, Slovakian politics is more important to understanding the setting and promise of Slovakia than other countries in this study. Mass physical education and culture has been an important part of Czechoslovakia for hundreds of years. Starting in 1720 when a nobleman donated his estates for education and sport to help poor children, the exercise movement for therapy and fellowship was founded (Jaros 1992). Exercise institutions had been in existence since 1659 but only as amusement or pastime, not for the improvement of physical health or skill. The primary gymnastic and fraternal organization, Sokol, became formalized in 1862 with the purpose of the development of mind, body, and spirit through gymnastic competition and fellowship. The objective was to become a better person and be part of something that allowed everyone to make a worthy contribution to the betterment of the country. (When political ideals instead of gymnastics became a focus of the students in Prague in 1848, several schools disbanded rather than become tainted or diluted from their main objectives.)

So this organization of gaining and maintaining freedom as a people through common ideals of fellowship, health, and physical education is instilled deep in the national character. A caution is that there is the possibility for perversion into a modern type of national socialism in Slovakia more than in other countries where this history does not exist, as evidenced after the WWI peace conferences and the opposition of Father Andrej Hlinka to the Treaty of Trianon, which created Czechoslovakia. This feeling persisted through the interwar period and into the German dominated puppet state presided over by Father Josef Tiso, Hlinka's successor as head of the Slovak People's Party, later, the People's (Catholic) Party. A recent article in *The Economist* (2010) where the Prime Minister is promoting patriotism as a reinforcement of independent could be considered application of this charactertistic.

Purposes and Methods of Study

The purpose of this study of Slovakia is to describe and explain the relationships between country or business risk and FDI inflows. The contrast of the old ethos of collectivism and national feelings (both of the forced Communist variety and the historic cultural traits) with the attempts at transition to a market and capitalistic culture (emphasizing self-responsibility and self-determination) is highlighted. A diversity of sources, including banks, ratings agencies, investment companies, and expert testimonies provide the composite investment picture for Slovakia. The context of classical liberalism features institutions that promote risk-taking and the reward of performance while creating and maintaining individual liberties. Certain traits of capitalism are therefore present in the culture and background of Slovakia, and that voluntary pursuit of private enterprise, which creates an overall betterment of society, is one trait that serves Slovaks well.

Carl Menger (1840-1921), a professor of political economy at the University of Vienna and founder of the Austrian School of economics, published Principles of Economics in 1871 and introduced the concept of marginal analysis. Even more relevant to this study, he viewed economics as a study of purposeful human choice, the relationships between means and ends. Menger explained prices as the outcome of purposeful, voluntary interaction of buyers and sellers, each satisfying his own subjective evaluations of the usefulness of goods and services. This is today called marginal utility. Trade is the result of people deliberately trying to improve their well-being.

The Austrian School promotes market economies, private property, and peaceful international relations, and opposes government solutions to corporate or individual problems (Ludwig von Mises Institute). The Central European economies in transition in this study can find direct application of these principles to their circumstances as they work into the global arena of trade and commerce. This idea is expanded upon in Chapter V.

Description of the Information Obtained and Sources

Slovakia's economy grew at a record rate of nearly ten percent from Q3 2005 to Q3 2006. New production, especially in electrical equipment manufacturing and transportation equipment manufacturing, was largely responsible (BA-CA 2007). FDI only partly covered the current account deficit, totaling 5.8 percent of GDP in 2006. With the halting of privatization, FDI is likely to decrease to 4.2 percent of GDP in 2007 (BA-CA 2007). Political risk in Slovakia is being watched closely by ratings agencies in 2007 due to the shift in power to the political left.

The major export markets of Slovakia are to Germany (26 percent), Czech Republic (14 percent), Austria (7 percent), Italy (6.6 percent), Poland (6.3 percent), and Hungary (5.6 percent). Majority of imports come from Germany (21 percent), Czech Republic (12.7 percent), Russia (10.7 percent), Poland (4.1 percent), and Italy (4.7 percent). FDI inflows come from Korea (31 percent), Germany (30 percent), Czech Republic (8 percent), Switzerland (7.6 percent), Austria (7.5 percent), and The Netherlands (7.2 percent). (The large inflows from Korea resulted from the Hyundai (Kia) plant.)

The Slovak koruna recently experienced a rare event for accession countries to the EU. A revaluation was permitted by the European Commission (EC) in mid-March as an inflation countermeasure and economic growth temper. This move on its own would likely attract further FDI inflows (Zhou 2007).

The first interview source for Slovakia is from a former minister of the government who had responsibility for negotiating bilateral agreements between Slovakia and the EU, NATO, and OECD. There are many more positive trends than negative ones over the past decade. The few negatives include general unawareness of opportunities in Slovakia (partly due to a lack of public relations on Slovakia's side), corruption, and the uncertainty about reversals of the free market reforms of the past nine years by the new leftist prime minister. The key to eliminating nearly all business risk in Slovakia for a foreign investor is to prepare thoroughly, perform due diligence, and seek a serious Slovak partner. Factors most inviting to FDI are the following: stable and increasing GDP growth, low inflation, low labor and other production costs, EU membership, good geographic location close to major Western markets like Germany, near large potential markets to the east like Ukraine and Russia, good transportation infrastructure in western Slovakia, well-educated workforce (although high unemployment), very favorable tax and investment incentives for large investors, attractive wage and training subsidies, and start up cost subsidies.

Vulnerabilities that could affect investor confidence include: the political climate, a brain drain from the country, and social tension. This tension is specifically about employment opportunities, where there is a large market for young (under thirty years old) workers but much more of a closed market for those over forty-five years. So unemployment is mostly affecting skilled and experienced people just before retirement, leading to problems in the social structure and pension areas.

FDI seeks labor and other production cost benefits, and there are parallels with start ups in China, India, and Southeast Asia. Within the Central European region, Slovakia is a prime choice for FDI. Overall infrastructure changes of the past decade are the reason. In Slovakia, versus Poland, Hungary, and Czech Republic, for example, economic growth started later (2003) and under different conditions. Slower FDI inflows and higher unemployment had to do some with political uncertainty and some with internal industrial and agricultural structural problems. The deep and wide changes in entrepreneurship policies (privatization), social policies (education and health), and infrastructure created the exceptionally favorable macroeconomic environment, including low inflation and a stable currency. A key point to realize is that GDP growth in Slovakia is due greatly to intensive or internal factors versus the extensive or external factors, which are responsible for growth in surrounding countries. An example is the flat 19 percent tax, inspiring confidence in investors and savers alike.

The next policy move is to relate the macro environment to the micro, and the summer election of 2006 has stalled this. The people, having lost patience with reforms, voted the country back toward a more socialistic government. Nevertheless, Slovakia is already seeing positive results from transition policies, and with no chance of one political party to have a majority, coalition governance is the way of political life. This is a stabilizing factor. Even with the new left government, an equivalent example might be a move from a Thatcher-type or US Republican party-type to a Blair-type or US Democratic party-type style. All parties see the favorable effects of FDI. Slovakia also receives, as do other EU countries, sizable amounts of EU structural funds, with the key for Slovakia being how these funds are used. If infrastructure is developed and industrial research and development is supported, the economy can continue long-term growth.

Land ownership hurdles for investors have been cleared in a unique way. Historically, all children of a deceased landowner inherit the land in Slovakia, as opposed to German Habsburg law in Czech Republic, where only the oldest son is the inheritor. So if a company wants to buy land in Slovakia, it must deal with many people. But because Slovak developers already own a great deal of land usable for industry, titles are cleaner. Further, legislation is passed in Slovakia that allows the government to force a sale from private owners to the government so it can resell to investors, the government interest of increasing employment being served.

Lastly, this source sees Slovakia as no greater risk compared to other countries in the region. The risk he sees as greater is to the foreign investor who is not familiar or not doing enough research to appraise the real situation. Slovak legislation regarding finance and investor protection is fully harmonized with the

EU. A recent problem Slovakia faces is a tax system so favorable to foreign investors that old EU states (especially Germany) complain that Slovakia is stealing their entrepreneurs.

The next set of answers relating country or business risk to FDI in Slovakia is from an economist and bond fund manager responsible for country risk on all portfolio positions, including Slovak sovereign and some corporate bonds. Slovakia has typically generated interest around its heated politics and sometimes razor-thin governing coalitions. The return of the left to government recently had a depressing effect on foreign confidence at first, but in fact, the new government has kept in place nearly all the reforms enacted by the prior conservative coalition, although it has not built on them further. As such, Slovakia remains a good place to invest. With a lack of modern industry, more technological advancement is needed.

The riskiness of Slovakia has declined over the past ten years. A key point is that the leftist government has not tried to undo the liberalizations made under the rightist coalition. The continuation of policy is reassuring. Problems with the Hungarian minority remain and sometimes spill over into problems with Hungary. FDI into Hungarian-speaking areas may thus be more problematic than in other areas. If conservatives come back into power, this issue may become more important since conservatives have very little political support from that area and might try to steer investment into other areas more in their sphere of support. This is an internal issue.

Unique to Slovakia is that Slovakia had a great deal of smokestack industry when Communism fell, and so has a large and well-trained workforce who know their business in this industry. This is not true for Slovenia or Croatia and only to a lesser extent for Hungary. Leaders know that they need to promote change in order to become competitive with countries that have been functioning as market economies for decades. Looking at a different industry, Slovakia has beautiful vacation areas in the mountains with excellent ski resorts. This is not so in Hungary and only partly so in Croatia and Slovenia.

Factors that most invite FDI to Slovakia and make Slovakia friendly as a host country for FDI are also rooted in history. As the poorer relation of Czechoslovakia (see the Context section of this case), Slovakia made the decision to part ways with Czech Republic though it was not in their economic interest to do so. So the Slovaks are taking the opportunity to show the world what they can do on their own. A personal visit six years ago found great openness among all levels of society, from government officials to shopkeepers. Like all the countries in this study, many people speak German, and in Slovakia they do not mind using it, as opposed to other countries still trying to live down bad experiences from 65 years ago.

Vulnerabilities that might change investor confidence include internal political rivalries and the Hungarian question. But it is clear to the political leaders of all parties that Slovakia needs foreign help to continue to develop and they will do what is necessary to get this help. No changes in tax legislation or zoning laws are foreseen that would work to the disadvantage of foreigners. Mostly foreseen is harmonization with the EU to continue smoothly. Protectionism within the EU could make Slovaks and other accession countries believe they are not so welcome as competitors to existing industry and agriculture. Slovakia, more than any other accession country, knows it needs to change and seems willing to bear the burden of doing so.

The following responses are from an economist with an international financial NGO who is director of the European Department and responsible for country risk assessments. Themes of the past decade include the following ideas. After the Argentine default – the last big international default – country risk is now thought of as longer-term, with less concern about one currency due to the EU and monetary convergence. In fact, there is practically "no country risk" anymore, even for Turkey. The old concept of foreign exchange and foreign debt servicing has given way to more concern of reducing fiscal deficits and government spending as countries transition to market economies and enter the EU and EMS. There is a big compression of external debt spreads. A new financial infrastructure is in place for the accession countries, including Slovakia, as a policy requirement of EMU.

There are relatively low-cost risks in Slovakia, with strong growth and a stronger business environment developed over the past years. Slovakia is friendly to FDI because of the business environment, and German companies have been outsourcing to Central Europe in general, adding stability and diversity to the economic base. Slovakia is a big center for automobile production and is better at managing its fiscal deficit than many other countries in the region. A political hurdle is modernizing its industry without government subsidization. The strong growth rate should be a plus in attempting to do that.

Vulnerabilities include populist politicians (e.g., women have been paid 10,000 Euros to have a baby), helping pensioners with cost of living problems, and the possible reversal of market oriented policies.

A leading educator of free market economics and president of an educational foundation points out as a real concern that Slovakia's nationalistic government is xenophobic and at times seems national socialist in its statements. With the requirement of a certain amount of privatization by the EU, officially, Slovakia has the start of a pro-privatization sector. But the government can own shares in companies, even though there is a percent limit. Another vulnerability this source sees is a possible change in the current flat tax for investors. In the attempt to transition to a market economy, a major philosophical hurdle is that the EU has certain social safety net standards that require minimum government expenditures. This does not seem in step with privatization goals and relieving fiscal burdens associated with national health care, public housing, and social security.

The last source is a commercial banker with a global bank in Slovakia who identifies the main themes regarding business risk and FDI as political stability arising from Slovakia's accession talks, prospects of entering the Eurozone in 2009, two consecutive terms of a rightist government that put many beneficial reforms in place, and the discussions of lower taxes, government involvement in attracting FDI, and cheap, skilled labor. Benefits to Slovakia from its accession to the EU are that it became better known to investors, business and country risk has decreased, and there are better prospects for FDI overall. Rating agencies' credit ratings are cited as further reasons for confidence, constrained only by the country's moderate wealth levels and unclear picture of future economic and fiscal policy.

Unique to Slovakia are the following factors: geographical location in the CEE; cheap labor of high quality; strongest economic growth in the region giving positive and realistic prospects of entering the Eurozone; partially industrialized background; strong FDI presence already – in the auto industry, VW, Peugot, KIA, and their suppliers and sub-suppliers, which creates know-how spillover out of which other investors in this or related sectors can benefit; flat tax regime.

Other concepts considered important about risk and its effects on FDI are that the two successive terms of the rightist government created one of the most reformist economies in the entire EU. Attempts to turn that direction by the new government might be perceived as negative. Also important to the risk and FDI relationship is the idea of finishing the started reforms and avoiding populist decisions.

Personal Assertions and Changes in Naturalistic Generalizations

It may be typical Slovak emotion and rhetoric that caused first a stir, then a calming after the 2006 election of a leftist government. So much good has been done over the past ten years by putting reforms in place that there must have been (so far) some reflection by the leftists about the benefits of the reforms. It has been quiet regarding reversals or a turn in direction from them.

The peaceful land of Slovakia is rich in its history of fellowship and fraternal benevolence, national physical education for all ages, and a desire to help contribute to a larger whole. When the veil of Communism fell and a free Czechoslovakia emerged, the Slovak sector appears to have been less scourged than the Czech counterpart. This is only perhaps because of the more lighthearted approach to life and living, which can be learned through its folklore history. But something in the national spirit caused a resurgence of freedom and determination to regain some standing in the world. By all standards, Slovakia has made great strides in its social, economic, and political systems and moved to the top of the ratings, exceeding in several areas many current EU member states.

Personal connections and understanding of the author lead to an insider optimism about the economy (with a warning on social expenditures), the political frontier (with stability a continued condition due to the glow of past reforms still shining on the current landscape), and the social structure (again with a warning about restarting pension reform and increasing privatization for services like health care and education). Knowing the nature of the Slovak, his desire for political independence, private enterprise, and fraternal fellowship, the process of reform will likely resume before any real damage is done to the deficit or a serious drain put on the robust economy. This is said with historic context and current technical expertise.

Closing Comments, Conclusions, and Lessons

Summarizing all sources turns out to be rather succinct for Slovakia. Country risk is low due to a stable political outlook (even with a new leftist government), superior reforms that are holding although not progressing, an economy that is well-positioned internally to continue its growth without any significant problems, a well-educated workforce poised to resolve its own problems and contribute valuable thinking and resources to the EU and other eastern neighbors.

One surprise result obtained from this overall field research for Slovakia is that the naturalistic generalization from the initial surveys of the general financial, academic, and news press did not match the optimism or accuracy of the expert interview sources. The experts related a truly positive outlook, which is reflected with this "full-flavored" field study comprised of multiple sources and a variety of input. The experts that are interviewed here show with current financial, economic, and political insights that the context that began this study could not fully account for the power of the Slovaks' ability to tap their historic spiritual wells and work toward world standing once again.

The statistical section of the analysis for Slovakia showed the strongest effect on FDI from the XR, but from the cointergration analysis, all variables except CPI cointegrated with FDI. So if the government does make headway with CA deficits and builds a favorable environment for SM growth and encourage a stable XR and LR, the qualitative conclusions will be supported by the statistical result, and vice-versa.

Czech Republic

Context

Czech Republic (or simply, Czech) has the largest economy of the field study countries and ranks twentieth by GDP among the fifty European countries (IMF 2006). Bordering Austria, Germany, Poland, and Slovakia, the Czech Republic is also positioned as a commercial bridge from Western to Eastern Europe. With somewhat of a more hard-nosed attitude toward business than some other countries in the region, the Czechs are likely to modernize their industrial base rapidly and propel themselves as an economic power into the global economic arena. As with their accession peers, the Czech government must create a climate conducive to private enterprise so the characteristics of private property rights and individual responsibility can grow. This same climate will attract investors and allow an accumulation of savings and investment that makes possible technological and economic development.

Following years of Communist rule, the reduction in the huge social safety net to the private sector and the cuts in government spending have created some feeling of resentment about institutional reform. Naturally, when many aspects of life that previously were subsidized now require private money or new choices, people feel some difference to their pocketbooks. Until the government can explain the new path with its long term benefits for all citizens, doubts remain. The biggest short term risk for Czech is that the current government, lacking a majority, will have difficulty continuing reforms due to a coalition rule. These reforms include pension and health care, sticking points in many transition nations. The instability keeps fiscal policy unbalanced and continues large budget deficits despite good economic growth. Entry to the Eurozone has been formally postponed to at least 2011.

Good news about the Czech Republic includes a sharply lower rate of inflation due to a stronger koruna, structural changes in place that increase productivity, and sharply lower food prices in the recent year. Further positive news is increased domestic demand, strong international relations with the United States and others (including Czech participation in both the Afghanistan and Iraqi campaigns), and industrial production that is leading growth and providing for the strong export demand for Czech products. The current account deficit narrowed in 2005, reflecting greatly increased flows of FDI, including government sales of its stake in the telecoms industry and increases in investment to the auto sector. The Czech Republic enacted a flat tax of 15 percent (effective in 2009), a brave move, which by itself is favorable to further FDI inflows. Prime Minister Mirek Topolanek's problems with forming an effective government seem (for the moment) balanced with the large amount of privatization already completed, falling unemployment, and low inflation. Also, the stability that membership in the EU and NATO provides must be considered.

Major export markets are to Germany (36 percent), Slovakia (8.4 percent), Austria (6 percent), Poland (5 percent), UK (4.7 percent), France (4.6 percent), and Italy (4 percent). Major imports come from Germany (31 percent), Slovakia (5.3 percent), China (5.2 percent), Poland (5 percent), France (4.7 percent), Russia (4 percent), and Austria (4 percent) (Czech Ministry of Industry and Trade 2007). Concentrations of FDI inflows during 2006 came from Luxemburg (22 percent), Germany (19 percent), Austria (14 percent), The Netherlands (11 percent), Cyprus (9 percent), UK (9 percent), Slovakia (5 percent), France (4.6 percent), USA (4 percent), Korea (2 percent), and Japan (2 percent) (Czech National Bank 2007).

Purpose and Methods of Study

The purpose of this field study is to describe and explain the relationships between country or business risk in Czech and FDI inflows. Several types of information contribute to this study, including the general and financial press, government, bank, and various agency reports, and a variety of first hand interviews. Government officials, bankers, professors, and international financial institution managers are the experts who contribute to a full composite investment picture for Czech.

Grassroots initiations have started turnarounds in several areas, including energy and finance. An example of ownership, negotiation, and a drive for transparency results in a success story of western training for a Czech-born entrepreneur. A story in the July 11, 2006 Financial Times tells of Zdenek Bakala, who after leaving a career of investment banking, began acquiring coal companies, restructured OKD (the largest coal company in Czech), and is now working with the Polish government to arrange a takeover of two large Polish coal mines in Poland to create a firm that would be listed on both the Prague and London stock exchanges. A key to seeing the hidden value of a company that seemed obscure in an unfashionable industry was his knowledge of the company from his investment banking time. He is pushing for openness in records and financial management. He is improving the company's financial structure, management and trading, and streamlining the operating structure. He is planning potential acquisitions in Russia and Ukraine, but the company already seems primed for listing on two exchanges, one west and one east.

This achievement is a reason for this field study. As markets become even more transparent and government involvement lessens in the economy, the freedom for others to find opportunities and conclude their own successes (as Mr. Bakala did) will increase. This study and the others in this section are building a theory from the ground up, or a Grounded Theory, of the region and the investment setting.

Description of the Information Obtained and Sources

The first interview source for Czech is a corporate banker in Czech who has been on site for five years. Themes of the past decade are: improving country and business risk has attracted FDI; largest FDI per capita in the region; political support to FDI; competition from other countries in the region and parts east with even lower corporate taxes and cheaper labor. Czech has a low level of country risk, and short term political instability has not influenced the appetite of foreign investors.

Unique to Czech is its geographic location in the CEE region, its cheap labor with high quality workforce, and the historic industrial background of the country. Also, previous FDI is bringing new investors from related industries, i.e., other auto investors have followed investment from automobile firms Skoda, VW, and Toyota.

Cultural, political, and economic characteristics that make Czech friendly as a host country for FDI include overall political stability and government support and incentives for FDI; the positive economic development of the country; cheap and skilled labor; good infrastructure; an industrial tradition.

Vulnerabilities to changes in investor confidence at this time are longer-term political instability if it materializes, a change in the flat tax if it occurs, red tape, bureaucracy, and corruption. Other concepts that could affect the relationship between country or business risk and FDI are simplifying the legal framework, creating labor legislation, and enacting further tax reform.

A next input comes from a professor who was present at the start of market reforms, has advised the government in several policy areas, and is currently head of a case-study organization. His general overall opinion is that agreements and contracts are not kept. There seems to be no sense of binding rules. There is still too much old Communist thinking and no initiative at the ordinary working level. A conference that was run a few years ago brought out an attitude that is still distrustful and primarily money-oriented in a negative sense.

The contrast between a city like Brno, which is more countrified and Prague, which seems to contain more "fast operators" is drawn. Throughout much of Czech, understanding of the financial system is low. Naturally, in small countries there are not many huge companies, just smaller ones. So the use of even basic financial mechanisms like letters of credit has not developed. Also, many companies or shops do not use credit cards, and this small financial convenience, common in the West, prevents companies from integrating into the mainstream of western business. Culturally, the propensity to invest in Germany, Czech, and The Netherlands is low because the reputation is thrifty. This also holds for small town businesses and entrepreneurs.

A concept unique to Czech Republic based on its recent history is that before WWII, Czech had a lot of manufacturing and management skills. They knew how to manufacture, and that feeling is still there. Czechs are stable, keeping a low profile until the older generation goes by, and then hoping for a fresh start. This is to say that corruption is decreasing through election choices and continued harmonization with EU policies, and much of Central and Eastern Europe has reached a maturity in their democracies where immunity from justice is no longer the norm for public officials or the average person.

The head of a libertarian think tank and educational foundation who has lectured in Prague feels that country risk is low in Czech. This country has been good at reforms over the past decade and there is a favorable business and service sector, including the Bohemian art class. Czech has a desire to be part of the West and is open to FDI as a way to integrate with the West. Vulnerabilities to changes in investor confidence are: the divided government and that the president is gridlocked on moving legislation through parliament; privatization has halted, signifying that the country can't get closer to a market oriented system, and it is not clear yet where resources will go; there is no way to sever the welfare state – fiscal hurdles like national health care, public housing, and social security create a block to lowering deficits and allowing incentives to private enterprise.

Positively, joining the EU has kept Czech and other countries "safe" and has attracted FDI. The accession countries could not have good access to EU markets without joining, which in the libertarian view is a necessary evil.

A final assessment is from an economist and former portfolio manager of Czech securities, responsible for country risk on all positions. Czech Republic bonds have traded through German government bonds (Czech yields are below German yields) for some time, limiting potential returns. Czech had a well-trained workforce when the wall came down and its technological advancement was among the best in the Comecon. This may have given a false sense of the need to restructure. The proximity of Czech to Germany and Austria and the long historic connection (Prague had the first German-speaking university, ahead of Heidelberg) made it an easy sell for investment in the German and Austrian boardrooms. This despite the fact that a macroeconomic policy favoring full employment over structural adjustments made the change in relative wages and prices to world market standards very slow and hesitating.

Riskiness is low in Czech because of well-advanced adjustments to EU membership. Entry to the Eurozone should be less of a problem than for many other countries seeking entry. But Czech is already starting to lose out to countries farther east (and in Asia) when being considered for FDI where low wages are an important part of the investment. The real danger is that microeconomic adjustment might not be completed so that Czech turns into another EU member seeking subsidies without ever being willing or politically able to restructure. Should this happen, subtle means of unfriendly behavior toward foreigners could easily emerge.

Unique to Czech is that Czech is closer to the German speaking countries of Central Europe both physically and culturally. This provides a level of trust for corporations with limited knowledge of the area. In addition, it is full of historic sites, including Prague itself, that provide great opportunities for the tourism industry. So the sum of most inviting factors to foreign investors are the proximity to the rest of the EU, Czech's cultural compatibility with key markets, and its well-trained workforce.

Vulnerabilities to changes in investor confidence are minor annoyances such as Austria's objections to Czech nuclear plants near its border that could discourage investments in the energy sector. It is also possible that local industrial interests, which are more developed in Czech than in some other former Comecon countries, may work to keep competition out by lobbying the government of the day on technical issues. On the whole, these concerns should not be a major factor in determining further FDI inflows to Czech.

Other considerations about FDI and country risk have to do with other CEE countries and their timing on entering the common currency. As some countries stop to re-evaluate their timing of entry, the EU may want an example to show that convergence is possible and helpful for all concerned. Czech is a good candidate for this role, as its workforce is already relatively well paid and its agricultural sector much smaller than most other accession candidates. For this to work, the Czech government will want to continue to do all that is necessary for its convergence into Europe.

Personal Assertions and Naturalistic Generalizations

For certain internal and external reasons, Czech seems likely to keep moving ahead with EU harmonization and without much effort once the political uncertainty is conquered. This uncertainty seems tempered by the excellent potential of its markets and cultural ties to key economies like Germany and Austria. The lack of reforms into the microeconomy is countered with the advanced adjustments to EU membership. Relatively high wages are blunted by a 15 percent flat tax. Therefore, the setting and prospects are bright for the Czech economy and continued FDI.

The realistic Czechs will work through their internal uncertainty and create the environment for modernizing without the government overly subsidizing. The government is still the most important player in the Czech and other accession states, and this is, unfortunately, a good setting for corruption.

No strong assertions have surfaced that would be contrary to the context set out at the beginning of this country study. Economic potential is large, reminding one of an athlete waiting to compete in his event. The political environment is forcing a marking of time, with the athlete slowly getting out of shape, losing tone, as the start of the contest is continuously postponed. So the rules have been learned, the path made clear, the training done with relish, and now there is a lull. If that lull lasts too long, FDI will seek a more favorable, productive location. Czech is all primed, with many advantages and a focus on industry, its main event, and needs to hear the starting gun from the politicians reaching consensus on continuing reforms toward market practices, streamlining legal and labor issues, and promoting the spirit of entrepreneurship within the economy.

Closing Comments, Conclusions, and Lessons

Continuing the analogy of the athlete ready to run his race, the best conclusion in this case must be to start the contest and let the athlete do that for which he was trained. Being close to a situation often hides the forest for the trees, and perhaps an outside view from a friend would prompt a closing of ranks by the political parties in Czech, open the floodgates, and allow the economic waterfall of resources to flood through the system.

An all source summary would number the following statements among key points about the Czech Republic. The country has been successful in attracting FDI with government support and by its overall excellent economic performance. The economy has harmonized well with EU requirements and has put into place adjustments that matter greatly to outside markets, but lack in the domestic wage and price department. As evidenced in the statistical sections, CA and LR have strongest effects on FDI from both analyses. CPI cointegrated with FDI fairly significantly. Therefore, the recommendation for attracting even more FDI is to focus on these three domestic financial variables as tools of influence.

Fiscal fitness has begun with a flat tax, and now spending reductions are needed quickly in the social sectors. Reverting to reforms and reinvigorating the political scene with an urgency and freshness reminiscent of Vaclav Havel and the radical thinking that began the new era of freedom can resolve this. Although the objective is often clear, the means often confound, especially as a movement matures and must make longer-term policy decisions that are not as emotional as political revolution.

Field Studies Summary

All three of these countries are worth considering as destinations for FDI. All have low country or business risk, high quality workforces, and demonstrate stability as members of the EU and NATO. All also have a need to continue the process of privatization. After these factors, there are some differences, and the choice of where to invest likely depends on the investor's comfort level with the refinements in culture, size of economy, and political climate.

Tupy (2006) offers insights into the problem of corruption in the region, which he says has not been addressed. The move back to populist parties and socialism is a result of several factors. These include: the pervasiveness of corruption due to ineffective restraints on the political class; a lack of rule of law; too large a role by the state in the economy; the Communist involvement in business and politics; rigged privatization deals which undermine the moral values inherent in capitalism. People in Central Europe continue to believe that free markets are superior to socialism. Therefore, the move of political power to the left is explained by public discouragement with corruption in politics and business. Depken, LaFountain, and Butters (2006) discuss the effects of corruption on sovereign credit ratings and a country's creditworthiness. Their model shows that a one standard deviation decrease in corruption improves sovereign credit rating by almost a full category.

Tupy (2006) also states that the EU's burdensome regulatory structure, required social safety net spending, and its protective trade policies make it difficult to improve CA and budget sectors. Berger, Kopits, and Szekely (2007) show how fiscal performance of the Central European countries has deteriorated in recent years, in contrast to improvement in the Baltics. Conflict between the political economy of the accession process and the Maastricht guidelines might explain some digression from those criteria if a country has some healthier fiscal position. Aristovnik (2006) explains that current account deficits can be sustained if inflows of FDI are maintained, at least in the medium term. A new group of liberal leaders who can take a moral stand, reduce the role of government, visibly reduce corruption, and maintain foreign investor interest is the hope of these countries.

Slovakia is the more nationalistic, with its deep history of folkways and physical education as a means to fraternal benevolence and helping their own countrymen. This feeling is alive in the current thinking. Slovenia is more inward looking politically and protective of its small economy, which offers fewer FDI opportunities because of that small size. Yet Slovenia has already adopted the Euro and seems the most predictable. Czech Republic is the largest economy with more opportunities, more open to new ideas and FDI, and has been the most successful in attracting FDI. The micro economy poses bigger risks in Slovakia and Czech Republic in that reforms are not seeping down to that level. Macroeconomic reforms in these two countries are advanced, in place, and awaiting continuation. Tax is a last key issue, with Slovenia at the highest rate, Slovakia at a 19 percent flat tax, and Czech at a 15 percent flat tax.

The bottom line in the field studies is that a foreign investor must be comfortable with a host country's environment. Research and due diligence are primary for success in any of these countries. All these countries provide a fertile ground for foreign investment. If the investor can adapt better to uncertain politics, there is one setting. If there is an opportunity in a specialty industry in a small economy, there is another setting. That is the reality of these emerging economies in transition – that one place does not fit all but that all can certainly fit in some place.

Summary Comparison of Analyses

All three levels of analysis build to the conclusions reached in this work. Statistics lend support to the majority of the hypotheses. The chart analysis section introduces country risk into the overall picture and verifies much of the statistical results. And the qualitative field studies corroborate the other two methods while incorporating factors such as geography, legal and banking systems, social structure, and stages of economic development into the analysis.

This whole work is a history of developing markets finance in Central Europe with applications to present circumstances. The examination of the components of interest rates allows an investigation of the most sensitive aspects of macro financial sectors that affect FDI flows to the region. Further studies can include comparisons of interest rate spreads to discern which countries are controlling inflation, improving interest rate competitiveness, or how CA balances compare. Tax rates also have some effect where firms locate their activities and their profits. Nominal tax rates on corporate income in the EU average 26 percent versus nearly 40 percent in North America (Walker 2007). Slovakia, Poland, and Hungary all have tax rates under 20 percent (Walker 2007). Tax rates and FDI are other areas where much current research is being done, yet further research could include an analysis of the variables in this study combined with tax rates. More suggestions for further research are offered in Chapter V.

Chapter V
Summary and Conclusions

Introduction

"The pursuit of commerce reconciles nations, calms wars, strengthens peace, and commutes the private good of individuals into the common benefit of all." Hugh of Saint Victor (1096-1141) wrote this in his *Didascalicon* (c. 1127), which was innovative in adding to the medieval curriculum of study the "mechanical" arts, including commerce. At his time in history, a commercial revolution was crossing Europe and linking it with the rest of the world (Acton Institute 2007).

The basis for this analysis in international finance was laid by Hugh's philosophy and the development of the natural law tradition of Saint Thomas Aquinas and those who followed. Money is simply an advanced concept of a commodity, and the investment in foreign nations of both financial and direct assets has led to this dissertation at this time. The concepts of FDI, commercial, legal, banking, and social factors, and trading mechanisms such as securities, deposits, and forward agreements have been honed since the Middle Ages and brought to bear on this work.

Overview

Central Europe is a region transitioning from centrally planned to market economies. This region is in a unique position to test the effectiveness of market-oriented policies, which are the opposite of the policies of the past fifty years. Ideas like flat tax rates, low government involvement in the economy, and an emphasis on private enterprise as economic drivers seem made to order for this part of the world at this time.

The vibrancy and potential of these economies in transition provide turmoil and opportunity. Some politics are becoming more volatile. Citizens are becoming impatient with the trickle down theory of economic improvement for all, and in some cases, with the move to EU accession. (See the Field Studies for details on this subject.) Free trade policies sometimes seem as if they are becoming managed trade policies (Ebeling 2004). Yet FDI is increasing in much of the region from a variety of sources. Although there is much to settle in both the political and economic arenas, in addition to balancing internal social safety demands with budget deficit demands, volatility seems to be occurring within narrower parameters, as evidenced by the convergence of several of this study's variables even as they continue to fluctuate.

With all the inefficiencies left from central planning with which these countries began the newly independent era, the exceptional growth rates of the past fifteen years might not be surprising. Market reforms have resulted in improved managerial techniques, industry restructuring, and a great resource reallocation. From this point, Schadler, Mody, et al. (2006) are interested in determining if the past fifteen years of growth was unusual and due to initial post transitional effects in a favorable period or a scenario that will foster even further growth.

Contributions of This Research

The primary contributions of this research are twofold. One, the fresh look at the focus countries with current data and statistical methodology gives previous research a large measure of support in the correlations and provides new insights into cointegration of the variables. Two, the qualitative studies highlight original and primary sources resulting in the conclusions reached and ideas presented. Qualitative methodology has not been used in major international finance research up to now, and using it here may make the results of the research more accessible to those who know case and field study methodology but do not know international finance. Likewise, researchers who know the field of international finance may glean a new insight into variables that affect foreign investment from a qualitative point of view.

A wide yet still focused view of three field studies is presented here. One benefit of qualitative research is that the larger picture with a broader range of issues can be incorporated into the research. There is latitude to cover settings and contexts like legal, social, and political aspects of international finance and markets.

Limitations of This Research

A larger time span of transition would increase the credibility of these results. This is to say that updating this study in four to six years will be a worthwhile endeavor. With more time series, more and varied statistics can be run. In the qualitative area, opinions and input from the next group of leaders and workers can be gathered and used to confirm or adjust the results in this study.

Suggestions for Further Research

Already noted is the idea of using spreads, or differentials, of the interest rate components in this study to make cross-country comparisons. Also useful would be applying the current methodology to the next wave of potential accession countries to the EU to determine policy adjustments that would increase their chances of accession. A survey of conditions would likely be needed to assess the timing and readiness, and the qualitative methods used to create the field studies could be replicated if a researcher had access to qualified expert sources.

Another aspect of research that could build on this work's qualitative analysis would be a study done using the Austrian approach to the problem of variables affecting FDI. Austrian concepts fit well with developments in emerging market nations, considering the constant state of flux and adjustments to the countries' own internal economic conditions plus the conforming pressures to external global trade and commercial standards. Austrian economics employs the concepts of logic, human choice and action, and competition. It has an emphasis on entrepreneurship, the market process, and the contribution of business to society.

The thought process of this branch of economics could be used as a template for further refinements in recommendations to policymakers. It shows that economics is not about amassing data, but is about identifying universal facts (such as unlimited wants and scarce resources), applying them to circumstances and conditions (such as markets in transition), and obtaining results (such as an array of subjective ranking of preferences) (Ludwig von Mises Institute 2005).

Eugen von Boehm-Bawerk (1884) demonstrated in his "Positive Theory of Capital" that capital is not homogenous but an intricate and diverse structure with a time dimension, and that a growing economy is not just a consequence of increased capital investment but also of longer and longer processes of production (Ludwig von Mises Institute 2005). These factors could be the lens in a useful, innovative research extension about capital and FDI.

Recommendations to Policymakers

Recommendations to policymakers resulting from this study include an increased and continued application of free market policies in all areas – economic, social, legal, financial, and political. The numbers in the statistical analysis and the composite results of the field studies point toward increased satisfaction and stability of all sectors examined as openness, privatization, and free movement of resources are allowed. Specifically, by focusing on and improving the condition of the variables in this study that most affect FDI, namely the exchange rate, the current account, the stock market, and the long-term lending rate, policymakers could most benefit their countries' economies.

Vaclav Klaus, President of Czech Republic, notes the dissent within the EU about ratifying the EU Constitution (Lloyd 2006). One size does not fit all, even among developed Western economies like France and The Netherlands, which held referendums about ratification. The new accession countries naturally value the benefits of membership that the EU offers, particularly increased economic stability, which leads to further FDI inflows.

FDI is necessary for many countries' continued economic growth and continued freedom, allowing them to follow their own paths to independence. The USA is tremendously dependent on foreign capital to finance its domestic and international growth. No matter how advanced an economy, or perhaps the *more* advanced an economy, the more important foreign trade and investment are to that economy in bringing it to the next level of advancement. Revisiting the thought of Hugh of Saint Victor, trade and commerce are the best proven solutions to peaceful economic growth and advancement.

A further recommendation to policymakers is to investigate the school of Austrian economics and its applicability to economies in transition. Politicians and policymakers should consider Austrian concepts and methods as a long-term philosophy with long-term benefits to the nation and society. See the section of Suggestions for Further Research for more explanation on this economic school of thought.

Conclusion

A practical reason to promote a more stable financial environment in these transition economies is to attract financial flows to help fund the many required activities and programs of accession to EU membership. A further reason to promote a more stable financial environment in these countries is to improve standards of living and quality of life. Therefore, the study of relationships among country risk, investor expectations, and financial variables as defined in this book directly helps the focus countries improve liquidity and transparency of markets and the overall move toward freer, more independent, and more democratic societies. With transparency come less corruption, improved laws, and an even better view to determining policy.

The increased need for capital in the emerging economies in this study can only come from investors outside the region at this time. Using and improving domestic markets is important for long term benefits, yet current needs must come from FDI, other financial inflows, syndicated loans, and flexible financing mechanisms. So there is the need for foreign investors to view these countries as secure destinations for investments. Access to varied capital markets also allows the nations to acquire or sell foreign assets as the need arises, thereby increasing stability. And with the increased use of local and regional markets, participants in those markets, fiscal and monetary authorities, and foreign policymakers will all benefit from the increased information provided by the markets.

Changes in growth rates, relationships, needs, market dynamics, and demographics all demand ongoing research to monitor the economic picture and provide policymakers with updated information. The transition economies are key players now in the global circular flow of resources and products, and will increase in importance in the decades to come.

Appendices

Appendix A

Questions Used as a Basis for Interviews[1]

The purpose of this case study is to describe and understand relationships between country or business risk in the focus country and Foreign Direct Investment (FDI). This research is part of a study in international finance and will produce policy papers and journal articles at a later time. This study seeks your opinions and comments to create a case for use in the classroom as well as partially satisfy requirements for a book on the topic.

Answers to the questions need not be extensive. All answers, information, and opinions are important so that a general investment picture can be created for the focus country. The process of transition to a market economy means things continue to change. This case study may be able to be used as a model to predict what other countries may encounter as they move toward freer markets as your country is doing.

Definitions

Country risk – a level of risk to investments in the focus country based on economic, political, social, legal, or general business conditions.

Foreign Direct Investment (FDI) – investments in buildings, companies, factories, mines, or land by non-citizens.

[1] Note: the same questions were used for the field studies on Slovenia, Slovakia, and the Czech Republic.

Questions

- What is your primary function at this time? For example, are you a professor, businessman, government official. . .
- What is your experience over the past decade in business, education, research, or government with country risk or business risk in the focus country or the region?
- What themes have you detected over the past decade or so regarding country or business risk and its effect on Foreign Direct Investment (FDI) in the focus country?
- At this time, how do you view the riskiness of the focus country to foreign investors? What evidence supports your view?
- What is unique to the focus country in this area? That is, why would an investor favor your country over Croatia or Slovenia or Hungary?[2]
- What cultural, political, or economic characteristics do you feel most invite FDI to your country? What factors make your country friendly as a host country for FDI?
- What aspects of your country seem vulnerable to changes in investor confidence?
- What other concepts do you consider important about country risk, business risk, or the importance of FDI to your country as it continues to harmonize with the EU and other Western economies?

---

[2] Country names were changed as the focus country changed.

Appendix B

Raw Data Distributions – Tests

Croatia:

Date: 11/27/06 Time: 11:55

Sample (adjusted): 1997Q2 2006Q1

Included observations: 36 after adjustments

Trend assumption: Linear deterministic trend
Series: CRFDI CRCUAC CREXRDOL CRSM LOG(CRCPI) CRLR

Lags interval (in first differences): 1 to 1

Unrestricted Cointegration Rank Test (Trace)

Hypothesized No. of CE(s)	Eigenvalue	Trace Statistic	0.05 Critical Value	Prob.**
None *	0.832937	127.2457	95.75366	0.0001
At most 1	0.484820	62.82788	69.81889	0.1590
At most 2	0.416143	38.95126	47.85613	0.2622
At most 3	0.363419	19.57970	29.79707	0.4518
At most 4	0.084812	3.320499	15.49471	0.9505
At most 5	0.003604	0.129989	3.841466	0.7184

Trace test indicates 1 cointegrating eqn(s) at the 0.05 level

* denotes rejection of the hypothesis at the 0.05 level

**MacKinnon-Haug-Michelis (1999) p-values

Unrestricted Cointegration Rank Test (Maximum Eigenvalue)

Hypothesized No. of CE(s)	Eigenvalue	Max-Eigen Statistic	0.05 Critical Value	Prob.**
None *	0.832937	64.41779	40.07757	0.0000
At most 1	0.484820	23.87663	33.87687	0.4646
At most 2	0.416143	19.37156	27.58434	0.3863
At most 3	0.363419	16.25920	21.13162	0.2101
At most 4	0.084812	3.190510	14.26460	0.9332

At most 5	0.003604	0.129989	3.841466	0.7184

Max-eigenvalue test indicates 1 cointegrating eqn(s) at the 0.05 level
* denotes rejection of the hypothesis at the 0.05 level
**MacKinnon-Haug-Michelis (1999) p-values

Unrestricted Cointegrating Coefficients (normalized by b'*S11*b=I):

CRFDI	CRCUAC	CREXRDOL	CRSM	LOG(CRCPI)	CRLR
-0.001678	-0.001626	0.262334	-0.000274	1.431573	0.076169
0.002289	2.13E-06	0.023901	-7.05E-05	-15.66644	-0.096031
0.006190	-0.000392	-0.099626	0.000613	-12.63256	-0.456111
-0.002710	-0.000195	-1.031720	-0.002339	-9.675842	-0.922536
-0.001283	-7.13E-05	1.384779	0.002793	-7.880072	0.020452
-0.000877	-0.000135	0.011493	0.004201	-15.37977	-0.165230

Unrestricted Adjustment Coefficients (alpha):

D(CRFDI)	29.58142	-56.79457	-118.9694	99.54629	0.817048	0.969309
D(CRCUAC)	1183.479	-85.60215	351.4894	-169.0821	-58.61223	8.474552
D(CREXRDOL)	0.024857	0.110677	-0.041471	-0.008050	-0.077825	0.000864
D(CRSM)	-33.94687	-49.43048	9.246518	23.95525	-18.39844	3.126516
D(LOG(CRCPI))	-0.003420	0.004122	0.000628	0.001493	-0.000127	0.000339
D(CRLR)	-0.284407	0.029568	0.391184	0.485528	-0.014554	-0.023729

1 Cointegrating Equation(s): Log likelihood -693.4819

Normalized cointegrating coefficients (standard error in parentheses)

CRFDI	CRCUAC	CREXRDOL	CRSM	LOG(CRCPI)	CRLR
1.000000	0.968758	-156.3384	0.163425	-853.1487	-45.39313
	(0.08497)	(88.2540)	(0.28173)	(1353.61)	(52.8146)

Adjustment coefficients (standard error in parentheses)

D(CRFDI)	-0.049637
	(0.08292)
D(CRCUAC)	-1.985862
	(0.27131)
D(CREXRDOL)	-4.17E-05
	(0.00010)
D(CRSM)	0.056962
	(0.03720)
D(LOG(CRCPI))	5.74E-06

	(2.8E-06)
D(CRLR)	0.000477
	(0.00035)

2 Cointegrating Equation(s):	Log likelihood	-681.5436

Normalized cointegrating coefficients (standard error in parentheses)

CRFDI	CRCUAC	CREXRDOL	CRSM	LOG(CRCPI)	CRLR
1.000000	0.000000	10.60139	-0.030983	-6849.450	-41.94676
		(148.338)	(0.47572)	(2246.65)	(88.1757)
0.000000	1.000000	-172.3236	0.200678	6189.682	-3.557518
		(177.997)	(0.57083)	(2695.85)	(105.806)

Adjustment coefficients (standard error in parentheses)

D(CRFDI)	-0.179650	-0.048208
	(0.13691)	(0.07841)
D(CRCUAC)	-2.181821	-1.924002
	(0.45662)	(0.26152)
D(CREXRDOL)	0.000212	-4.02E-05
	(0.00016)	(9.2E-05)
D(CRSM)	-0.056193	0.055077
	(0.05706)	(0.03268)
D(LOG(CRCPI))	1.52E-05	5.57E-06
	(4.1E-06)	(2.4E-06)
D(CRLR)	0.000545	0.000462
	(0.00059)	(0.00034)

3 Cointegrating Equation(s):	Log likelihood	-671.8578

Normalized cointegrating coefficients (standard error in parentheses)

CRFDI	CRCUAC	CREXRDOL	CRSM	LOG(CRCPI)	CRLR
1.000000	0.000000	0.000000	0.009263	-5383.485	-50.95507
			(0.26085)	(1594.60)	(50.4231)
0.000000	1.000000	0.000000	-0.453524	-17639.30	142.8708
			(1.59251)	(9734.97)	(307.832)
0.000000	0.000000	1.000000	-0.003796	-138.2804	0.849729
			(0.01121)	(68.5297)	(2.16699)

Adjustment coefficients (standard error in parentheses)

D(CRFDI)	-0.916117	-0.001556	18.25525
	(0.29063)	(0.07136)	(12.0191)

D(CRCUAC)	-0.005967	-2.061831	273.4029
	(0.99784)	(0.24502)	(41.2658)
D(CREXRDOL)	-4.51E-05	-2.39E-05	0.013298
	(0.00038)	(9.3E-05)	(0.01573)
D(CRSM)	0.001047	0.051452	-11.00806
	(0.13638)	(0.03349)	(5.64010)
D(LOG(CRCPI))	1.91E-05	5.32E-06	-0.000861
	(9.9E-06)	(2.4E-06)	(0.00041)
D(CRLR)	0.002966	0.000309	-0.112875
	(0.00131)	(0.00032)	(0.05426)

4 Cointegrating Equation(s):	Log likelihood	-663.7282

Normalized cointegrating coefficients (standard error in parentheses)

CRFDI	CRCUAC	CREXRDOL	CRSM	LOG(CRCPI)	CRLR
1.000000	0.000000	0.000000	0.000000	-5633.251	-51.18389
				(1347.25)	(51.8026)
0.000000	1.000000	0.000000	0.000000	-5411.024	154.0734
				(3555.93)	(136.728)
0.000000	0.000000	1.000000	0.000000	-35.92010	0.943503
				(18.3812)	(0.70677)
0.000000	0.000000	0.000000	1.000000	26962.77	24.70110
				(9646.82)	(370.927)

Adjustment coefficients (standard error in parentheses)

D(CRFDI)	-1.185885	-0.020968	-84.44864	-0.309888
	(0.28077)	(0.06449)	(40.9679)	(0.09325)
D(CRCUAC)	0.452241	-2.028860	447.8482	0.292524
	(1.04810)	(0.24074)	(152.932)	(0.34810)
D(CREXRDOL)	-2.33E-05	-2.23E-05	0.021603	-2.12E-05
	(0.00041)	(9.4E-05)	(0.05971)	(0.00014)
D(CRSM)	-0.063872	0.046780	-35.72317	-0.037557
	(0.14298)	(0.03284)	(20.8634)	(0.04749)
D(LOG(CRCPI))	1.50E-05	5.03E-06	-0.002401	-2.46E-06
	(1.0E-05)	(2.4E-06)	(0.00153)	(3.5E-06)
D(CRLR)	0.001651	0.000214	-0.613804	-0.000820
	(0.00124)	(0.00029)	(0.18117)	(0.00041)

5 Cointegrating Equation(s):	Log likelihood	-662.1330

Normalized cointegrating coefficients (standard error in parentheses)

CRFDI	CRCUAC	CREXRDOL	CRSM	LOG(CRCPI)	CRLR
1.000000	0.000000	0.000000	0.000000	0.000000	142.2351
					(49.2986)
0.000000	1.000000	0.000000	0.000000	0.000000	339.8622
					(88.7731)
0.000000	0.000000	1.000000	0.000000	0.000000	2.176828
					(0.48887)
0.000000	0.000000	0.000000	1.000000	0.000000	-901.0720
					(274.828)
0.000000	0.000000	0.000000	0.000000	1.000000	0.034335
					(0.00863)

Adjustment coefficients (standard error in parentheses)

D(CRFDI)	-1.186933	-0.021026	-83.31721	-0.307606	1465.373
	(0.28504)	(0.06455)	(67.0240)	(0.14192)	(908.749)
D(CRCUAC)	0.527463	-2.024679	366.6832	0.128824	692.9858
	(1.06085)	(0.24023)	(249.449)	(0.52820)	(3382.16)
D(CREXRDOL)	7.66E-05	-1.68E-05	-0.086167	-0.000239	-0.483300
	(0.00040)	(9.1E-05)	(0.09424)	(0.00020)	(1.27777)
D(CRSM)	-0.040259	0.048092	-61.20095	-0.088943	522.1889
	(0.14284)	(0.03235)	(33.5865)	(0.07112)	(455.385)
D(LOG(CRCPI))	1.52E-05	5.04E-06	-0.002577	-2.81E-06	-0.090847
	(1.1E-05)	(2.4E-06)	(0.00250)	(5.3E-06)	(0.03384)
D(CRLR)	0.001669	0.000215	-0.633958	-0.000860	-10.39524
	(0.00126)	(0.00029)	(0.29636)	(0.00063)	(4.01817)

Vector Autoregression Estimates
Date: 11/27/06 Time: 11:57
Sample (adjusted): 1997Q4 2006Q1
Included observations: 34 after adjustments
Standard errors in ( ) & t-statistics in [ ]

	CRFDI	CRCUAC	CREXRDOL	CRSM	LOG(CRCPI)	CRLR
CRFDI(-1)	0.262066	-0.097088	0.000896	0.126861	-4.30E-06	0.001187
	(0.32911)	(0.47001)	(0.00039)	(0.18324)	(8.2E-06)	(0.00150)
	[0.79628]	[-0.20657]	[2.27057]	[0.69231]	[-0.52422]	[0.79361]
CRFDI(-2)	-0.275203	-0.021453	-0.000477	-0.135197	6.14E-06	0.000416
	(0.36660)	(0.52354)	(0.00044)	(0.20411)	(9.1E-06)	(0.00167)
	[-0.75069]	[-0.04098]	[-1.08661]	[-0.66236]	[0.67138]	[0.24983]
CRFDI(-3)	-0.216583	0.567847	0.000823	0.190495	1.04E-05	-0.000813

	(0.38716)	(0.55290)	(0.00046)	(0.21556)	(9.7E-06)	(0.00176)
	[-0.55942]	[1.02704]	[1.77336]	[0.88372]	[1.07960]	[-0.46198]
CRFDI(-4)	-0.452288	0.067537	-0.000595	-0.030271	1.24E-05	-0.001008
	(0.31528)	(0.45025)	(0.00038)	(0.17554)	(7.9E-06)	(0.00143)
	[-1.43456]	[0.15000]	[-1.57446]	[-0.17244]	[1.57310]	[-0.70346]
CRCUAC(-1)	0.213767	-0.992145	0.000435	0.015039	-8.49E-06	0.000229
	(0.24780)	(0.35389)	(0.00030)	(0.13797)	(6.2E-06)	(0.00113)
	[0.86265]	[-2.80358]	[1.46604]	[0.10900]	[-1.37377]	[0.20287]
CRCUAC(-2)	0.069930	-1.029657	0.000296	0.036784	-5.42E-06	0.000413
	(0.27299)	(0.38986)	(0.00033)	(0.15199)	(6.8E-06)	(0.00124)
	[0.25616]	[-2.64112]	[0.90364]	[0.24201]	[-0.79600]	[0.33272]
CRCUAC(-3)	0.210598	-0.986643	0.000627	0.044160	-9.12E-06	0.000287
	(0.27006)	(0.38568)	(0.00032)	(0.15036)	(6.7E-06)	(0.00123)
	[0.77981]	[-2.55822]	[1.93550]	[0.29369]	[-1.35438]	[0.23415]
CRCUAC(-4)	0.092582	0.058837	0.000407	0.022012	-7.99E-06	0.000131
	(0.31656)	(0.45207)	(0.00038)	(0.17625)	(7.9E-06)	(0.00144)
	[0.29247]	[0.13015]	[1.07211]	[0.12489]	[-1.01191]	[0.09082]
CREXRDOL(-1)	-68.30871	328.6205	0.666776	162.8999	0.002761	0.514183
	(212.862)	(303.986)	(0.25513)	(118.516)	(0.00531)	(0.96755)
	[-0.32091]	[1.08104]	[2.61344]	[1.37449]	[0.52043]	[0.53143]
CREXRDOL(-2)	-80.55711	319.2980	0.132302	-147.6413	-0.006880	-1.451017
	(218.548)	(312.106)	(0.26195)	(121.682)	(0.00545)	(0.99339)
	[-0.36860]	[1.02304]	[0.50507]	[-1.21334]	[-1.26295]	[-1.46067]
CREXRDOL(-3)	156.1968	-22.35730	0.137854	63.67691	0.013926	-0.450844
	(245.819)	(351.053)	(0.29464)	(136.866)	(0.00613)	(1.11735)
	[0.63541]	[-0.06369]	[0.46788]	[0.46525]	[2.27254]	[-0.40349]
CREXRDOL(-4)	-134.6890	-299.0296	-0.174949	-171.5564	-0.005311	0.572635
	(169.659)	(242.288)	(0.20335)	(94.4617)	(0.00423)	(0.77117)
	[-0.79388]	[-1.23419]	[-0.86033]	[-1.81615]	[-1.25587]	[0.74255]
CRSM(-1)	-1.245063	1.271051	0.000418	0.699591	5.07E-05	-0.000407
	(0.72536)	(1.03588)	(0.00087)	(0.40386)	(1.8E-05)	(0.00330)
	[-1.71648]	[1.22703]	[0.48047]	[1.73226]	[2.80375]	[-0.12333]
CRSM(-2)	1.226375	-1.843385	0.000257	0.481241	-1.91E-05	-0.000885

	(0.77540)	(1.10734)	(0.00093)	(0.43172)	(1.9E-05)	(0.00352)
	[1.58161]	[-1.66470]	[0.27700]	[1.11470]	[-0.98995]	[-0.25108]
CRSM(-3)	-0.129844	-1.559104	-0.001611	-0.588430	-2.82E-05	-0.000204
	(1.10857)	(1.58314)	(0.00133)	(0.61722)	(2.8E-05)	(0.00504)
	[-0.11713]	[-0.98482]	[-1.21276]	[-0 95335]	[-1.02104]	[-0.04040]
CRSM(-4)	-0.111463	1.005178	0.001580	0.373590	-4.50E-07	0.001806
	(0.62690)	(0.89527)	(0.00075)	(0.34904)	(1.6E-05)	(0.00285)
	[-0.17780]	[1.12276]	[2.10298]	[1.07033]	[-0.02881]	[0.63384]
LOG(CRCPI (-1))	6312.226	-3386.364	4.691262	-6409.587	0.570560	-1.051919
	(7408.47)	(10580.0)	(8.87971)	(4124.86)	(0.18468)	(33.6746)
	[0.85203]	[-0.32007]	[0.52831]	[-1.55389]	[3.08950]	[-0.03124]
LOG(CRCPI (-2))	-7548.555	9567.975	-7.805847	859.6933	-0.027340	-25.97382
	(9904.36)	(14144.4)	(11.8713)	(5514.51)	(0.24689)	(45.0195)
	[-0.76214]	[0.67645]	[-0.65754]	[0.15590]	[-0.11073]	[-0.57695]
LOG(CRCPI (-3))	-3034.208	11042.80	17.41745	5548.089	0.533764	9.998457
	(10068.1)	(14378.2)	(12.0675)	(5605.68)	(0.25098)	(45.7638)
	[-0.30137]	[0.76802]	[1.44333]	[0.98973]	[2.12675]	[0.21848]
LOG(CRCPI (-4))	7555.549	-17416.95	-15.54447	-175.5792	-0.198917	-3.610003
	(8029.55)	(11466.9)	(9.62413)	(4470.66)	(0.20016)	(36.4977)
	[0.94097]	[-1.51888]	[-1.61516]	[-0.03927]	[-0.99379]	[-0.09891]
CRLR(-1)	19.29029	-41.87131	-0.145557	-54.73718	-0.001239	0.296199
	(70.2553)	(100.331)	(0.08421)	(39.1164)	(0.00175)	(0.31934)
	[0.27457]	[-0.41733]	[-1.72856]	[-1.39934]	[-0.70724]	[0.92754]
CRLR(-2)	-75.99120	64.92155	0.077313	10.47282	-2.53E-05	0.305729
	(73.3957)	(104.816)	(0.08797)	(40.8650)	(0.00183)	(0.33361)
	[-1.03536]	[0.61939]	[0.87885]	[0.25628]	[-0.01382]	[0.91641]
CRLR(-3)	77.44742	-1.062962	0.160355	13.61038	-0.000617	-0.267833
	(72.6547)	(103.758)	(0.08708)	(40.4524)	(0.00181)	(0.33025)
	[1.06597]	[-0.01024]	[1.84140]	[0.33645]	[-0.34057]	[-0.81101]
CRLR(-4)	-3.524911	-110.0071	-0.051073	-30.52654	0.002658	-0.374543
	(81.0359)	(115.727)	(0.09713)	(45.1188)	(0.00202)	(0.36834)
	[-0.04350]	[-0.95058]	[-0.52582]	[-0.67658]	[1.31576]	[-1.01683]

C	-13377.55	-1121.359	6.579720	2438.596	0.509044	114.7332
	(10870.1)	(15523.6)	(13.0288)	(6052.23)	(0.27097)	(49.4093)
	[-1.23067]	[-0.07224]	[0.50501]	[0.40293]	[1.87860]	[2.32209]
R-squared	0.688124	0.975585	0.971558	0.970927	0.998144	0.912104
Adj. R-squared	-0.143544	0.910478	0.895712	0.893398	0.993196	0.677715
Sum sq. resids	603144.8	1230085.	0.866487	186974.4	0.000375	12.46148
S.E. equation	258.8747	369.6973	0.310284	144.1351	0.006453	1.176694
F-statistic	0.827402	14.98439	12.80965	12.52343	201.7205	3.891407
Log likelihood	-214.5643	-226.6799	14.14046	-194.6541	145.8195	-31.18069
Akaike AIC	14.09202	14.80470	0.638796	12.92083	-7.107030	3.304747
Schwarz SC	15.21434	15.92702	1.761120	14.04316	-5.984706	4.427071
Mean dependent	337.4014	-481.9369	7.030865	1140.347	4.644425	12.45289
S.D. dependent	242.0823	1235.611	0.960821	441.4554	0.078235	2.072733

Determinant resid covariance (dof adj.)	78455774
Determinant resid covariance	26990.22
Log likelihood	-462.9184
Akaike information criterion	36.05402
Schwarz criterion	42.78797

Czech Republic:

Vector Autoregression Estimates
Date: 11/27/06 Time: 11:08
Sample (adjusted): 1996Q1 2005Q4
Included observations: 40 after adjustments
Standard errors in ( ) & t-statistics in [ ]

	CZFDI	CZCUAC	CZEXRDOL	CZSM	LOG(CZCPI)	CZLR
CZFDI(-1)	-0.520678	0.059387	0.000954	-0.005057	3.75E-06	-3.44E-05
	(0.25184)	(0.08041)	(0.00054)	(0.01423)	(1.8E-06)	(0.00013)
	[-2.06747]	[0.73852]	[1.76517]	[-0.35538]	[2.04453]	[-0.26469]
CZFDI(-2)	0.146591	0.065565	-0.000614	-0.001336	-2.02E-06	0.000275
	(0.20554)	(0.06563)	(0.00044)	(0.01161)	(1.5E-06)	(0.00011)
	[0.71320]	[0.99903]	[-1.39301]	[-0.11503]	[-1.34859]	[2.58649]

CZFDI(-3)	0.117436	0.314416	0.000584	0.012852	2.35E-07	2.37E-05
	(0.28023)	(0.08948)	(0.00060)	(0.01583)	(2.0E-06)	(0.00014)
	[0.41906]	[3.51385]	[0.97096]	[0.81169]	[0.11519]	[0.16345]
CZFDI(-4)	-0.111818	-0.179753	0.000114	-0.018218	-3.58E-06	-1.94E-05
	(0.27530)	(0.08790)	(0.00059)	(0.01555)	(2.0E-06)	(0.00014)
	[-0.40617]	[-2.04489]	[0.19221]	[-1.17122]	[-1.78711]	[-0.13658]
CZCUAC(-1)	0.553425	-0.041017	-0.002679	0.006607	-4.80E-06	-9.66E-05
	(0.64433)	(0.20574)	(0.00138)	(0.03641)	(4.7E-06)	(0.00033)
	[0.85891]	[-0.19937]	[-1.93740]	[0.18149]	[-1.02183]	[-0.29032]
CZCUAC(-2)	0.168816	0.255686	0.001136	0.038473	5.57E-06	-0.000796
	(0.52818)	(0.16865)	(0.00113)	(0.02984)	(3.8E-06)	(0.00027)
	[0.31962]	[1.51610]	[1.00252]	[1.28922]	[1.44739]	[-2.91974]
CZCUAC(-3)	-1.181065	-0.405645	-0.001115	-0.021488	-1.67E-07	-0.000580
	(0.58276)	(0.18608)	(0.00125)	(0.03293)	(4.2E-06)	(0.00030)
	[-2.02668]	[-2.18001]	[-0.89160]	[-0.65261]	[-0.03932]	[-1.92755]
CZCUAC(-4)	-1.272407	0.666970	0.002316	-0.021286	1.46E-05	-0.000624
	(0.70323)	(0.22454)	(0.00151)	(0.03973)	(5.1E-06)	(0.00036)
	[-1.80938]	[2.97036]	[1.53498]	[-0.53572]	[2.84503]	[-1.71722]
CZEXRDOL(-1)	-175.9990	71.03517	0.988579	-0.546322	0.003152	-0.042912
	(124.081)	(39.6192)	(0.26625)	(7.01066)	(0.00090)	(0.06408)
	[-1.41842]	[1.79295]	[3.71295]	[-0.07793]	[3.48709]	[-0.66961]
CZEXRDOL(-2)	154.7352	-14.40024	-0.276198	-9.696311	-0.001974	0.116228
	(139.274)	(44.4702)	(0.29885)	(7.86905)	(0.00101)	(0.07193)
	[1.11102]	[-0.32382]	[-0.92420]	[-1.23221]	[-1.94530]	[1.61584]
CZEXRDOL(-3)	215.1911	76.44306	0.580166	6.921131	0.001508	-0.011234
	(148.449)	(47.4000)	(0.31854)	(8.38748)	(0.00108)	(0.07667)
	[1.44959]	[1.61272]	[1.82133]	[0.82517]	[1.39462]	[-0.14653]
CZEXRDOL(-4)	222.2897	-86.40454	-0.396065	-10.32573	-0.003473	0.009028
	(149.091)	(47.6048)	(0.31992)	(8.42372)	(0.00109)	(0.07700)
	[1.49097]	[-1.81504]	[-1.23802]	[-1.22579]	[-3.19790]	[0.11725]

CZSM(-1)	6.936441	3.942855	-0.008521	0.916693	1.71E-05	0.000330
	(3.91496)	(1.25005)	(0.00840)	(0.22120)	(2.9E-05)	(0.00202)
	[1.77178]	[3.15416]	[-1.01427]	[4.14423]	[0.60118]	[0.16315]
CZSM(-2)	3.924094	-4.368768	-0.001178	-0.057646	-4.41E-05	-0.001864
	(5.71565)	(1.82501)	(0.01226)	(0.32294)	(4.2E-05)	(0.00295)
	[0.68655]	[-2.39383]	[-0.09607]	[-0.17851]	[-1.05808]	[-0.63140]
CZSM(-3)	-2.472188	-0.341769	0.009809	-0.101476	6.74E-06	0.000434
	(5.71758)	(1.82563)	(0.01227)	(0.32305)	(4.2E-05)	(0.00295)
	[-0.43238]	[-0.18721]	[0.79954]	[-0.31412]	[0.16186]	[0.14707]
CZSM(-4)	-3.628591	1.737737	0.007260	0.143989	2.55E-05	0.000187
	(4.46607)	(1.42602)	(0.00958)	(0.25234)	(3.3E-05)	(0.00231)
	[-0.81248]	[1.21859]	[0.75753]	[0.57063]	[0.78351]	[0.08124]
LOG(CZCPI(-1))	1416.809	8157.709	19.96290	-732.3360	0.895281	7.475839
	(23558.5)	(7522.24)	(50.5515)	(1331.07)	(0.17162)	(12.1672)
	[0.06014]	[1.08448]	[0.39490]	[-0.55019]	[5.21655]	[0.61442]
LOG(CZCPI(-2))	-39135.24	-17588.09	-69.43691	543.1217	-0.291582	10.11547
	(28431.6)	(9078.23)	(61.0081)	(1606.40)	(0.20712)	(14.6840)
	[-1.37647]	[-1.93739]	[-1.13816]	[0.33810]	[-1.40776]	[0.68888]
LOG(CZCPI(-3))	2752.419	4812.318	7.613170	1410.225	0.009114	-14.89058
	(25544.7)	(8156.45)	(54.8135)	(1443.29)	(0.18609)	(13.1930)
	[0.10775]	[0.59000]	[0.13889]	[0.97709]	[0.04898]	[-1.12867]
LOG(CZCPI(-4))	26361.25	8266.404	42.28134	-1177.843	0.417751	-11.53408
	(21401.7)	(6833.57)	(45.9234)	(1209.21)	(0.15591)	(11.0533)
	[1.23174]	[1.20968]	[0.92069]	[-0.97406]	[2.67942]	[-1.04350]
CZLR(-1)	-550.3707	233.3963	-0.325095	-32.94628	0.014532	0.227628
	(452.966)	(144.633)	(0.97197)	(25.5929)	(0.00330)	(0.23394)
	[-1.21504]	[1.61372]	[-0.33447]	[-1.28732]	[4.40397]	[0.97301]
CZLR(-2)	-182.5751	8.283216	0.631671	15.28636	-0.007326	0.155065
	(471.693)	(150.612)	(1.01215)	(26.6510)	(0.00344)	(0.24361)
	[-0.38706]	[0.05500]	[0.62409]	[0.57358]	[-2.13192]	[0.63652]

CZLR(-3)	1050.456	97.85327	-0.600445	0.791723	0.006165	0.308743
	(498.814)	(159.272)	(1.07035)	(28.1833)	(0.00363)	(0.25762)
	[2.10591]	[0.61438]	[-0.56098]	[0.02809]	[1.69650]	[1.19844]
CZLR(-4)	-199.7200	-74.89129	0.804757	-0.211757	-0.010619	0.001507
	(395.384)	(126.247)	(0.84841)	(22.3395)	(0.00288)	(0.20420)
	[-0.50513]	[-0.59321]	[0.94855]	[-0.00948]	[-3.68682]	[0.00738]
C	22782.10	-21709.26	-7.858930	478.6435	-0.101356	38.45252
	(23294.2)	(7437.85)	(49.9843)	(1316.14)	(0.16970)	(12.0307)
	[0.97802]	[-2.91875]	[-0.15723]	[0.36367]	[-0.59727]	[3.19619]

R-squared	0.768984	0.908559	0.946676	0.988828	0.998666	0.990847
Adj. R-squared	0.399358	0.762253	0.861358	0.970952	0.996532	0.976201
Sum sq. resids	11772105	1200203.	54.20347	37580.36	0.000625	3.140094
S.E. equation	885.8933	282.8666	1.900938	50.05354	0.006454	0.457536
F-statistic	2.080440	6.210010	11.09581	55.31619	467.9916	67.65617
Log likelihood	-308.6048	-262.9400	-62.83485	-193.6647	164.5830	-5.865004
Akaike AIC	16.68024	14.39700	4.391742	10.93323	-6.979148	1.543250
Schwarz SC	17.73579	15.45255	5.447292	11.98878	-5.923598	2.598800
Mean dependent	1245.778	-930.2825	31.02800	625.0108	4.594119	8.608158
S.D. dependent	1143.072	580.1290	5.105287	293.6797	0.109595	2.965852

Determinant resid covariance (dof adj.)	1.72E+09
Determinant resid covariance	4783778.
Log likelihood	-648.1601
Akaike information criterion	39.90800
Schwarz criterion	46.24130

Date: 11/27/06 Time: 11:15

Sample (adjusted): 1995Q3 2005Q4

Included observations: 42 after adjustments

Trend assumption: Linear deterministic trend

Series: CZFDI CZCUAC CZEXRDOL CZSM LOG(CZCPI) CZLR

Lags interval (in first differences): 1 to 1

Unrestricted Cointegration Rank Test (Trace)

Hypothesized No. of CE(s)	Eigenvalue	Trace Statistic	0.05 Critical Value	Prob.**
None *	0.625559	118.2721	95.75366	0.0006
At most 1 *	0.498800	77.01466	69.81889	0.0119
At most 2 *	0.453120	48.00316	47.85613	0.0484
At most 3	0.287400	22.65506	29.79707	0.2634
At most 4	0.173887	8.423999	15.49471	0.4212
At most 5	0.009502	0.401006	3.841466	0.5266

Trace test indicates 3 cointegrating eqn(s) at the 0.05 level
* denotes rejection of the hypothesis at the 0.05 level
**MacKinnon-Haug-Michelis (1999) p-values

Unrestricted Cointegration Rank Test (Maximum Eigenvalue)

Hypothesized No. of CE(s)	Eigenvalue	Max-Eigen Statistic	0.05 Critical Value	Prob.**
None *	0.625559	41.25747	40.07757	0.0366
At most 1	0.498800	29.01150	33.87687	0.1707
At most 2	0.453120	25.34809	27.58434	0.0941
At most 3	0.287400	14.23107	21.13162	0.3464
At most 4	0.173887	8.022993	14.26460	0.3764
At most 5	0.009502	0.401006	3.841466	0.5266

Max-eigenvalue test indicates 1 cointegrating eqn(s) at the 0.05 level
* denotes rejection of the hypothesis at the 0.05 level
**MacKinnon-Haug-Michelis (1999) p-values

Unrestricted Cointegrating Coefficients (normalized by b'*S11*b=I):

CZFDI	CZCUAC	CZEXRDOL	CZSM	LOG(CZCPI)	CZLR
-0.000548	0.001884	-0.283029	-8.43E-05	4.058667	-0.321287
0.001324	-0.002236	-0.046164	-0.002544	-1.703120	-0.065805
0.000537	0.001687	-0.129760	-0.004736	12.64023	0.186067
0.000728	-0.000116	-0.120704	-0.000594	0.078048	0.363533
-0.000417	-0.000835	-0.037068	0.000416	14.38984	0.551581
1.76E-06	0.000662	0.216020	0.007441	-3.101953	0.091384

Unrestricted Adjustment Coefficients (alpha):

D(CZFDI)	232.0857	-524.8061	-228.2619	-323.7579	164.4714	2.130359
D(CZCUAC)	-242.2870	42.85771	-115.9795	-17.83022	131.3904	8.401490
D(CZEXRDOL)	-0.118254	0.190934	-0.551607	0.494434	-0.035106	0.123920
D(CZSM)	32.67426	9.631820	-6.308539	4.617194	8.736360	-1.324937
D(LOG(CZCPI))	-0.004132	-0.002696	-0.003118	0.002547	0.000154	-0.000168
D(CZLR)	-0.009400	0.160796	-0.203759	-0.119383	-0.100534	-0.016185

1 Cointegrating Equation(s): Log likelihood -846.1192

Normalized cointegrating coefficients (standard error in parentheses)

CZFDI	CZCUAC	CZEXRDOL	CZSM	LOG(CZCPI)	CZLR
1.000000	-3.440458	516.8462	0.153863	-7411.640	586.7117
	(0.76339)	(97.2008)	(2.04324)	(4794.10)	(183.016)

Adjustment coefficients (standard error in parentheses)

D(CZFDI)	-0.127092
	(0.10374)
D(CZCUAC)	0.132678
	(0.03943)
D(CZEXRDOL)	6.48E-05
	(0.00017)
D(CZSM)	-0.017893
	(0.00377)
D(LOG(CZCPI))	2.26E-06
	(8.0E-07)
D(CZLR)	5.15E-06
	(5.0E-05)

2 Cointegrating Equation(s): Log likelihood -831.6134

Normalized cointegrating coefficients (standard error in parentheses)

CZFDI	CZCUAC	CZEXRDOL	CZSM	LOG(CZCPI)	CZLR
1.000000	0.000000	-566.3180	-3.919329	4615.039	-662.7359
		(127.067)	(2.88416)	(5627.54)	(257.687)
0.000000	1.000000	-314.8314	-1.183910	3495.663	-363.1632
		(57.6766)	(1.30914)	(3008.28)	(116.966)

Adjustment coefficients (standard error in parentheses)

D(CZFDI)	-0.822156	1.610581

	(0.23890)	(0.48736)
D(CZCUAC)	0.189440	-0.552292
	(0.10267)	(0.20945)
D(CZEXRDOL)	0.000318	-0.000650
	(0.00044)	(0.00090)
D(CZSM)	-0.005136	0.040025
	(0.00958)	(0.01954)
D(LOG(CZCPI))	-1.31E-06	-1.76E-05
	(2.0E-06)	(4.0E-06)
D(CZLR)	0.000218	-0.000377
	(0.00012)	(0.00025)

3 Cointegrating Equation(s): Log likelihood -818.9394

Normalized cointegrating coefficients (standard error in parentheses)

CZFDI	CZCUAC	CZEXRDOL	CZSM	LOG(CZCPI)	CZLR
1.000000	0.000000	0.000000	-4.429761	8040.122	264.1818
			(1.00506)	(2852.01)	(124.365)
0.000000	1.000000	0.000000	-1.467672	5399.758	152.1353
			(0.58312)	(1654.70)	(72.1548)
0.000000	0.000000	1.000000	-0.000901	6.047985	1.636744
			(0.00412)	(11.6846)	(0.50952)

Adjustment coefficients (standard error in parentheses)

D(CZFDI)	-0.944649	1.225460	-11.84055
	(0.24796)	(0.54695)	(51.0007)
D(CZCUAC)	0.127201	-0.747972	81.64513
	(0.10532)	(0.23231)	(21.6619)
D(CZEXRDOL)	2.16E-05	-0.001580	0.096231
	(0.00045)	(0.00098)	(0.09170)
D(CZSM)	-0.008521	0.029381	-8.873802
	(0.01009)	(0.02226)	(2.07538)
D(LOG(CZCPI))	-2.98E-06	-7.02E-06	0.001699
	(1.9E-06)	(4.3E-06)	(0.00040)
D(CZLR)	0.000109	-0.000721	0.021677
	(0.00012)	(0.00027)	(0.02482)

4 Cointegrating Equation(s): Log likelihood -811.8239

Normalized cointegrating coefficients (standard error in parentheses)

CZFDI	CZCUAC	CZEXRDOL	CZSM	LOG(CZCPI)	CZLR
1.000000	0.000000	0.000000	0.000000	-280.2070	992.1906

				(8804.85)	(395.053)
0.000000	1.000000	0.000000	0.000000	2643.059	393.3399
				(3333.79)	(149.579)
0.000000	0.000000	1.000000	0.000000	4.355062	1.784871
				(11.7209)	(0.52589)
0.000000	0.000000	0.000000	1.000000	-1878.280	164.3449
				(2056.54)	(92.2720)

Adjustment coefficients (standard error in parentheses)

D(CZFDI)	-1.180336	1.263113	27.23844	2.588875
	(0.25796)	(0.51414)	(51.3150)	(0.82347)
D(CZCUAC)	0.114222	-0.745898	83.79732	0.471303
	(0.11651)	(0.23222)	(23.1771)	(0.37193)
D(CZEXRDOL)	0.000382	-0.001638	0.036551	0.001843
	(0.00047)	(0.00094)	(0.09396)	(0.00151)
D(CZSM)	-0.005160	0.028844	-9.431117	-0.000117
	(0.01109)	(0.02211)	(2.20666)	(0.03541)
D(LOG(CZCPI))	-1.13E-06	-7.32E-06	0.001391	2.05E-05
	(2.0E-06)	(4.0E-06)	(0.00040)	(6.5E-06)
D(CZLR)	2.19E-05	-0.000707	0.036087	0.000628
	(0.00013)	(0.00026)	(0.02567)	(0.00041)

5 Cointegrating Equation(s): Log likelihood -807.8124

Normalized cointegrating coefficients (standard error in parentheses)

CZFDI	CZCUAC	CZEXRDOL	CZSM	LOG(CZCPI)	CZLR
1.000000	0.000000	0.000000	0.000000	0.000000	1012.961
					(232.446)
0.000000	1.000000	0.000000	0.000000	0.000000	197.4181
					(68.8791)
0.000000	0.000000	1.000000	0.000000	0.000000	1.462044
					(0.28879)
0.000000	0.000000	0.000000	1.000000	0.000000	303.5760
					(70.9657)
0.000000	0.000000	0.000000	0.000000	1.000000	0.074127
					(0.01275)

Adjustment coefficients (standard error in parentheses)

D(CZFDI)	-1.248916	1.125829	21.14187	2.657282	1291.931
	(0.26106)	(0.52043)	(50.7302)	(0.81159)	(2939.70)
D(CZCUAC)	0.059435	-0.855569	78.92698	0.525951	-633.0671
	(0.11336)	(0.22599)	(22.0290)	(0.35242)	(1276.53)
D(CZEXRDOL)	0.000396	-0.001609	0.037852	0.001829	-8.244159

	(0.00049)	(0.00097)	(0.09451)	(0.00151)	(5.47650)
D(CZSM)	-0.008803	0.021552	-9.754954	0.003517	162.5436
	(0.01112)	(0.02217)	(2.16102)	(0.03457)	(125.227)
D(LOG(CZCPI))	-1.19E-06	-7.44E-06	0.001385	2.05E-05	-0.049180
	(2.1E-06)	(4.2E-06)	(0.00040)	(6.5E-06)	(0.02345)
D(CZLR)	6.38E-05	-0.000623	0.039814	0.000586	-4.343560
	(0.00013)	(0.00026)	(0.02516)	(0.00040)	(1.45772)

Hungary:

Date: 11/27/06 Time: 11:24
Sample (adjusted): 1995Q3 2006Q1
Included observations: 43 after adjustments
Trend assumption: Linear deterministic trend
Series: HFDI HCUAC HEXRDOL HSM LOG(HCPI)
HLR
Lags interval (in first differences): 1 to 1

Unrestricted Cointegration Rank Test (Trace)

Hypothesized No. of CE(s)	Eigenvalue	Trace Statistic	0.05 Critical Value	Prob.**
None *	0.682974	125.0657	95.75366	0.0001
At most 1 *	0.567764	75.66853	69.81889	0.0158
At most 2	0.343534	39.60086	47.85613	0.2371
At most 3	0.268170	21.50284	29.79707	0.3270
At most 4	0.169080	8.077958	15.49471	0.4571
At most 5	0.002634	0.113420	3.841466	0.7363

Trace test indicates 2 cointegrating eqn(s) at the 0.05 level
* denotes rejection of the hypothesis at the 0.05 level
**MacKinnon-Haug-Michelis (1999) p-values

Unrestricted Cointegration Rank Test (Maximum Eigenvalue)

Hypothesized No. of CE(s)	Eigenvalue	Max-Eigen Statistic	0.05 Critical Value	Prob.**
None *	0.682974	49.39715	40.07757	0.0034
At most 1 *	0.567764	36.06767	33.87687	0.0269
At most 2	0.343534	18.09801	27.58434	0.4870
At most 3	0.268170	13.42488	21.13162	0.4139
At most 4	0.169080	7.964537	14.26460	0.3823
At most 5	0.002634	0.113420	3.841466	0.7363

Max-eigenvalue test indicates 2 cointegrating eqn(s) at the 0.05 level
* denotes rejection of the hypothesis at the 0.05 level
**MacKinnon-Haug-Michelis (1999) p-values

Unrestricted Cointegrating Coefficients (normalized by b'*S11*b=I):

HFDI	HCUAC	HEXRDOL	HSM	LOG(HCPI)	HLR
-0.002155	0.000383	0.010957	0.000448	13.09030	0.180067
-0.001288	0.000917	-0.022596	4.43E-05	-1.684009	-0.204610
-0.000514	0.002054	0.023010	0.000206	-24.57363	0.351795
-0.000703	-0.002823	0.016091	-0.000291	58.99273	-0.530244
0.001022	0.001211	-0.031599	-0.000105	71.45645	-0.853928
-0.001473	-0.000718	-0.014749	-0.000273	1.596577	-0.104612

Unrestricted Adjustment Coefficients (alpha):

D(HFDI)	515.9696	238.6463	-79.40399	-8.759859	-112.0206	-9.192703
D(HCUAC)	72.29325	-59.73257	-21.51938	121.5217	-30.92642	7.184563
D(HEXRDOL)	4.822190	-2.085169	0.545678	-2.906061	0.175991	0.347571
D(HSM)	-376.6007	73.39631	-561.8545	-210.7107	-69.43965	15.44276
D(LOG(HCPI))	-0.001398	0.004746	0.002016	-0.001229	-0.001697	0.000122
D(HLR)	0.002408	0.532047	-0.030194	0.070604	0.129456	0.001707

1 Cointegrating Equation(s):	Log likelihood	-1058.519

Normalized cointegrating coefficients (standard error in parentheses)

HFDI	HCUAC	HEXRDOL	HSM	LOG(HCPI)	HLR
1.000000	-0.177691	-5.083535	-0.207936	-6073.288	-83.54247
	(0.20702)	(2.70205)	(0.03280)	(5164.36)	(57.9924)

Adjustment coefficients (standard error in parentheses)

D(HFDI)	-1.112116
	(0.21518)
D(HCUAC)	-0.155820
	(0.10953)
D(HEXRDOL)	-0.010394
	(0.00359)
D(HSM)	0.811721
	(0.41201)
D(LOG(HCPI))	3.01E-06
	(3.3E-06)

D(HLR)	-5.19E-06
	(0.00029)

2 Cointegrating Equation(s):	Log likelihood	-1040.486

Normalized cointegrating coefficients (standard error in parentheses)

HFDI	HCUAC	HEXRDOL	HSM	LOG(HCPI)	HLR
1.000000	0.000000	-12.61536	-0.265731	-8530.556	-164.2329
		(4.00318)	(0.03671)	(7321.82)	(83.9090)
0.000000	1.000000	-42.38725	-0.325256	-13828.89	-454.1056
		(11.7307)	(0.10758)	(21455.5)	(245.883)

Adjustment coefficients (standard error in parentheses)

D(HFDI)	-1.419588	0.416343
	(0.22931)	(0.09071)
D(HCUAC)	-0.078861	-0.027060
	(0.12506)	(0.04947)
D(HEXRDOL)	-0.007707	-6.43E-05
	(0.00408)	(0.00161)
D(HSM)	0.717157	-0.076965
	(0.47899)	(0.18948)
D(LOG(HCPI))	-3.10E-06	3.81E-06
	(3.2E-06)	(1.3E-06)
D(HLR)	-0.000691	0.000489
	(0.00025)	(9.7E-05)

3 Cointegrating Equation(s):	Log likelihood	-1031.436

Normalized cointegrating coefficients (standard error in parentheses)

HFDI	HCUAC	HEXRDOL	HSM	LOG(HCPI)	HLR
1.000000	0.000000	0.000000	-0.175963	-8598.145	-18.07962
			(0.02145)	(4827.27)	(44.1473)
0.000000	1.000000	0.000000	-0.023640	-14055.99	36.96518
			(0.03926)	(8836.08)	(80.8096)
0.000000	0.000000	1.000000	0.007116	-5.357689	11.58534
			(0.00177)	(399.281)	(3.65159)

Adjustment coefficients (standard error in parentheses)

D(HFDI)	-1.378766	0.253249	-1.566065
	(0.23153)	(0.20609)	(3.07656)
D(HCUAC)	-0.067798	-0.071260	1.646687
	(0.12731)	(0.11332)	(1.69174)

D(HEXRDOL)	-0.007988	0.001057	0.112509
	(0.00416)	(0.00370)	(0.05528)
D(HSM)	1.006006	-1.230999	-18.71299
	(0.42402)	(0.37743)	(5.63438)
D(LOG(HCPI))	-4.14E-06	7.96E-06	-7.62E-05
	(3.2E-06)	(2.8E-06)	(4.2E-05)
D(HLR)	-0.000675	0.000427	-0.012691
	(0.00025)	(0.00022)	(0.00334)

4 Cointegrating Equation(s):	Log likelihood	-1024.724

Normalized cointegrating coefficients (standard error in parentheses)

HFDI	HCUAC	HEXRDOL	HSM	LOG(HCPI)	HLR
1.000000	0.000000	0.000000	0.000000	-12541.51	166.5545
				(9305.62)	(84.0451)
0.000000	1.000000	0.000000	0.000000	-14585.78	61.77054
				(7807.92)	(70.5184)
0.000000	0.000000	1.000000	0.000000	154.1067	4.118989
				(530.375)	(4.79017)
0.000000	0.000000	0.000000	1.000000	-22410.17	1049.276
				(60036.7)	(542.231)

Adjustment coefficients (standard error in parentheses)

D(HFDI)	-1.372605	0.277980	-1.707018	0.228023
	(0.24005)	(0.32783)	(3.40215)	(0.05185)
D(HCUAC)	-0.153264	-0.414340	3.602076	-0.009991
	(0.12020)	(0.16415)	(1.70354)	(0.02596)
D(HEXRDOL)	-0.005944	0.009261	0.065748	0.003026
	(0.00411)	(0.00562)	(0.05828)	(0.00089)
D(HSM)	1.154200	-0.636121	-22.10351	-0.219828
	(0.42938)	(0.58639)	(6.08535)	(0.09274)
D(LOG(HCPI))	-3.27E-06	1.14E-05	-9.60E-05	3.55E-07
	(3.3E-06)	(4.5E-06)	(4.6E-05)	(7.0E-07)
D(HLR)	-0.000725	0.000227	-0.011554	-2.11E-06
	(0.00026)	(0.00035)	(0.00366)	(5.6E-05)

5 Cointegrating Equation(s):	Log likelihood	-1020.742

Normalized cointegrating coefficients (standard error in parentheses)

HFDI	HCUAC	HEXRDOL	HSM	LOG(HCPI)	HLR
1.000000	0.000000	0.000000	0.000000	0.000000	63.43780
					(16.7476)

0.000000	1.000000	0.000000	0.000000	0.000000	-58.15415
					(16.6177)
0.000000	0.000000	1.000000	0.000000	0.000000	5.386059
					(0.93484)
0.000000	0.000000	0.000000	1.000000	0.000000	865.0193
					(107.106)
0.000000	0.000000	0.000000	0.000000	1.000000	-0.008222
					(0.00059)

Adjustment coefficients (standard error in parentheses)

D(HFDI)	-1.487131	0.142318	1.832690	0.239767	-217.8038
	(0.25148)	(0.33792)	(4.34192)	(0.05154)	(8545.48)
D(HCUAC)	-0.184882	-0.451793	4.579311	-0.006750	6534.744
	(0.12792)	(0.17189)	(2.20862)	(0.02622)	(4346.85)
D(HEXRDOL)	-0.005764	0.009474	0.060187	0.003007	-105.6347
	(0.00440)	(0.00592)	(0.07605)	(0.00090)	(149.675)
D(HSM)	1.083207	-0.720216	-19.90930	-0.212551	-8638.924
	(0.45883)	(0.61653)	(7.92185)	(0.09403)	(15591.2)
D(LOG(HCPI))	-5.01E-06	9.37E-06	-4.24E-05	5.33E-07	-0.269596
	(3.4E-06)	(4.6E-06)	(5.9E-05)	(7.0E-07)	(0.11538)
D(HLR)	-0.000592	0.000384	-0.015645	-1.57E-05	13.29311
	(0.00027)	(0.00036)	(0.00466)	(5.5E-05)	(9.17034)

Vector Autoregression Estimates
Date: 11/27/06 Time: 11:26
Sample (adjusted): 1996Q1 2006Q1
Included observations: 41 after adjustments
Standard errors in ( ) & t-statistics in [ ]

	HFDI	HCUAC	HEXRDOL	HSM	LOG(HCPI)	HLR
HFDI(-1)	0.424345	0.325479	-0.010017	0.905201	-1.22E-06	-0.000461
	(0.31677)	(0.16883)	(0.00679)	(0.70225)	(5.4E-06)	(0.00042)
	[1.33962]	[1.92786]	[-1.47523]	[1.28900]	[-0.22629]	[-1.08520]
HFDI(-2)	0.050794	0.111761	-0.007864	0.526671	-5.77E-07	-0.000322
	(0.29381)	(0.15660)	(0.00630)	(0.65137)	(5.0E-06)	(0.00039)
	[0.17288]	[0.71368]	[-1.24863]	[0.80856]	[-0.11554]	[-0.81774]
HFDI(-3)	0.240116	0.114196	-0.010093	0.222317	5.75E-07	-2.38E-05
	(0.26870)	(0.14321)	(0.00576)	(0.59569)	(4.6E-06)	(0.00036)
	[0.89362]	[0.79739]	[-1.75231]	[0.37321]	[0.12583]	[-0.06599]

HFDI(-4)	0.074564	-0.057101	-0.004268	-0.120634	-5.24E-06	-0.000450
	(0.23249)	(0.12391)	(0.00498)	(0.51542)	(4.0E-06)	(0.00031)
	[0.32071]	[-0.46081]	[-0.85637]	[-0.23405]	[-1.32429]	[-1.44353]
HCUAC (-1)	-0.447917	0.236235	-0.004879	-0.461275	2.15E-06	0.000309
	(0.44351)	(0.23638)	(0.00951)	(0.98322)	(7.5E-06)	(0.00059)
	[-1.00994]	[0.99939]	[-0.51318]	[-0.46915]	[0.28554]	[0.52038]
HCUAC (-2)	0.110078	0.431544	0.023523	-1.245539	2.39E-07	-0.000360
	(0.43146)	(0.22996)	(0.00925)	(0.95652)	(7.3E-06)	(0.00058)
	[0.25513]	[1.87662]	[2.54345]	[-1.30215]	[0.03257]	[-0.62231]
HCUAC (-3)	0.511106	-0.254175	-0.007109	-1.625797	-1.66E-06	4.08E-05
	(0.40647)	(0.21664)	(0.00871)	(0.90111)	(6.9E-06)	(0.00054)
	[1.25743]	[-1.17326]	[-0.81587]	[-1.80421]	[-0.23943]	[0.07485]
HCUAC (-4)	-0.112713	0.289745	-0.002695	-0.624822	-4.58E-06	-0.000416
	(0.36420)	(0.19411)	(0.00781)	(0.80740)	(6.2E-06)	(0.00049)
	[-0.30948]	[1.49268]	[-0.34525]	[-0.77386]	[-0.73977]	[-0.85290]
HEXRDOL (-1)	-13.19718	1.502348	0.684416	15.19230	0.000223	0.010463
	(10.1412)	(5.40503)	(0.21738)	(22.4823)	(0.00017)	(0.01359)
	[-1.30135]	[0.27795]	[3.14847]	[0.67575]	[1.28997]	[0.76975]
HEXRDOL (-2)	19.10463	14.99335	0.101864	-37.49848	4.30E-05	-0.005256
	(13.3744)	(7.12829)	(0.28669)	(29.6502)	(0.00023)	(0.01793)
	[1.42845]	[2.10336]	[0.35532]	[-1.26470]	[0.18883]	[-0.29321]
HEXRDOL (-3)	21.03787	-10.06766	0.376709	-4.434807	-0.000132	-0.002019
	(13.5288)	(7.21057)	(0.29000)	(29.9925)	(0.00023)	(0.01813)
	[1.55504]	[-1.39624]	[1.29901]	[-0.14786]	[-0.57301]	[-0.11131]
HEXRDOL (-4)	-30.09269	-7.704266	-0.115705	27.78698	-0.000207	-0.027140
	(16.6355)	(8.86639)	(0.35659)	(36.8799)	(0.00028)	(0.02230)
	[-1.80894]	[-0.86893]	[-0.32448]	[0.75345]	[-0.73095]	[-1.21717]
HSM(-1)	0.061014	0.004756	0.001471	0.342496	-7.84E-07	-0.000361
	(0.10222)	(0.05448)	(0.00219)	(0.22662)	(1.7E-06)	(0.00014)
	[0.59688]	[0.08729]	[0.67133]	[1.51134]	[-0.45096]	[-2.63202]

HSM(-2)	0.099642	-0.142807	0.002463	0.575163	1.49E-06	0.000332
	(0.14580)	(0.07771)	(0.00313)	(0.32324)	(2.5E-06)	(0.00020)
	[0.68340]	[-1.83769]	[0.78816]	[1.77938]	[0.60108]	[1.69675]
HSM(-3)	-0.179953	0.011366	-0.003831	-0.126549	-7.74E-07	-0.000105
	(0.16881)	(0.08997)	(0.00362)	(0.37424)	(2.9E-06)	(0.00023)
	[-1.06601]	[0.12633]	[-1.05870]	[-0.33815]	[-0.26959]	[-0.46292]
HSM(-4)	0.087381	0.024713	0.005589	-0.435477	-3.00E-06	-6.30E-05
	(0.13654)	(0.07277)	(0.00293)	(0.30270)	(2.3E-06)	(0.00018)
	[0.63995]	[0.33958]	[1.90957]	[-1.43862]	[-1.29350]	[-0.34411]
LOG(HCPI (-1))	-10029.70	-10734.56	-26.44242	24793.19	0.900295	26.67391
	(15011.8)	(8000.99)	(321.786)	(33280.2)	(0.25535)	(20.1210)
	[-0.66812]	[-1.34165]	[-0.08217]	[0.74498]	[3.52569]	[1.32567]
LOG(HCPI (-2))	13273.56	14256.64	151.1885	-16780.77	-0.260322	-22.10778
	(20288.3)	(10813.3)	(434.890)	(44977.9)	(0.34511)	(27.1934)
	[0.65425]	[1.31844]	[0.34765]	[-0.37309]	[-0.75432]	[-0.81298]
LOG(HCPI (-3))	-14013.37	-1393.481	-41.37642	-34698.07	0.011510	0.733533
	(17966.1)	(9575.55)	(385.112)	(39829.6)	(0.30560)	(24.0808)
	[-0.77999]	[-0.14552]	[-0.10744]	[-0.87116]	[0.03766]	[0.03046]
LOG(HCPI (-4))	10355.72	-1148.332	-331.8401	23523.48	0.100384	25.50186
	(12222.4)	(6514.27)	(261.992)	(27096.2)	(0.20790)	(16.3822)
	[0.84728]	[-0.17628]	[-1.26660]	[0.86815]	[0.48284]	[1.55668]
HLR(-1)	94.60766	-182.1215	-1.290946	288.2976	0.003286	1.100917
	(159.324)	(84.9164)	(3.41519)	(353.211)	(0.00271)	(0.21355)
	[0.59381]	[-2.14472]	[-0.37800]	[0.81622]	[1.21241]	[5.15533]
HLR(-2)	-148.4604	94.78208	-1.034459	-348.5395	-0.003516	-0.565869
	(243.323)	(129.686)	(5.21574)	(539.431)	(0.00414)	(0.32614)
	[-0.61014]	[0.73086]	[-0.19833]	[-0.64612]	[-0.84941]	[-1.73507]
HLR(-3)	-14.64708	-129.8845	8.549241	-499.7101	0.000231	0.214080
	(246.695)	(131.483)	(5.28803)	(546.907)	(0.00420)	(0.33066)
	[-0.05937]	[-0.98784]	[1.61672]	[-0.91370]	[0.05501]	[0.64744]
HLR(-4)	36.37590	131.1534	-0.718971	482.8744	-0.000132	-0.288418
	(130.238)	(69.4140)	(2.79171)	(288.729)	(0.00222)	(0.17456)

	[0.27930]	[1.88944]	[-0.25754]	[1.67242]	[-0.05979]	[-1.65222]
C	2708.525	-3084.602	1064.805	18045.27	1.207027	-129.0966
	(46418.8)	(24740.3)	(995.010)	(102907)	(0.78959)	(62.2173)
	[0.05835]	[-0.12468]	[1.07015]	[0.17535]	[1.52868]	[-2.07493]
R-squared	0.804088	0.926982	0.972747	0.980747	0.990705	0.995108
Adj. R-squared	0.510219	0.817455	0.931867	0.951867	0.976764	0.987769
Sum sq. resids	3869600.	1099225.	1778.002	19018293	0.001120	6.951844
S.E. equation	491.7825	262.1098	10.54159	1090.249	0.008365	0.659159
F-statistic	2.736215	8.463481	23.79532	33.95990	71.06030	135.6023
Log likelihood	-293.0058	-267.2056	-135.4548	-325.6469	157.2440	-21.79789
Akaike AIC	15.51248	14.25393	7.827063	17.10473	-6.450929	2.282824
Schwarz SC	16.55734	15.29879	8.871924	18.14959	-5.406068	3.327685
Mean dependent	1013.476	-601.1951	224.8459	9114.521	4.700408	14.87074
S.D. dependent	702.7034	613.4764	40.38570	4969.425	0.054878	5.960245

Determinant resid covariance (dof adj.)	8.86E+12
Determinant resid covariance	3.13E+10
Log likelihood	-844.4670
Akaike information criterion	48.51058
Schwarz criterion	54.77975

Lithuania:

Date: 11/27/06 Time: 11:33

Sample (adjusted): 2000Q2 2006Q1

Included observations: 24 after adjustments

Trend assumption: Linear deterministic trend
Series: LIFDI LICUAC LIEXRDOL LISM LOG(LICPI) LILR

Lags interval (in first differences): 1 to 1

Unrestricted Cointegration Rank Test (Trace)

Hypothesized No. of CE(s)	Eigenvalue	Trace Statistic	0.05 Critical Value	Prob.**
None *	0.950832	183.3133	95.75366	0.0000

At most 1 *	0.841663	111.0129	69.81889	0.0000
At most 2 *	0.738403	66.78012	47.85613	0.0003
At most 3 *	0.606933	34.59729	29.79707	0.0130
At most 4	0.397565	12.18669	15.49471	0.1482
At most 5	0.001003	0.024093	3.841466	0.8766

Trace test indicates 4 cointegrating eqn(s) at the 0.05 level
* denotes rejection of the hypothesis at the 0.05 level
**MacKinnon-Haug-Michelis (1999) p-values

Unrestricted Cointegration Rank Test (Maximum Eigenvalue)

Hypothesized No. of CE(s)	Eigenvalue	Max-Eigen Statistic	0.05 Critical Value	Prob.**
None *	0.950832	72.30037	40.07757	0.0000
At most 1 *	0.841663	44.23276	33.87687	0.0021
At most 2 *	0.738403	32.18283	27.58434	0.0119
At most 3 *	0.606933	22.41060	21.13162	0.0329
At most 4	0.397565	12.16259	14.26460	0.1047
At most 5	0.001003	0.024093	3.841466	0.8766

Max-eigenvalue test indicates 4 cointegrating eqn(s) at the 0.05 level
* denotes rejection of the hypothesis at the 0.05 level
**MacKinnon-Haug-Michelis (1999) p-values

Unrestricted Cointegrating Coefficients (normalized by b'*S11*b=I):

LIFDI	LICUAC	LIEXRDOL	LISM	LOG(LICPI)	LILR
-0.005731	0.007470	-7.187653	-0.013272	121.7098	1.029020
-0.010031	0.011683	1.341588	0.020469	-59.47460	-0.164145
-0.001997	0.011315	-1.003612	0.014556	-89.83141	-0.581142
-0.011391	-0.004861	0.619892	-0.015105	99.41996	-0.234791
0.001433	0.015500	-0.066860	0.006346	19.52876	-0.218044
0.000425	0.008888	-1.198405	0.000460	-72.89950	-0.251872

Unrestricted Adjustment Coefficients (alpha):

D(LIFDI)	-6.019399	66.46905	30.55935	57.08700	-27.62466	0.783966
D(LICUAC)	-1.017402	-5.588006	-42.32237	4.851673	-27.45051	-0.149900
D(LIEXRDOL)	0.045088	0.029534	0.022810	-0.062227	-0.000228	0.000433
D(LISM)	22.69131	-12.73034	-2.226377	9.343306	0.233014	0.212588
D(LOG(LICPI))	-0.001637	0.000938	0.002391	-0.001323	-0.001300	0.000151
D(LILR)	-0.074096	-0.139446	0.196413	-0.001613	-0.143376	-2.63E-05

1 Cointegrating Equation(s):	Log likelihood	-254.8409			

Normalized cointegrating coefficients (standard error in parentheses)

LIFDI	LICUAC	LIEXRDOL	LISM	LOG(LICPI)	LILR
1.000000	-1.303520	1254.215	2.315880	-21237.34	-179.5595
	(0.24804)	(73.2249)	(0.32505)	(1930.03)	(12.4972)

Adjustment coefficients (standard error in parentheses)

D(LIFDI)	0.034496
	(0.17203)
D(LICUAC)	0.005831
	(0.09524)
D(LIEXRDOL)	-0.000258
	(0.00013)
D(LISM)	-0.130039
	(0.02918)
D(LOG(LICPI))	9.38E-06
	(8.9E-06)
D(LILR)	0.000425
	(0.00051)

2 Cointegrating Equation(s):	Log likelihood	-232.7246			

Normalized cointegrating coefficients (standard error in parentheses)

LIFDI	LICUAC	LIEXRDOL	LISM	LOG(LICPI)	LILR
1.000000	0.000000	-11775.98	-38.58230	233805.3	1659.775
		(923.393)	(3.44931)	(23208.7)	(162.696)
0.000000	1.000000	-9996.164	-31.37519	195657.3	1411.052
		(743.491)	(2.77729)	(18687.0)	(130.998)

Adjustment coefficients (standard error in parentheses)

D(LIFDI)	-0.632270	0.731596
	(0.28881)	(0.34667)
D(LICUAC)	0.061885	-0.072885
	(0.19133)	(0.22965)
D(LIEXRDOL)	-0.000555	0.000682
	(0.00025)	(0.00030)
D(LISM)	-0.002338	0.020779
	(0.04592)	(0.05513)
D(LOG(LICPI))	-2.77E-08	-1.27E-06
	(1.8E-05)	(2.1E-05)

D(LILR)	0.001823	-0.002183
	(0.00095)	(0.00114)

	Log likelihood	
3 Cointegrating Equation(s):	likelihood	-216.6332

Normalized cointegrating coefficients (standard error in parentheses)

LIFDI	LICUAC	LIEXRDOL	LISM	LOG(LICPI)	LILR
1.000000	0.000000	0.000000	0.302769	-10362.50	-99.26613
			(0.39440)	(3070.45)	(15.5702)
0.000000	1.000000	0.000000	1.632802	-11607.06	-82.12786
			(0.29069)	(2263.05)	(11.4759)
0.000000	0.000000	1.000000	0.003302	-20.73439	-0.149375
			(0.00018)	(1.43198)	(0.00726)

Adjustment coefficients (standard error in parentheses)

D(LIFDI)	-0.693286	1.077367	101.7697
	(0.27907)	(0.42602)	(175.675)
D(LICUAC)	0.146388	-0.551752	42.29118
	(0.14937)	(0.22802)	(94.0277)
D(LIEXRDOL)	-0.000600	0.000940	-0.307348
	(0.00025)	(0.00037)	(0.15460)
D(LISM)	0.002107	-0.004411	-177.9417
	(0.04615)	(0.07045)	(29.0495)
D(LOG(LICPI))	-4.80E-06	2.58E-05	0.010627
	(1.7E-05)	(2.5E-05)	(0.01046)
D(LILR)	0.001431	3.97E-05	0.148376
	(0.00077)	(0.00118)	(0.48579)

	Log	
4 Cointegrating Equation(s):	likelihood	-205.4278

Normalized cointegrating coefficients (standard error in parentheses)

LIFDI	LICUAC	LIEXRDOL	LISM	LOG(LICPI)	LILR
1.000000	0.000000	0.000000	0.000000	-13628.06	-187.0705
				(4087.94)	(28.2443)
0.000000	1.000000	0.000000	0.000000	-29217.88	-555.6469
				(12213.8)	(84.3871)
0.000000	0.000000	1.000000	0.000000	-56.34931	-1.106988
				(21.8687)	(0.15109)
0.000000	0.000000	0.000000	1.000000	10785.65	290.0040
				(6643.61)	(45.9019)

Adjustment coefficients (standard error in parentheses)

D(LIFDI)	-1.343592	0.799877	137.1575	1.022976
	(0.31141)	(0.35330)	(141.091)	(0.61292)
D(LICUAC)	0.091120	-0.575335	45.29869	-0.790216
	(0.20732)	(0.23521)	(93.9302)	(0.40804)
D(LIEXRDOL)	0.000109	0.001242	-0.345922	0.001278
	(0.00023)	(0.00026)	(0.10389)	(0.00045)
D(LISM)	-0.104327	-0.049828	-172.1499	-0.735271
	(0.05179)	(0.05875)	(23.4636)	(0.10193)
D(LOG(LICPI))	1.03E-05	3.22E-05	0.009807	9.57E-05
	(2.3E-05)	(2.6E-05)	(0.01021)	(4.4E-05)
D(LILR)	0.001450	4.75E-05	0.147377	0.001012
	(0.00108)	(0.00122)	(0.48749)	(0.00212)

5 Cointegrating Equation(s):	Log likelihood	-199.3466

Normalized cointegrating coefficients (standard error in parentheses)

LIFDI	LICUAC	LIEXRDOL	LISM	LOG(LICPI)	LILR
1.000000	0.000000	0.000000	0.000000	0.000000	32.03985
					(8.01391)
0.000000	1.000000	0.000000	0.000000	0.000000	-85.88528
					(13.3769)
0.000000	0.000000	1.000000	0.000000	0.000000	-0.201010
					(0.02397)
0.000000	0.000000	0.000000	1.000000	0.000000	116.5937
					(14.4582)
0.000000	0.000000	0.000000	0.000000	1.000000	0.016078
					(0.00183)

Adjustment coefficients (standard error in parentheses)

D(LIFDI)	-1.383164	0.371681	139.0045	0.847670	-2294.917
	(0.29134)	(0.42913)	(131.499)	(0.58223)	(3400.55)
D(LICUAC)	0.051797	-1.000831	47.13404	-0.964417	3956.674
	(0.17501)	(0.25779)	(78.9938)	(0.34976)	(2042.78)
D(LIEXRDOL)	0.000108	0.001239	-0.345907	0.001277	-4.508921
	(0.00023)	(0.00034)	(0.10390)	(0.00046)	(2.68674)
D(LISM)	-0.103994	-0.046216	-172.1654	-0.733792	4652.347
	(0.05198)	(0.07656)	(23.4606)	(0.10387)	(606.691)
D(LOG(LICPI))	8.41E-06	1.21E-05	0.009894	8.75E-05	-0.626872
	(2.2E-05)	(3.2E-05)	(0.00992)	(4.4E-05)	(0.25649)
D(LILR)	0.001244	-0.002175	0.156963	0.000103	-21.32912
	(0.00091)	(0.00133)	(0.40888)	(0.00181)	(10.5737)

Vector Autoregression Estimates
Date: 11/27/06 Time: 11:35
Sample (adjusted): 2000Q3 2006Q1
Included observations: 23 after adjustments
Standard errors in ( ) & t-statistics in [ ]

	LIFDI	LICUAC	LIEXRDOL	LISM	LOG(LICPI)	LILR
LIFDI(-1)	1.418278	0.540189	-0.000808	0.254458	-2.14E-05	0.002636
	(0.35215)	(0.34016)	(0.00027)	(0.07522)	(3.2E-05)	(0.00148)
	[4.02750]	[1.58806]	[-3.02426]	[3.38297]	[-0.66742]	[1.78340]
LIFDI(-2)	-0.302740	-0.297668	0.000627	-0.262878	4.91E-05	0.001239
	(0.28104)	(0.27147)	(0.00021)	(0.06003)	(2.6E-05)	(0.00118)
	[-1.07720]	[-1.09648]	[2.94264]	[-4.37910]	[1.92222]	[1.05019]
LIFDI(-3)	0.706933	0.655784	-0.002033	0.205106	-9.86E-05	0.000461
	(0.47002)	(0.45401)	(0.00036)	(0.10039)	(4.3E-05)	(0.00197)
	[1.50405]	[1.44441]	[-5.70358]	[2.04301]	[-2.30638]	[0.23350]
LICUAC(-1)	1.129512	-0.152589	0.000310	-0.067472	5.60E-05	-0.002984
	(0.31596)	(0.30520)	(0.00024)	(0.06749)	(2.9E-05)	(0.00133)
	[3.57483]	[-0.49996]	[1.29456]	[-0.99976]	[1.94754]	[-2.24979]
LICUAC(-2)	-2.555318	-0.671636	0.001456	-0.044647	-3.57E-05	-0.003430
	(0.47141)	(0.45536)	(0.00036)	(0.10069)	(4.3E-05)	(0.00198)
	[-5.42058]	[-1.47496]	[4.07266]	[-0.44340]	[-0.83268]	[-1.73359]
LICUAC(-3)	-0.252138	-0.700504	0.001466	-0.033037	9.18E-05	0.003067
	(0.44459)	(0.42945)	(0.00034)	(0.09496)	(4.0E-05)	(0.00187)
	[-0.56713]	[-1.63117]	[4.34677]	[-0.34789]	[2.27051]	[1.64385]
LIEXRDOL(-1)	839.3730	520.9759	-1.195257	253.8968	-0.054950	-0.873879
	(461.740)	(446.017)	(0.35019)	(98.6258)	(0.04199)	(1.93801)
	[1.81785]	[1.16806]	[-3.41317]	[2.57434]	[-1.30871]	[-0.45091]
LIEXRDOL(-2)	109.9665	-85.33814	1.005486	-306.5029	0.049517	-1.072243
	(312.265)	(301.632)	(0.23683)	(66.6985)	(0.02840)	(1.31064)
	[0.35216]	[-0.28292]	[4.24568]	[-4.59535]	[1.74383]	[-0.81811]
LIEXRDOL(-3)	-1086.102	131.7232	-0.512482	-84.62444	-0.090195	-0.047843
	(364.521)	(352.108)	(0.27646)	(77.8601)	(0.03315)	(1.52996)
	[-2.97954]	[0.37410]	[-1.85375]	[-1.08688]	[-2.72102]	[-0.03127]

LISM(-1)	-0.898109	1.513014	-0.003533	0.581071	-0.000348	-0.005731
	(1.42079)	(1.37241)	(0.00108)	(0.30347)	(0.00013)	(0.00596)
	[-0.63212]	[1.10245]	[-3.27837]	[1.91473]	[-2.69598]	[-0.96100]
LISM(-2)	1.022226	-2.796042	0.003128	-0.487485	9.48E-05	0.005619
	(1.34680)	(1.30094)	(0.00102)	(0.28767)	(0.00012)	(0.00565)
	[0.75900]	[-2.14925]	[3.06241]	[-1.69460]	[0.77389]	[0.99404]
LISM(-3)	-3.085611	-0.186799	0.000294	0.061176	0.000185	-0.006762
	(1.52967)	(1.47758)	(0.00116)	(0.32573)	(0.00014)	(0.00642)
	[-2.01718]	[-0.12642]	[0.25302]	[0.18724]	[1.33042]	[-1.05319]
LOG(LICPI (-1))	-394.1676	503.6584	20.41805	-2509.906	1.716481	-5.482323
	(4669.99)	(4510.97)	(3.54178)	(997.491)	(0.42466)	(19.6009)
	[-0.08440]	[0.11165]	[5.76491]	[-2.51622]	[4.04199]	[-0.27970]
LOG(LICPI (-2))	-22351.89	-5291.950	-12.80525	4989.998	-1.639730	-18.87130
	(5365.89)	(5183.17)	(4.06956)	(1146.13)	(0.48794)	(22.5217)
	[-4.16555]	[-1.02099]	[-3.14659]	[4.35377]	[-3.36049]	[-0.83792]
LOG(LICPI (-3))	25736.93	6363.323	13.74007	1157.091	2.198589	34.87413
	(7791.00)	(7525.71)	(5.90880)	(1664.13)	(0.70847)	(32.7004)
	[3.30342]	[0.84554]	[2.32536]	[0.69531]	[3.10329]	[1.06647]
LILR(-1)	-287.3065	-4.311002	0.009998	41.43966	-0.007826	0.341677
	(80.6769)	(77.9297)	(0.06119)	(17.2323)	(0.00734)	(0.33862)
	[-3.56120]	[-0.05532]	[0.16340]	[2.40477]	[-1.06682]	[1.00904]
LILR(-2)	261.4954	59.96867	0.304090	-16.97982	0.026623	0.716690
	(113.261)	(109.404)	(0.08590)	(24.1921)	(0.01030)	(0.47538)
	[2.30878]	[0.54814]	[3.54010]	[-0.70187]	[2.58491]	[1.50762]
LILR(-3)	19.89815	-74.48756	-0.072089	-10.01507	-0.007456	0.232925
	(65.3735)	(63.1474)	(0.04958)	(13.9635)	(0.00594)	(0.27439)
	[0.30438]	[-1.17958]	[-1.45399]	[-0.71723]	[-1.25429]	[0.84890]
C	-13354.81	-9612.411	-93.60374	-16309.74	-5.586710	-45.17908
	(34196.7)	(33032.2)	(25.9352)	(7304.27)	(3.10965)	(143.530)
	[-0.39053]	[-0.29100]	[-3.60914]	[-2.23291]	[-1.79657]	[-0.31477]
R-squared	0.953620	0.980679	0.998727	0.998585	0.986058	0.997588
Adj. R-squared	0.744909	0.893735	0.993000	0.992215	0.923317	0.986732

Sum sq. resids	13964.68	13029.83	0.008032	637.1133	0.000115	0.246008
S.E. equation	59.08612	57.07413	0.044812	12.62055	0.005373	0.247996
F-statistic	4.569100	11.27947	174.3898	156.7702	15.71636	91.89739
Log likelihood	-106.3367	-105.5399	58.90181	-70.83230	107.6869	19.55008
Akaike AIC	10.89884	10.82955	-3.469722	7.811504	-7.711904	-0.047833
Schwarz SC	11.83686	11.76757	-2.531705	8.749521	-6.773887	0.890184
Mean dependent	153.0489	-304.2609	3.282948	197.3252	4.624621	6.990029
S.D. dependent	116.9871	175.0834	0.535615	143.0351	0.019403	2.153009

Determinant resid covariance (dof adj.)	0.000000
Determinant resid covariance	0.000000

Poland:

Date: 11/27/06 Time: 11:38

Sample (adjusted): 1995Q3 2006Q1

Included observations: 43 after adjustments

Trend assumption: Linear deterministic trend

Series: PLFDI PLCUAC PLEXRDOL PLSM LOG(PLCPI) PLLR

Lags interval (in first differences): 1 to 1

Unrestricted Cointegration Rank Test (Trace)

Hypothesized No. of CE(s)	Eigenvalue	Trace Statistic	0.05 Critical Value	Prob.**
None *	0.623839	119.8023	95.75366	0.0004
At most 1 *	0.495724	77.75954	69.81889	0.0101
At most 2 *	0.448523	48.32039	47.85613	0.0452
At most 3	0.245311	22.72872	29.79707	0.2596
At most 4	0.184403	10.62638	15.49471	0.2355
At most 5	0.042367	1.861491	3.841466	0.1725

Trace test indicates 3 cointegrating eqn(s) at the 0.05 level

* denotes rejection of the hypothesis at the 0.05 level

**MacKinnon-Haug-Michelis (1999) p-values

Unrestricted Cointegration Rank Test (Maximum Eigenvalue)

Hypothesized		Max-Eigen	0.05

No. of CE(s)	Eigenvalue	Statistic	Critical Value	Prob.**
None *	0.623839	42.04276	40.07757	0.0297
At most 1	0.495724	29.43915	33.87687	0.1547
At most 2	0.448523	25.59167	27.58434	0.0880
At most 3	0.245311	12.10234	21.13162	0.5376
At most 4	0.184403	8.764885	14.26460	0.3062
At most 5	0.042367	1.861491	3.841466	0.1725

Max-eigenvalue test indicates 1 cointegrating eqn(s) at the 0.05 level
* denotes rejection of the hypothesis at the 0.05 level
**MacKinnon-Haug-Michelis (1999) p-values

Unrestricted Cointegrating Coefficients (normalized by b'*S11*b=I):

PLFDI	PLCUAC	PLEXRDOL	PLSM	LOG(PLCPI)	PLLR
0.004614	-0.002020	-2.776015	-0.002833	-17.26416	0.055118
0.004915	0.003572	3.667083	0.000436	43.89932	-0.169481
0.000132	0.000600	-0.742540	0.002359	-23.51466	0.329403
0.000972	-0.000641	0.201025	-2.61E-05	50.88766	-0.366790
-0.000715	-0.001945	1.576195	0.001067	20.76186	-0.109001
-0.001715	-0.000552	0.877000	-0.003907	14.82258	-0.103884

Unrestricted Adjustment Coefficients (alpha):

D(PLFDI)	-168.0982	-157.6579	1.062949	-27.38174	-50.29934	-13.52635
D(PLCUAC)	72.13113	-83.00152	-39.47972	41.05748	114.3900	29.11805
D(PLEXRD OL)	0.063014	-0.040297	0.070692	0.006761	0.025280	-0.010876
D(PLSM)	19.11508	-24.98450	-36.29865	37.91326	-42.20074	-0.805192
D(LOG(PL CPI))	0.002304	0.000307	-0.004777	-0.001919	-0.000105	-0.001236
D(PLLR)	-0.193634	0.199983	-0.195133	0.269766	0.097467	-0.136186

1 Cointegrating Equation(s): Log likelihood -777.2906

Normalized cointegrating coefficients (standard error in parentheses)

PLFDI	PLCUAC	PLEXRDOL	PLSM	LOG(PLCPI)	PLLR
1.000000	-0.437947	-601.7124	-0.613977	-3742.076	11.94700
	(0.12621)	(141.837)	(0.15514)	(2131.47)	(15.3043)

Adjustment coefficients (standard error in parentheses)

D(PLFDI)	-0.775525
	(0.23170)
D(PLCUAC)	0.332779
	(0.26828)
D(PLEXRDOL)	0.000291
	(0.00012)
D(PLSM)	0.088188
	(0.11015)
D(LOG(PLCPI))	1.06E-05
	(8.0E-06)
D(PLLR)	-0.000893
	(0.00077)

2 Cointegrating Equation(s): Log likelihood -762.5710

Normalized cointegrating coefficients (standard error in parentheses)

PLFDI	PLCUAC	PLEXRDOL	PLSM	LOG(PLCPI)	PLLR
1.000000	0.000000	-94.88825	-0.349786	1023.762	-5.512289
		(84.8427)	(0.10997)	(1615.69)	(11.8370)
0.000000	1.000000	1157.274	0.603250	10882.23	-39.86625
		(148.353)	(0.19228)	(2825.14)	(20.6977)

Adjustment coefficients (standard error in parentheses)

D(PLFDI)	-1.550351	-0.223466
	(0.28694)	(0.17468)
D(PLCUAC)	-0.075141	-0.442195
	(0.38040)	(0.23158)
D(PLEXRDOL)	9.27E-05	-0.000271
	(0.00017)	(0.00010)
D(PLSM)	-0.034601	-0.127858
	(0.15839)	(0.09643)
D(LOG(PLCPI))	1.21E-05	-3.56E-06
	(1.2E-05)	(7.1E-06)
D(PLLR)	8.95E-05	0.001106
	(0.00110)	(0.00067)

3 Cointegrating Equation(s): Log likelihood -749.7752

Normalized cointegrating coefficients (standard error in parentheses)

PLFDI	PLCUAC	PLEXRDOL	PLSM	LOG(PLCPI)	PLLR
1.000000	0.000000	0.000000	-0.485950	3034.407	-29.10124
			(0.12703)	(1118.02)	(10.0641)
0.000000	1.000000	0.000000	2.263929	-13639.95	247.8287
			(0.76624)	(6743.81)	(60.7060)
0.000000	0.000000	1.000000	-0.001435	21.18962	-0.248597
			(0.00066)	(5.82152)	(0.05240)

Adjustment coefficients (standard error in parentheses)

D(PLFDI)	-1.550210	-0.222828	-112.2906
	(0.28699)	(0.17653)	(198.316)
D(PLCUAC)	-0.080361	-0.465876	-475.2953
	(0.37781)	(0.23240)	(261.069)
D(PLEXRDOL)	0.000102	-0.000229	-0.375193
	(0.00015)	(9.0E-05)	(0.10157)
D(PLSM)	-0.039401	-0.149632	-117.7308
	(0.15293)	(0.09407)	(105.677)
D(LOG(PLCPI))	1.15E-05	-6.42E-06	-0.001722
	(1.0E-05)	(6.4E-06)	(0.00715)
D(PLLR)	6.37E-05	0.000988	1.415779
	(0.00108)	(0.00066)	(0.74544)

4 Cointegrating Equation(s): Log likelihood -743.7240

Normalized cointegrating coefficients (standard error in parentheses)

PLFDI	PLCUAC	PLEXRDOL	PLSM	LOG(PLCPI)	PLLR
1.000000	0.000000	0.000000	0.000000	10805.89	-57.96614
				(3055.13)	(26.2179)
0.000000	1.000000	0.000000	0.000000	-49845.50	382.3036
				(13379.2)	(114.815)
0.000000	0.000000	1.000000	0.000000	44.13852	-0.333834
				(8.71678)	(0.07480)
0.000000	0.000000	0.000000	1.000000	15992.35	-59.39889
				(6497.84)	(55.7620)

Adjustment coefficients (standard error in parentheses)

D(PLFDI)	-1.576827	-0.205289	-117.7950	0.410709
	(0.28824)	(0.17757)	(197.324)	(0.15708)

D(PLCUAC)	-0.040450	-0.492176	-467.0417	-0.334688
	(0.37877)	(0.23334)	(259.301)	(0.20642)
D(PLEXRD OL)	0.000109	-0.000233	-0.373834	-2.94E-05
	(0.00015)	(9.1E-05)	(0.10152)	(8.1E-05)
D(PLSM)	-0.002546	-0.173917	-110.1093	-0.151658
	(0.14822)	(0.09131)	(101.466)	(0.08077)
D(LOG(PL CPI))	9.64E-06	-5.19E-06	-0.002108	-1.76E-05
	(1.0E-05)	(6.3E-06)	(0.00700)	(5.6E-06)
D(PLLR)	0.000326	0.000816	1.470008	0.000168
	(0.00104)	(0.00064)	(0.71519)	(0.00057)

5 Cointegrating Equation(s): Log likelihood -739.3416

Normalized cointegrating coefficients (standard error in parentheses)

PLFDI	PLCUAC	PLEXRDOL	PLSM	LOG(PLCPI)	PLLR
1.000000	0.000000	0.000000	0.000000	0.000000	24.43568
					(5.69040)
0.000000	1.000000	0.000000	0.000000	0.000000	2.199869
					(16.7294)
0.000000	0.000000	1.000000	0.000000	0.000000	0.002750
					(0.02026)
0.000000	0.000000	0.000000	1.000000	0.000000	62.55299
					(11.7912)
0.000000	0.000000	0.000000	0.000000	1.000000	-0.007626
					(0.00099)

Adjustment coefficients (standard error in parentheses)

D(PLFDI)	-1.540859	-0.107470	-197.0766	0.357044	-6481.695
	(0.28391)	(0.19172)	(204.043)	(0.16011)	(3156.56)
D(PLCUAC)	-0.122248	-0.714635	-286.7407	-0.212644	503.6279
	(0.35709)	(0.24113)	(256.632)	(0.20137)	(3970.10)
D(PLEXRD OL)	9.05E-05	-0.000282	-0.333987	-2.47E-06	-3.650278
	(0.00015)	(9.9E-05)	(0.10508)	(8.2E-05)	(1.62561)
D(PLSM)	0.027631	-0.091848	-176.6259	-0.196682	479.8935
	(0.14079)	(0.09507)	(101.186)	(0.07940)	(1565.35)
D(LOG(PL CPI))	9.72E-06	-4.99E-06	-0.002274	-1.77E-05	-0.013777
	(1.0E-05)	(6.9E-06)	(0.00739)	(5.8E-06)	(0.11426)
D(PLLR)	0.000256	0.000626	1.623636	0.000272	32.46192
	(0.00104)	(0.00071)	(0.75058)	(0.00059)	(11.6114)

Vector Autoregression Estimates
Date: 11/27/06 Time: 11:41
Sample (adjusted): 1996Q1 2006Q1
Included observations: 41 after adjustments
Standard errors in ( ) & t-statistics in [ ]

	PLFDI	PLCUAC	PLEXRDOL	PLSM	LOG(PLC PI)	PLLR
PLFDI(-1)	-0.226388	0.032847	0.000125	-0.021878	1.93E-06	-0.000617
	(0.23393)	(0.30705)	(0.00016)	(0.13881)	(8.8E-06)	(0.00101)
	[-0.96775]	[0.10698]	[0.77089]	[-0.15762]	[0.21826]	[-0.61228]
PLFDI(-2)	-0.579001	0.163391	-0.000283	-0.042373	7.50E-06	-0.000263
	(0.23553)	(0.30914)	(0.00016)	(0.13975)	(8.9E-06)	(0.00101)
	[-2.45831]	[0.52853]	[-1.73677]	[-0.30319]	[0.84368]	[-0.25957]
PLFDI(-3)	-0.530218	0.674042	-8.33E-05	-0.072107	-1.70E-05	-0.001850
	(0.26672)	(0.35008)	(0.00018)	(0.15826)	(1.0E-05)	(0.00115)
	[-1.98793]	[1.92540]	[-0.45159]	[-0.45562]	[-1.68937]	[-1.61091]
PLFDI(-4)	0.341603	0.299707	-5.44E-05	-0.067338	-9.26E-06	-0.001224
	(0.25239)	(0.33127)	(0.00017)	(0.14976)	(9.5E-06)	(0.00109)
	[1.35347]	[0.90471]	[-0.31206]	[-0.44964]	[-0.97126]	[-1.12646]
PLCUAC(-1)	-0.078306	0.092101	-7.86E-05	-0.098914	4.88E-06	0.000478
	(0.18344)	(0.24077)	(0.00013)	(0.10885)	(6.9E-06)	(0.00079)
	[-0.42688]	[0.38253]	[-0.62001]	[-0.90874]	[0.70489]	[0.60503]
PLCUAC(-2)	0.024263	0.201709	-0.000236	-0.064438	-1.54E-05	-0.000565
	(0.16765)	(0.22004)	(0.00012)	(0.09948)	(6.3E-06)	(0.00072)
	[0.14473]	[0.91667]	[-2.03329]	[-0.64777]	[-2.43113]	[-0.78277]
PLCUAC(-3)	0.348256	0.282392	0.000136	-0.036078	-2.00E-05	-0.001729
	(0.21560)	(0.28299)	(0.00015)	(0.12793)	(8.1E-06)	(0.00093)
	[1.61528]	[0.99790]	[0.91326]	[-0.28201]	[-2.45708]	[-1.86271]
PLCUAC(-4)	-0.019360	0.031406	8.13E-05	-0.109464	5.95E-06	0.001443
	(0.17697)	(0.23228)	(0.00012)	(0.10501)	(6.7E-06)	(0.00076)
	[-0.10939]	[0.13521]	[0.66451]	[-1.04243]	[0.89055]	[1.89384]
PLEXRDOL(-1)	414.4012	216.2492	0.697333	219.1279	-0.021036	0.146072
	(420.887)	(552.434)	(0.29096)	(249 741)	(0.01589)	(1.81253)

	[0.98459]	[0.39145]	[2.39670]	[0.87742]	[-1.32371]	[0.08059]
PLEXRDOL(-2)	-86.90951	-871.0521	0.272573	-271.9789	0.028523	2.511551
	(422.037)	(553.942)	(0.29175)	(250.423)	(0.01594)	(1.81748)
	[-0.20593]	[-1.57246]	[0.93427]	[-1.08608]	[1.78996]	[1.38189]
PLEXRDOL(-3)	-652.1211	243.7844	-0.303554	-329.9650	0.011281	1.316177
	(423.215)	(555.489)	(0.29256)	(251.122)	(0.01598)	(1.82255)
	[-1.54087]	[0.43886]	[-1.03756]	[-1.31396]	[0.70593]	[0.72216]
PLEXRDOL(-4)	328.5101	892.9812	0.355277	-63.70966	-0.033919	-2.397988
	(383.419)	(503.255)	(0.26505)	(227.509)	(0.01448)	(1.65118)
	[0.85679]	[1.77441]	[1.34040]	[-0.28003]	[-2.34292]	[-1.45229]
PLSM(-1)	0.386049	0.583390	0.000576	0.316704	-1.36E-05	-0.001194
	(0.41495)	(0.54464)	(0.00029)	(0.24622)	(1.6E-05)	(0.00179)
	[0.93035]	[1.07115]	[2.00814]	[1.28628]	[-0.87056]	[-0.66842]
PLSM(-2)	0.597364	-1.094021	3.27E-05	-0.062531	2.21E-05	0.002303
	(0.41336)	(0.54255)	(0.00029)	(0.24527)	(1.6E-05)	(0.00178)
	[1.44515]	[-2.01644]	[0.11427]	[-0.25494]	[1.41335]	[1.29400]
PLSM(-3)	-0.026884	0.169860	-0.000287	0.315385	-8.49E-06	-0.000172
	(0.53139)	(0.69748)	(0.00037)	(0.31531)	(2.0E-05)	(0.00229)
	[-0.05059]	[0.24354]	[-0.78226]	[1.00023]	[-0.42317]	[-0.07523]
PLSM(-4)	0.305159	-0.463954	-0.000168	0.350768	-3.46E-05	0.000344
	(0.47524)	(0.62378)	(0.00033)	(0.28199)	(1.8E-05)	(0.00205)
	[0.64211]	[-0.74378]	[-0.51236]	[1.24388]	[-1.92689]	[0.16793]
LOG(PLCPI(-1))	5903.469	-3318.270	-0.276033	4219.509	0.589195	34.21950
	(6367.52)	(8357.66)	(4.40180)	(3778.28)	(0.24042)	(27.4214)
	[0.92712]	[-0.39703]	[-0.06271]	[1.11678]	[2.45065]	[1.24791]
LOG(PLCPI(-2))	-9864.515	-2007.090	-3.625092	-946.0709	0.170402	8.702906
	(7508.55)	(9855.31)	(5.19059)	(4455.33)	(0.28351)	(32.3352)
	[-1.31377]	[-0.20366]	[-0.69840]	[-0.21235]	[0.60105]	[0.26915]
LOG(PLCPI(-3))	254.5475	1954.498	1.857261	-468.2953	-0.180127	-43.19791
	(6982.56)	(9164.93)	(4.82698)	(4143.23)	(0.26365)	(30.0701)
	[0.03645]	[0.21326]	[0.38477]	[-0.11303]	[-0.68322]	[-1.43658]

LOG(PLCPI(-4))	-5868.221	17595.10	0.182950	-3115.309	0.177151	36.39910
	(5704.79)	(7487.80)	(3.94367)	(3385.04)	(0.21540)	(24.5674)
	[-1.02865]	[2.34984]	[0.04639]	[-0.92032]	[0.82243]	[1.48160]
PLLR(-1)	-7.683829	5.715754	0.002895	-46.64736	0.004590	1.145371
	(51.4061)	(67.4729)	(0.03554)	(30.5028)	(0.00194)	(0.22138)
	[-0.14947]	[0.08471]	[0.08146]	[-1.52928]	[2.36504]	[5.17383]
PLLR(-2)	-14.03199	-10.88366	0.010911	48.13622	-0.003357	-0.512603
	(72.2276)	(94.8020)	(0.04993)	(42.8576)	(0.00273)	(0.31104)
	[-0.19427]	[-0.11480]	[0.21852]	[1.12317]	[-1.23080]	[-1.64801]
PLLR(-3)	-19.81631	59.55411	0.003016	-70.89718	-0.001150	-0.012317
	(70.9374)	(93.1086)	(0.04904)	(42.0920)	(0.00268)	(0.30549)
	[-0.27935]	[0.63962]	[0.06150]	[-1.68434]	[-0.42933]	[-0.04032]
PLLR(-4)	117.8157	-157.1789	0.011225	47.64316	-0.000212	0.081140
	(56.1134)	(73.6514)	(0.03879)	(33.2959)	(0.00212)	(0.24165)
	[2.09960]	[-2.13409]	[0.28938]	[1.43090]	[-0.10004]	[0.33577]
C	43084.17	-66474.55	8.018158	3537.895	1.222200	-170.3916
	(24602.8)	(32292.3)	(17.0077)	(14598.5)	(0.92895)	(105.951)
	[1.75119]	[-2.05853]	[0.47144]	[0.24235]	[1.31568]	[-1.60821]
R-squared	0.771883	0.790770	0.957042	0.919880	0.990153	0.992834
Adj. R-squared	0.429708	0.476925	0.892605	0.799700	0.975382	0.982084
Sum sq. resids	854726.0	1472501.	0.408458	300937.0	0.001219	15.85133
S.E. equation	231.1285	303.3666	0.159777	137.1443	0.008727	0.995343
F-statistic	2.255811	2.519618	14.85240	7.654172	67.03478	92.36111
Log likelihood	-262.0482	-273.1989	36.30674	-240.6487	155.5088	-38.69495
Akaike AIC	14.00235	14.54629	-0.551548	12.95847	-6.366284	3.107071
Schwarz SC	15.04721	15.59115	0.493313	14.00333	-5.321423	4.151932
Mean dependent	450.2683	-555.3902	3.666063	1157.448	4.675535	16.25807
S.D. dependent	306.0587	419.4553	0.487554	306.4340	0.055620	7.436265

Determinant resid covariance (dof adj.)	55932384
Determinant resid covariance	197551.4
Log likelihood	-599.0308
Akaike information criterion	36.53809
Schwarz criterion	42.80726

Slovakia:

Date: 11/27/06 Time: 11:44
Sample (adjusted): 1995Q3 2005Q4
Included observations: 42 after adjustments
Trend assumption: Linear deterministic trend (restricted)
Series: SLFDI SLCUAC SLEXRDOL SLSM LOG(SLCPI) SLLR
Lags interval (in first differences): 1 to 1

Unrestricted Cointegration Rank Test (Trace)

Hypothesized No. of CE(s)	Eigenvalue	Trace Statistic	0.05 Critical Value	Prob.**
None *	0.644357	122.6381	117.7082	0.0234
At most 1	0.456007	79.21731	88.80380	0.2012
At most 2	0.351359	53.64694	63.87610	0.2673
At most 3	0.315490	35.46612	42.91525	0.2264
At most 4	0.273688	19.54596	25.87211	0.2498
At most 5	0.135500	6.115388	12.51798	0.4458

Trace test indicates 1 cointegrating eqn(s) at the 0.05 level
* denotes rejection of the hypothesis at the 0.05 level
**MacKinnon-Haug-Michelis (1999) p-values

Unrestricted Cointegration Rank Test (Maximum Eigenvalue)

Hypothesized No. of CE(s)	Eigenvalue	Max-Eigen Statistic	0.05 Critical Value	Prob.**
None	0.644357	43.42082	44.49720	0.0652
At most 1	0.456007	25.57037	38.33101	0.6306
At most 2	0.351359	18.18082	32.11832	0.7881
At most 3	0.315490	15.92016	25.82321	0.5518
At most 4	0.273688	13.43057	19.38704	0.2945
At most 5	0.135500	6.115388	12.51798	0.4458

Max-eigenvalue test indicates no cointegration at the 0.05 level
* denotes rejection of the hypothesis at the 0.05 level
**MacKinnon-Haug-Michelis (1999) p-values

Unrestricted Cointegrating Coefficients (normalized by b'*S11*b=I):

SLFDI	SLCUAC	SLEXRDOL	SLSM	LOG(SLCPI)	SLLR	@TREND(95Q2)
-0.001821	0.000688	0.223014	0.004710	-52.45439	-0.181427	0.919341
-0.001171	-0.002435	-0.232262	-0.015534	34.97724	-0.256430	-0.635613
3.10E-05	-0.000475	0.091430	-0.006815	-58.93495	-0.341198	0.965236
1.49E-05	-0.000975	0.039798	0.016684	28.39531	0.193544	-0.577582
0.000407	0.000480	-0.009250	0.006972	7.133778	-0.148304	-0.162072
4.57E-06	0.000341	-0.196989	-0.009155	-16.26348	0.046087	0.355857

Unrestricted Adjustment Coefficients (alpha):

D(SLFDI)	612.2162	157.2974	-202.1845	-116.0592	21.70015	-20.80915
D(SLCUAC)	-338.2265	84.85262	115.5020	9.667224	-281.6759	-42.42726
D(SLEXRDOL)	-0.204404	0.199734	-0.401219	0.690767	-0.322236	0.249330
D(SLSM)	-4.446569	1.553374	-9.122779	-10.39745	5.699936	2.550559
D(LOG(SLCPI))	-0.005332	-0.005366	0.002399	-0.001226	-0.005567	0.002111
D(SLLR)	0.212063	0.391984	0.350767	-0.108963	0.156923	0.199658

1 Cointegrating Equation(s): Log likelihood -863.9424

Normalized cointegrating coefficients (standard error in parentheses)

SLFDI	SLCUAC	SLEXRDOL	SLSM	LOG(SLCPI)	SLLR	@TREND(95Q2)
1.000000	-0.377792	-122.4837	-2.586619	28808.98	99.64336	-504.9203
	(0.20184)	(27.4033)	(1.83863)	(6246.41)	(32.8511)	(110.045)

Adjustment coefficients (standard error in parentheses)

D(SLFDI)	-1.114702
	(0.20359)
D(SLCUAC)	0.615831
	(0.20246)
D(SLEXRDOL)	0.000372
	(0.00053)
D(SLSM)	0.008096
	(0.00862)
D(LOG(SLCPI))	9.71E-06
	(4.9E-06)
D(SLLR)	-0.000386
	(0.00033)

2 Cointegrating Equation(s): Log likelihood -851.1572

Normalized cointegrating coefficients (standard error in parentheses)

SLFDI	SLCUAC	SLEXRDOL	SLSM	LOG(SLCPI)	SLLR	@TREND(95Q2)
1.000000	0.000000	-73.15844	-0.149628	19787.26	117.9843	-343.8363
		(19.9888)	(1.59014)	(4649.67)	(29.9904)	(80.9383)
0.000000	1.000000	130.5619	6.450612	-23880.13	48.54757	426.3825
		(22.1490)	(1.76200)	(5152.17)	(33.2316)	(89.6855)

Adjustment coefficients (standard error in parentheses)

D(SLFDI)	-1.298954	0.038060
	(0.23493)	(0.27460)
D(SLCUAC)	0.516438	-0.439298
	(0.23866)	(0.27896)
D(SLEXRDOL)	0.000138	-0.000627
	(0.00063)	(0.00074)
D(SLSM)	0.006277	-0.006842
	(0.01024)	(0.01196)
D(LOG(SLCPI))	1.60E-05	9.40E-06
	(5.5E-06)	(6.4E-06)
D(SLLR)	-0.000845	-0.000809
	(0.00037)	(0.00043)

3 Cointegrating Equation(s):	Log likelihood	-842.0668

Normalized cointegrating coefficients (standard error in parentheses)

SLFDI	SLCUAC	SLEXRDOL	SLSM	LOG(SLCPI)	SLLR	@TREND(95Q2)
1.000000	0.000000	0.000000	-1.908490	-13514.81	-33.16228	209.7470
			(2.46887)	(8704.22)	(59.2919)	(155.166)
0.000000	1.000000	0.000000	9.589558	35552.29	318.2907	-561.5679
			(3.88027)	(13680.3)	(93.1879)	(243.872)
0.000000	0.000000	1.000000	-0.024042	-455.2048	-2.066016	7.566910
			(0.02934)	(103.433)	(0.70457)	(1.84386)

Adjustment coefficients (standard error in parentheses)

D(SLFDI)	-1.305214	0.134153	81.51284
	(0.22263)	(0.26475)	(34.4172)
D(SLCUAC)	0.520015	-0.494193	-84.57699
	(0.23480)	(0.27922)	(36.2985)
D(SLEXRDOL)	0.000126	-0.000436	-0.128659
	(0.00061)	(0.00073)	(0.09465)
D(SLSM)	0.005994	-0.002506	-2.186532
	(0.00966)	(0.01149)	(1.49342)

D(LOG(SLCPI))	1.61E-05	8.26E-06	0.000277
	(5.4E-06)	(6.4E-06)	(0.00083)
D(SLLR)	-0.000834	-0.000975	-0.011679
	(0.00034)	(0.00041)	(0.05314)

4 Cointegrating Equation(s):	Log likelihood	-834.1067

Normalized cointegrating coefficients (standard error in parentheses)

SLFDI	SLCUAC	SLEXRDOL	SLSM	LOG(SLCPI)	SLLR	@TREND(95Q2)
1.000000	0.000000	0.000000	0.000000	-7766.991	8.268703	108.7840
				(5423.56)	(40.1537)	(96.5392)
0.000000	1.000000	0.000000	0.000000	6671.304	110.1131	-54.26089
				(6765.98)	(50.0924)	(120.434)
0.000000	0.000000	1.000000	0.000000	-382.7978	-1.544098	6.295049
				(62.5300)	(0.46295)	(1.11303)
0.000000	0.000000	0.000000	1.000000	3011.712	21.70877	-52.90202
				(630.013)	(4.66435)	(11.2142)

Adjustment coefficients (standard error in parentheses)

D(SLFDI)	-1.306940	0.247261	76.89394	-0.118576
	(0.21843)	(0.27773)	(34.0040)	(2.44672)
D(SLCUAC)	0.520158	-0.503614	-84.19226	-3.536862
	(0.23478)	(0.29852)	(36.5499)	(2.62991)
D(SLEXRDOL)	0.000136	-0.001110	-0.101168	0.010194
	(0.00056)	(0.00071)	(0.08655)	(0.00623)
D(SLSM)	0.005840	0.007627	-2.600328	-0.156370
	(0.00886)	(0.01126)	(1.37861)	(0.09920)
D(LOG(SLCPI))	1.61E-05	9.46E-06	0.000228	2.14E-05
	(5.4E-06)	(6.8E-06)	(0.00084)	(6.0E-05)
D(SLLR)	-0.000836	-0.000869	-0.016016	-0.009299
	(0.00034)	(0.00043)	(0.05315)	(0.00382)

5 Cointegrating Equation(s):	Log likelihood	-827.3915

Normalized cointegrating coefficients (standard error in parentheses)

SLFDI	SLCUAC	SLEXRDOL	SLSM	LOG(SLCPI)	SLLR	@TREND(95Q2)
1.000000	0.000000	0.000000	0.000000	0.000000	173.0245	-1.077938
					(54.0823)	(20.4425)
0.000000	1.000000	0.000000	0.000000	0.000000	-31.40068	40.10286
					(55.6621)	(21.0396)
0.000000	0.000000	1.000000	0.000000	0.000000	6.575928	0.880481

					(2.13570)	(0.80727)
0.000000	0.000000	0.000000	1.000000	0.000000	-42.17660	-10.30219
					(16.6501)	(6.29352)
0.000000	0.000000	0.000000	0.000000	1.000000	0.021212	-0.014145
					(0.00577)	(0.00218)

Adjustment coefficients (standard error in parentheses)

D(SLFDI)	-1.298117	0.257676	76.69321	0.032728	-17836.60
	(0.22209)	(0.28172)	(33.9936)	(2.54408)	(9187.09)
D(SLCUAC)	0.405638	-0.638806	-81.58672	-5.500842	12167.36
	(0.21387)	(0.27129)	(32.7345)	(2.44985)	(8846.81)
D(SLEXRDOL)	5.04E-06	-0.001264	-0.098187	0.007947	58.66964
	(0.00055)	(0.00070)	(0.08455)	(0.00633)	(22.8501)
D(SLSM)	0.008157	0.010363	-2.653053	-0.116627	570.6485
	(0.00875)	(0.01110)	(1.33916)	(0.10022)	(361.919)
D(LOG(SLCPI))	1.38E-05	6.78E-06	0.000279	-1.74E-05	-0.123905
	(5.1E-06)	(6.4E-06)	(0.00077)	(5.8E-05)	(0.20915)
D(SLLR)	-0.000772	-0.000794	-0.017468	-0.008205	-20.06014
	(0.00034)	(0.00043)	(0.05239)	(0.00392)	(14.1578)

Vector Autoregression Estimates
Date: 11/27/06 Time: 11:48
Sample (adjusted): 1996Q1 2005Q4
Included observations: 40 after adjustments
Standard errors in ( ) & t-statistics in [ ]

	SLFDI	SLCUAC	SLEXRDOL	SLSM	LOG(SLCPI)	SLLR
SLFDI(-1)	0.478986	-0.059596	-0.000890	0.011110	4.92E-06	-0.000351
	(0.31316)	(0.27202)	(0.00060)	(0.01068)	(7.0E-06)	(0.00044)
	[1.52954]	[-0.21908]	[-1.47475]	[1.04075]	[0.70728]	[-0.79469]
SLFDI(-2)	-0.642484	0.156783	-0.000132	-0.005596	8.79E-06	-0.000271
	(0.30096)	(0.26143)	(0.00058)	(0.01026)	(6.7E-06)	(0.00042)
	[-2.13481]	[0.59972]	[-0.22724]	[-0.54543]	[1.31418]	[-0.63766]
SLFDI(-3)	0.246966	-0.109578	-0.000762	0.008119	-6.35E-06	0.000256
	(0.33791)	(0.29352)	(0.00065)	(0.01152)	(7.5E-06)	(0.00048)
	[0.73087]	[-0.37332]	[-1.16969]	[0.70487]	[-0.84588]	[0.53640]
SLFDI(-4)	-0.349048	0.058418	-2.15E-05	-0.017114	3.46E-06	-0.000617
	(0.30977)	(0.26909)	(0.00060)	(0.01056)	(6.9E-06)	(0.00044)
	[-1.12678]	[0.21710]	[-0.03600]	[-1.62061]	[0.50221]	[-1.41127]

SLCUAC(-1)	0.293951	0.064299	-0.000628	0.020638	-8.87E-06	-0.000741
	(0.41218)	(0.35804)	(0.00079)	(0.01405)	(9.2E-06)	(0.00058)
	[0.71316]	[0.17959]	[-0.78961]	[1.46878]	[-0.96832]	[-1.27406]
SLCUAC(-2)	-0.026155	0.272006	-9.86E-05	-0.004817	7.61E-06	-0.000311
	(0.42045)	(0.36523)	(0.00081)	(0.01433)	(9.3E-06)	(0.00059)
	[-0.06221]	[0.74476]	[-0.12167]	[-0.33606]	[0.81494]	[-0.52392]
SLCUAC(-3)	-0.036529	-0.369855	-0.000344	-0.008142	-4.97E-06	0.000217
	(0.41973)	(0.36460)	(0.00081)	(0.01431)	(9.3E-06)	(0.00059)
	[-0.08703]	[-1.01443]	[-0.42451]	[-0.56903]	[-0.53318]	[0.36662]
SLCUAC(-4)	-0.497064	0.212646	-4.84E-05	0.013196	2.26E-06	-0.001108
	(0.42288)	(0.36733)	(0.00082)	(0.01442)	(9.4E-06)	(0.00060)
	[-1.17544]	[0.57890]	[-0.05937]	[0.91542]	[0.24003]	[-1.85687]
SLEXRDOL (-1)	54.46088	-21.36049	0.760493	-1.763479	-0.000979	0.086693
	(100.153)	(86.9979)	(0.19311)	(3.41418)	(0.00223)	(0.14130)
	[0.54378]	[-0.24553]	[3.93803]	[-0.51652]	[-0.43984]	[0.61354]
SLEXRDOL (-2)	-135.2966	-45.70614	0.070293	0.374652	0.001266	-0.154473
	(136.690)	(118.736)	(0.26357)	(4.65972)	(0.00304)	(0.19285)
	[-0.98980]	[-0.38494]	[0.26670]	[0.08040]	[0.41686]	[-0.80101]
SLEXRDOL (-3)	216.6212	-43.04526	-0.084236	4.013599	-0.000339	-0.014061
	(151.195)	(131.335)	(0.29153)	(5.15416)	(0.00336)	(0.21331)
	[1.43273]	[-0.32775]	[-0.28894]	[0.77873]	[-0.10080]	[-0.06592]
SLEXRDOL (-4)	-95.09492	67.54240	0.196722	-6.043642	-0.001965	-0.130306
	(122.953)	(106.803)	(0.23708)	(4.19142)	(0.00273)	(0.17347)
	[-0.77343]	[0.63240]	[0.82978]	[-1.44191]	[-0.71901]	[-0.75119]
SLSM(-1)	-0.230695	1.939493	0.003465	0.832387	-0.000214	-0.021681
	(6.55149)	(5.69095)	(0.01263)	(0.22334)	(0.00015)	(0.00924)
	[-0.03521]	[0.34080]	[0.27432]	[3.72703]	[-1.46656]	[-2.34563]
SLSM(-2)	0.546532	1.471227	0.018611	0.029310	0.000259	0.012481
	(10.5997)	(9.20739)	(0.02044)	(0.36134)	(0.00024)	(0.01495)
	[0.05156]	[0.15979]	[0.91059]	[0.08111]	[1.10000]	[0.83458]
SLSM(-3)	-1.438303	-8.315830	-0.015305	-0.062543	-0.000132	-0.000242

	(11.1569)	(9.69141)	(0.02151)	(0.38033)	(0.00025)	(0.01574)
	[-0.12892]	[-0.85806]	[-0.71143]	[-0.16444]	[-0.53159]	[-0.01535]
SLSM(-4)	3.379053	-4.361148	-0.008766	-0.023116	-0.000115	-0.012029
	(9.44895)	(8.20782)	(0.01822)	(0.32211)	(0.00021)	(0.01333)
	[0.35761]	[-0.53134]	[-0.48111]	[-0.07176]	[-0.54939]	[-0.90234]
LOG(SLCPI (-1))	-2024.018	6534.045	9.098501	-184.4080	0.940837	-15.67376
	(12821.5)	(11137.4)	(24.7224)	(437.081)	(0.28493)	(18.0891)
	[-0.15786]	[0.58668]	[0.36803]	[-0.42191]	[3.30197]	[-0.86647]
LOG(SLCPI (-2))	-5378.521	-5941.535	0.003053	535.7184	0.209030	7.676721
	(16808.8)	(14600.9)	(32.4106)	(573.004)	(0.37354)	(23.7145)
	[-0.31998]	[-0.40693]	[9.4e-05]	[0.93493]	[0.55959]	[0.32371]
LOG(SLCPI (-3))	12540.10	-3942.319	-42.47406	680.3642	-0.466615	8.930218
	(16808.5)	(14600.7)	(32.4101)	(572.996)	(0.37354)	(23.7142)
	[0.74606]	[-0.27001]	[-1.31052]	[1.18738]	[-1.24919]	[0.37658]
LOG(SLCPI (-4))	-4818.964	3569.858	35.49301	-904.2081	0.350755	-2.475105
	(13071.3)	(11354.3)	(25.2040)	(445.595)	(0.29048)	(18.4415)
	[-0.36867]	[0.31440]	[1.40823]	[-2.02922]	[1.20749]	[-0.13421]
SLLR(-1)	-72.70298	62.12214	0.331740	5.449583	0.000553	0.758653
	(171.191)	(148.705)	(0.33009)	(5.83584)	(0.00380)	(0.24152)
	[-0.42469]	[0.41775]	[1.00500]	[0.93381]	[0.14527]	[3.14111]
SLLR(-2)	-58.34144	-44.53251	-0.508997	-0.599854	-9.06E-05	-0.117741
	(231.825)	(201.374)	(0.44700)	(7.90282)	(0.00515)	(0.32707)
	[-0.25166]	[-0.22114]	[-1.13869]	[-0.07590]	[-0.01760]	[-0.35999]
SLLR(-3)	68.59728	-77.04819	-0.323137	-11.64184	0.000501	0.077483
	(240.728)	(209.108)	(0.46417)	(8.20632)	(0.00535)	(0.33963)
	[0.28496]	[-0.36846]	[-0.69616]	[-1.41864]	[0.09362]	[0.22814]
SLLR(-4)	-30.43976	63.43385	0.843941	4.540586	-3.43E-05	-0.168838
	(149.901)	(130.212)	(0.28904)	(5.11008)	(0.00333)	(0.21149)
	[-0.20307]	[0.48716]	[2.91981]	[0.88855]	[-0.01028]	[-0.79834]
C	-1321.878	1082.797	-11.96430	-375.0949	-0.048358	24.16777
	(7116.98)	(6182.16)	(13.7229)	(242.615)	(0.15816)	(10.0409)
	[-0.18574]	[0.17515]	[-0.87185]	[-1.54605]	[-0.30575]	[2.40692]

R-squared	0.655929	0.687281	0.976368	0.974779	0.997066	0.979987
Adj. R-squared	0.105416	0.186930	0.938557	0.934424	0.992372	0.947965
Sum sq. resids	10631660	8022134.	39.52789	12355.08	0.005251	21.16209
S.E. equation	841.8891	731.3063	1.623328	28.69969	0.018709	1.187774
F-statistic	1.191487	1.373597	25.82212	24.15547	212.4142	30.60392
Log likelihood	-306.5669	-300.9343	-56.52008	-171.4164	122.0084	-44.02418
Akaike AIC	16.57834	16.29671	4.076004	9.820820	-4.850421	3.451209
Schwarz SC	17.63389	17.35226	5.131554	10.87637	-3.794871	4.506759
Mean dependent	653.4025	-938.1725	38.05940	177.9848	4.604409	13.53880
S.D. dependent	890.1115	811.0270	6.548906	112.0741	0.214220	5.206975

Determinant resid covariance (dof adj.)	4.11E+10
Determinant resid covariance	1.14E+08
Log likelihood	-711.6215
Akaike information criterion	43.08107
Schwarz criterion	49.41437

Slovenia:

Date: 11/27/06 Time: 11:51

Sample (adjusted): 1995Q3 2006Q1

Included observations: 43 after adjustments

Trend assumption: Linear deterministic trend
Series: SVFDI SVCUAC SVEXRDOL SVSM LOG(SVCPI) SVLR

Lags interval (in first differences): 1 to 1

Unrestricted Cointegration Rank Test (Trace)

Hypothesized No. of CE(s)	Eigenvalue	Trace Statistic	0.05 Critical Value	Prob.**
None *	0.757483	143.1582	95.75366	0.0000
At most 1 *	0.500834	82.24080	69.81889	0.0037
At most 2 *	0.465501	52.36373	47.85613	0.0178
At most 3	0.336256	25.42741	29.79707	0.1467
At most 4	0.135781	7.803456	15.49471	0.4866
At most 5	0.034922	1.528495	3.841466	0.2163

Trace test indicates 3 cointegrating eqn(s) at the 0.05 level
* denotes rejection of the hypothesis at the 0.05 level
**MacKinnon-Haug-Michelis (1999) p-values

Unrestricted Cointegration Rank Test (Maximum Eigenvalue)

Hypothesized No. of CE(s)	Eigenvalue	Max-Eigen Statistic	0.05 Critical Value	Prob.**
None *	0.757483	60.91742	40.07757	0.0001
At most 1	0.500834	29.87707	33.87687	0.1395
At most 2	0.465501	26.93632	27.58434	0.0604
At most 3	0.336256	17.62396	21.13162	0.1446
At most 4	0.135781	6.274961	14.26460	0.5782
At most 5	0.034922	1.528495	3.841466	0.2163

Max-eigenvalue test indicates 1 cointegrating eqn(s) at the 0.05 level
* denotes rejection of the hypothesis at the 0.05 level
**MacKinnon-Haug-Michelis (1999) p-values

Unrestricted Cointegrating Coefficients (normalized by b'*S11*b=I):

SVFDI	SVCUAC	SVEXRDOL	SVSM	LOG(SVCPI)	SVLR
0.003248	-0.019793	0.028517	0.001708	-10.20889	0.193583
0.001060	-0.003093	-0.109032	-0.003444	36.21324	0.066622
0.010579	0.003334	-0.030780	-0.001394	5.354997	-0.206331
0.000732	-0.010073	-0.020172	-0.002057	5.461588	-0.273195
-0.002944	0.006634	0.052326	0.003671	-33.10544	-0.184593
-0.002669	-0.001780	0.020026	0.000720	-6.480022	-0.209554

Unrestricted Adjustment Coefficients (alpha):

D(SVFDI)	-33.14144	-25.48349	-68.03034	-10.82604	12.18793	7.619521
D(SVCUAC)	58.03021	2.252615	-25.63517	5.682554	-12.88554	1.075437
D(SVEXRDOL)	-1.553642	1.462775	-2.536488	4.093428	1.710980	-0.446580
D(SVSM)	-81.80360	13.87010	-28.77836	1.405539	-51.91391	10.71276
D(LOG(SVCPI))	-0.000594	-0.004500	-0.000104	0.003103	-0.000516	-4.24E-05
D(SVLR)	0.091771	0.233599	0.334114	0.545532	0.077900	0.189498

1 Cointegrating Equation(s):	Log likelihood	-860.5996

Normalized cointegrating coefficients (standard error in parentheses)

SVFDI	SVCUAC	SVEXRDOL	SVSM	LOG(SVCPI)	SVLR
1.000000	-6.094640	8.781035	0.525913	-3143.576	59.60893
	(0.68429)	(3.59071)	(0.16051)	(1436.41)	(14.2676)

Adjustment coefficients (standard error in parentheses)

D(SVFDI)	-0.107628
	(0.06654)
D(SVCUAC)	0.188456
	(0.03407)
D(SVEXRDOL)	-0.005046
	(0.00538)
D(SVSM)	-0.265661
	(0.09094)
D(LOG(SVCPI))	-1.93E-06
	(4.6E-06)
D(SVLR)	0.000298
	(0.00083)

2 Cointegrating Equation(s):	Log likelihood	-845.6610

Normalized cointegrating coefficients (standard error in parentheses)

SVFDI	SVCUAC	SVEXRDOL	SVSM	LOG(SVCPI)	SVLR
1.000000	0.000000	-205.3412	-6.714235	68409.51	65.81311
		(37.3692)	(1.66907)	(14908.3)	(142.939)
0.000000	1.000000	-35.13288	-1.187953	11740.35	1.017973
		(6.21124)	(0.27742)	(2477.95)	(23.7583)

Adjustment coefficients (standard error in parentheses)

D(SVFDI)	-0.134644	0.734770
	(0.06844)	(0.40132)
D(SVCUAC)	0.190844	-1.155536
	(0.03582)	(0.21002)
D(SVEXRDOL)	-0.003495	0.026227
	(0.00559)	(0.03280)
D(SVSM)	-0.250957	1.576209
	(0.09533)	(0.55901)
D(LOG(SVCPI))	-6.70E-06	2.57E-05
	(4.1E-06)	(2.4E-05)
D(SVLR)	0.000546	-0.002539
	(0.00087)	(0.00508)

3 Cointegrating Equation(s):	Log likelihood	-832.1929

Normalized cointegrating coefficients (standard error in parentheses)

SVFDI	SVCUAC	SVEXRDOL	SVSM	LOG(SVCPI)	SVLR
1.000000	0.000000	0.000000	-0.023349	-456.2439	-16.55051
			(0.03795)	(251.795)	(7.84586)
0.000000	1.000000	0.000000	-0.043175	-42.26469	-13.07404
			(0.01312)	(87.0873)	(2.71362)
0.000000	0.000000	1.000000	0.032584	-335.3727	-0.401106
			(0.00339)	(22.4981)	(0.70104)

Adjustment coefficients (standard error in parentheses)

D(SVFDI)	-0.854358	0.507984	3.927363
	(0.18237)	(0.33313)	(1.91641)
D(SVCUAC)	-0.080359	-1.240993	2.198269
	(0.10613)	(0.19387)	(1.11529)
D(SVEXRDOL)	-0.030329	0.017771	-0.125721
	(0.01757)	(0.03209)	(0.18461)
D(SVSM)	-0.555412	1.480274	-2.959267
	(0.30547)	(0.55802)	(3.21013)
D(LOG(SVCPI))	-7.80E-06	2.53E-05	0.000477
	(1.3E-05)	(2.5E-05)	(0.00014)
D(SVLR)	0.004080	-0.001425	-0.033137
	(0.00275)	(0.00503)	(0.02891)

4 Cointegrating Equation(s):	Log likelihood	-823.3809

Normalized cointegrating coefficients (standard error in parentheses)

SVFDI	SVCUAC	SVEXRDOL	SVSM	LOG(SVCPI)	SVLR
1.000000	0.000000	0.000000	0.000000	-438.3188	-11.40077
				(192.688)	(7.51018)
0.000000	1.000000	0.000000	0.000000	-9.119090	-3.551585
				(81.1238)	(3.16187)
0.000000	0.000000	1.000000	0.000000	-360.3875	-7.587643
				(56.8474)	(2.21568)
0.000000	0.000000	0.000000	1.000000	767.6958	220.5526
				(1555.16)	(60.6138)

Adjustment coefficients (standard error in parentheses)

D(SVFDI)	-0.862285	0.617034	4.145749	0.148256
	(0.18162)	(0.36954)	(1.93263)	(0.07462)
D(SVCUAC)	-0.076198	-1.298233	2.083639	0.115396
	(0.10582)	(0.21531)	(1.12605)	(0.04348)
D(SVEXRDOL)	-0.027332	-0.023462	-0.208295	-0.012576

	(0.01583)	(0.03220)	(0.16843)	(0.00650)
D(SVSM)	-0.554383	1.466116	-2.987620	-0.150260
	(0.30613)	(0.62287)	(3.25751)	(0.12577)
D(LOG(SVCPI))	-5.53E-06	-5.93E-06	0.000414	8.25E-06
	(1.2E-05)	(2.5E-05)	(0.00013)	(5.0E-06)
D(SVLR)	0.004480	-0.006920	-0.044141	-0.002236
	(0.00256)	(0.00521)	(0.02722)	(0.00105)

5 Cointegrating Equation(s):	Log likelihood	-820.2434

Normalized cointegrating coefficients (standard error in parentheses)

SVFDI	SVCUAC	SVEXRDOL	SVSM	LOG(SVCPI)	SVLR
1.000000	0.000000	0.000000	0.000000	0.000000	3.147374
					(4.47814)
0.000000	1.000000	0.000000	0.000000	0.000000	-3.248915
					(1.52647)
0.000000	0.000000	1.000000	0.000000	0.000000	4.373899
					(1.90193)
0.000000	0.000000	0.000000	1.000000	0.000000	195.0722
					(26.6717)
0.000000	0.000000	0.000000	0.000000	1.000000	0.033191
					(0.00596)

Adjustment coefficients (standard error in parentheses)

D(SVFDI)	-0.898169	0.697884	4.783495	0.193000	-1411.419
	(0.18635)	(0.38195)	(2.09556)	(0.09489)	(819.796)
D(SVCUAC)	-0.038260	-1.383710	1.409390	0.068091	-190.5089
	(0.10654)	(0.21836)	(1.19805)	(0.05425)	(468.683)
D(SVEXRDOL)	-0.032369	-0.012112	-0.118766	-0.006295	20.96377
	(0.01603)	(0.03285)	(0.18025)	(0.00816)	(70.5135)
D(SVSM)	-0.401538	1.121739	-5.704069	-0.340847	2909.607
	(0.30005)	(0.61501)	(3.37422)	(0.15278)	(1320.01)
D(LOG(SVCPI))	-4.01E-06	-9.35E-06	0.000387	6.36E-06	-0.123459
	(1.2E-05)	(2.6E-05)	(0.00014)	(6.4E-06)	(0.05491)
D(SVLR)	0.004250	-0.006403	-0.040065	-0.001950	9.712232
	(0.00264)	(0.00542)	(0.02971)	(0.00135)	(11.6226)

Vector Autoregression Estimates
Date: 11/27/06 Time: 11:52
Sample (adjusted): 1996Q1 2006Q1
Included observations: 41 after adjustments
Standard errors in ( ) & t-statistics in [ ]

	SVFDI	SVCUAC	SVEXRDOL	SVSM	LOG(SVCPI)	SVLR
SVFDI(-1)	0.107846	-0.183518	-0.000889	-0.228022	-9.97E-06	0.002287
	(0.23196)	(0.11214)	(0.01526)	(0.24348)	(1.4E-05)	(0.00227)
	[0.46492]	[-1.63655]	[-0.05829]	[-0.93652]	[-0.73229]	[1.00525]
SVFDI(-2)	-0.168733	0.020638	-0.042094	-0.161472	-1.52E-05	0.001449
	(0.23022)	(0.11129)	(0.01514)	(0.24164)	(1.4E-05)	(0.00226)
	[-0.73294]	[0.18544]	[-2.78030]	[-0.66823]	[-1.12455]	[0.64174]
SVFDI(-3)	0.227711	0.079008	-0.021688	0.525374	5.44E-06	0.003783
	(0.25905)	(0.12523)	(0.01704)	(0.27191)	(1.5E-05)	(0.00254)
	[0.87903]	[0.63091]	[-1.27306]	[1.93219]	[0.35760]	[1.48890]
SVFDI(-4)	-0.009999	0.103158	-0.003439	0.283277	4.01E-05	0.004322
	(0.27771)	(0.13425)	(0.01826)	(0.29150)	(1.6E-05)	(0.00272)
	[-0.03601]	[0.76838]	[-0.18830]	[0.97180]	[2.45923]	[1.58683]
SVCUAC (-1)	0.606558	-0.302696	0.029478	-0.045560	-1.83E-05	-0.000171
	(0.45870)	(0.22174)	(0.03017)	(0.48146)	(2.7E-05)	(0.00450)
	[1.32235]	[-1.36507]	[0.97719]	[-0.09463]	[-0.67859]	[-0.03798]
SVCUAC (-2)	0.116493	-0.475349	0.028935	0.758695	2.11E-05	-0.003801
	(0.48585)	(0.23487)	(0.03195)	(0.50996)	(2.9E-05)	(0.00476)
	[0.23977]	[-2.02389]	[0.90560]	[1.48775]	[0.74180]	[-0.79763]
SVCUAC (-3)	-0.211225	-0.345206	0.041290	-1.346878	7.49E-06	-0.001445
	(0.43096)	(0.20834)	(0.02834)	(0.45235)	(2.5E-05)	(0.00423)
	[-0.49012]	[-1.65696]	[1.45685]	[-2.97750]	[0.29638]	[-0.34178]
SVCUAC (-4)	-0.424516	0.123370	-0.054269	1.077271	-4.50E-05	-0.007279
	(0.53123)	(0.25681)	(0.03494)	(0.55760)	(3.1E-05)	(0.00521)
	[-0.79912]	[0.48040]	[-1.55339]	[1.93199]	[-1.44284]	[-1.39707]
SVEXRD OL(-1)	3.777515	0.763100	0.153410	2.653417	0.000264	0.075862
	(3.27831)	(1.58481)	(0.21560)	(3.44103)	(0.00019)	(0.03215)
	[1.15227]	[0.48151]	[0.71156]	[0.77111]	[1.37359]	[2.35956]
SVEXRD OL(-2)	0.090766	2.361344	0.173097	6.586151	0.000318	-0.012145
	(3.38452)	(1.63615)	(0.22258)	(3.55250)	(0.00020)	(0.03319)

	[0.02682]	[1.44324]	[0.77768]	[1.85395]	[1.59941]	[-0.36590]
SVEXRD OL(-3)	3.781517	-1.435857	0.794528	-8.949780	0.000242	-0.011631
	(3.35438)	(1.62158)	(0.22060)	(3.52087)	(0.00020)	(0.03290)
	[1.12734]	[-0.88547]	[3.60169]	[-2.54193]	[1.22874]	[-0.35355]
SVEXRD OL(-4)	-4.436932	1.158853	-0.298315	-4.241905	-0.000400	-0.071524
	(4.11857)	(1.99101)	(0.27086)	(4.32299)	(0.00024)	(0.04039)
	[-1.07730]	[0.58204]	[-1.10138]	[-0.98124]	[-1.65357]	[-1.77076]
SVSM(-1)	0.069407	0.029220	-0.057240	1.291876	-2.14E-05	-0.000322
	(0.21078)	(0.10190)	(0.01386)	(0.22125)	(1.2E-05)	(0.00207)
	[0.32928]	[0.28676]	[-4.12920]	[5.83907]	[-1.73032]	[-0.15577]
SVSM(-2)	0.198151	0.170241	0.046362	-0.148763	4.91E-05	0.004177
	(0.30518)	(0.14753)	(0.02007)	(0.32032)	(1.8E-05)	(0.00299)
	[0.64930]	[1.15395]	[2.31006]	[-0.46441]	[2.74081]	[1.39551]
SVSM(-3)	0.078069	-0.044070	-0.000156	-0.340212	-3.47E-06	-0.005196
	(0.22219)	(0.10741)	(0.01461)	(0.23322)	(1.3E-05)	(0.00218)
	[0.35136]	[-0.41030]	[-0.01067]	[-1.45877]	[-0.26643]	[-2.38446]
SVSM(-4)	-0.261598	-0.016918	-0.006750	-0.101767	-2.14E-05	-0.000167
	(0.18098)	(0.08749)	(0.01190)	(0.18997)	(1.1E-05)	(0.00177)
	[-1.44542]	[-0.19337]	[-0.56707]	[-0.53571]	[-2.01768]	[-0.09412]
LOG(SVC PI(-1))	-2456.887	1682.250	187.5876	4770.985	0.725416	10.88036
	(4050.88)	(1958.28)	(266.404)	(4251.94)	(0.23769)	(39.7276)
	[-0.60651]	[0.85904]	[0.70415]	[1.12207]	[3.05195]	[0.27387]
LOG(SVC PI(-2))	1360.135	-1780.801	-153.0958	-11959.96	0.039033	-46.15080
	(4389.42)	(2121.94)	(288.668)	(4607.28)	(0.25755)	(43.0478)
	[0.30987]	[-0.83923]	[-0.53035]	[-2.59588]	[0.15155]	[-1.07208]
LOG(SVC PI(-3))	-2317.579	-619.3125	-696.3572	9744.514	-0.224995	-2.089836
	(5137.18)	(2483.42)	(337.845)	(5392.16)	(0.30143)	(50.3812)
	[-0.45114]	[-0.24938]	[-2.06118]	[1.80718]	[-0.74643]	[-0.04148]
LOG(SVC PI(-4))	2939.582	156.3194	741.2327	67.54153	0.343539	41.95683
	(3862.80)	(1867.36)	(254.035)	(4054.53)	(0.22665)	(37.8831)
	[0.76100]	[0.08371]	[2.91783]	[0.01666]	[1.51570]	[1.10753]

SVLR(-1)	-13.15475	-1.839885	1.024424	-62.37688	-0.000819	0.739674
	(18.9340)	(9.15311)	(1.24519)	(19.8738)	(0.00111)	(0.18569)
	[-0.69477]	[-0.20101]	[0.82271]	[-3.13865]	[-0.73722]	[3.98340]
SVLR(-2)	9.707738	13.95716	-2.977691	67.54282	-0.001266	-0.000302
	(25.3749)	(12.2668)	(1.66877)	(26.6343)	(0.00149)	(0.24886)
	[0.38257]	[1.13780]	[-1.78436]	[2.53593]	[-0.85058]	[-0.00121]
SVLR(-3)	-2.136633	10.92406	-0.429790	3.606784	0.000516	-0.034391
	(22.5716)	(10.9116)	(1.48441)	(23.6919)	(0.00132)	(0.22136)
	[-0.09466]	[1.00114]	[-0.28954]	[0.15224]	[0.38952]	[-0.15536]
SVLR(-4)	14.51202	6.005959	0.325849	-1.343882	0.000189	0.007374
	(13.9022)	(6.72063)	(0.91427)	(14.5922)	(0.00082)	(0.13634)
	[1.04386]	[0.89366]	[0.35640]	[-0.09210]	[0.23205]	[0.05409]
C	1352.451	1186.350	-234.1975	-10745.46	0.488795	-11.59740
	(7127.68)	(3445.67)	(468.749)	(7481.45)	(0.41822)	(69.9023)
	[0.18975]	[0.34430]	[-0.49962]	[-1.43628]	[1.16874]	[-0.16591]
R-squared	0.680146	0.752979	0.974626	0.995590	0.999361	0.972376
Adj. R-squared	0.200364	0.382446	0.936565	0.988976	0.998402	0.930941
Sum sq. resids	267181.4	62439.27	1155.553	294362.0	0.000920	25.69763
S.E. equation	129.2240	62.46963	8.498355	135.6378	0.007582	1.267321
F-statistic	1.417616	2.032154	25.60688	150.5220	1042.594	23.46722
Log likelihood	-238.2098	-208.4082	-126.6211	-240.1958	161.2729	-48.59943
Akaike AIC	12.83950	11.38577	7.396151	12.93638	-6.647459	3.590216
Schwarz SC	13.88436	12.43063	8.441012	13.98124	-5.602598	4.635077
Mean dependent	116.5333	-27.36098	194.7781	2577.676	4.639338	14.06563
S.D. dependent	144.5097	79.49349	33.74192	1291.862	0.189704	4.822540

Determinant resid covariance (dof adj.)	3.07E+09
Determinant resid covariance	10834967
Log likelihood	-681.1238
Akaike information criterion	40.54262
Schwarz criterion	46.81179

Bibliography

Acton Institute (2007). Academic Research Center, Studies in Ethics and Economics, In The Liberal Tradition. A History of Liberty – Collection of Biographies. Retrieved April 12, 2007 from http://www.acton.org/publicat/randl/liberal.php?id=33.

Appel, Gerald (2005). *Technical Analysis: Power Tools for Active Investors*. Upper Saddle River, New Jersey. Pearson Education, Inc., Financial Times/Prentice Hall.

Aristovnik, A. (2006). "Current Account Sustainability in Selected Transition Countries," William Davidson Institute Working Paper No. 844, retrieved on May 7, 2007 from http://ssrn.com/abstract=971017.

Arnold, Ivo, and Jan Lemmen (2001). "The Vulnerability of Banks to Government Default Risk in the EMU," *International Finance*, 4 (1); 101-125.

BA – CA (2007). Bank Austria-Credit Anstalt quarterly CEE report. Q1 2007.

Babbie, E. (2001). *The Practice of Social Research*. (9th ed.). Belmont, Cal.: Wadsworth/Thompson Learning.

Barberis, N. and Thaler, R. (2003). A Survey of Behavioral Finance, in *Handbook of the Economics of Finance*, Edited by G. Constantinides, M. Harris, and R. Stulz. Elsevier Science B.V.

———, Huang, M., and Thaler R. (2006). "Individual Preferences, Monetary Gambles, and Stock Market Participation: A Case for Narrow Framing," *The American Economic Review*, Nashville, 96 (4); 1069.

Barr, David, G., and Richard Priestly (2004). "Expected Returns, Risk and the Integration of International Bond Markets," *Journal of International Money and Finance*, 23; 71-97.

Bechev, I. (2006). "Segmented Market Efficiency Hypothesis," Retrieved May 6, 2007 from SSRN: http://ssrn.com/abstract=935049.

Bekaert, Geert (1995), "Market Integration and Investment Barriers in Emerging Equity Markets," *World Bank Economic Review*, 9; 75-107.

———, and Campbell R. Harvey (2002), Research in Emerging Markets Finance: Looking to the Future," *Emerging Markets Review*, 429-448.

———, (2003), "Emerging Markets Finance," *Journal of Empirical Finance*, 10; 3-35.

Berk, Jean Marc, and Laas H.W. Knot (1999). "Co-Movements in Long-Term Interest Rates and the Role of PPP-Based Exchange Rate Expectations," IMF Working Paper No. 99/81. Wasington, D.C. June.

Berg, B.L. (1998). *Qualitative Research Methods for the Social Sciences*. (3rd ed.). Boston: Allyn & Bacon.

Berger, H., George Kopits, and Istvan Szekely (2007). "Fiscal Indulgence in Central Europe: Loss of the External Anchor?" *Scottish Journal of Political Economy*, 54 (1); 116-135.

Bernanke, Ben, S. (2005). "Monetary Policy in a World of Mobile Capital," *Cato Journal*, 25 (1).

———, and Frederic S. Mishkin (1997). "Inflation Targeting: A New Framework for Monetary Policy?" NBER Working paper 5893. Cambridge, Mass. January 1997.

Bernoth, Kerstin, Jurgen von Hagen, and Ludger Schuknecht (2003). "Sovereign Risk Premia in the European Government Bond Market," ECB Working Paper No. 369, June 2004.

Bevan, Alan, A., and Saul Estrin (2004). The Determinants of Foreign Direct investment into European Transitional Economies," *Journal of Comparative Economics*, 32 (4); 775-787.

Brada, Josef C., and Ali M. Kutan (2002), "Balkan and Mediterranean Candidates for European Union Membership," *Eastern European Economics Armonk*, 40 (4): 31.

———, and Taner M. Yigit, (2004). "The Effects of Transition and Political Instability on Foreign Direct Investment Inflows: Central Europe and the Balkans," ZEI Working Paper No. B33. Center for European integration Studies. Bonn, Germany.

Bratislava Stock Exchange Retrieved 1 November 2006 (for the year 1995) http://www.bsse.sk/Obchodovanie/Indexy/_IndexHistoria.aspx?LANG=EN&Idx=SAX&Od=3.%207.%201995%200:00:00&Do=28.%206.%201996%200:00:00

Brooks, Robert, Robert W. Faff, David Hillier, and Joseph Hillier, 2004, "The National Market Impact of Sovereign Rating Changes," *The Journal of Banking and Finance*, 28: 233-250.

Bruggemann, R. and Trenkler, C. (2005). "Are Eastern European Countries Catching up? Time Series Evidence for Czech Republic, Hungary, and Poland," Humbolt-Universitat Berlin, SFB 649 Discussion Paper 2005-014. March, 2005.

Bruha, J. and Jiyi Podpiera (2007). "Transition Economy Convergence in a Two-Country Model: Implications for Monetary Integration," ECB Working paper No. 740, march 2007.

Buch, Claudia M., Robert M. Kokta, and Daniel Piazolo (2002), "Foreign Direct Investment in Europe: Is There Redirection from the South to the East?" *Journal of Comparative Economics,* 31; 91-109.

Buch, Claudia M., and Lusine Lusinyan (2001), "Short-Term Capital, Economic Transformation, and EU Accession," Kiel Institute of World Economics and European University Institute.

Busse, M. and Hefeker, C. (2005). "Political Risk, Institutions and Foreign Direct Investment," HWWA Discussion paper No. 315. April 2005.

Cantor, Richard, and Frank Packer (1995). "Sovereign Credit Ratings," Federal Reserve Bank of New York *Current Issues in Economics and Finance*, 1 (3); June.

———, (1996). "Determinants and Impact of Sovereign Credit Ratings," Federal Reserve Bank of New York *Economic Policy Review,* 2 (2); 37-53.

Carstensen, K. and Toubal, F. (2003). "Foreign Direct Investment in Central and Eastern European Countries: A Dynamic Panel Analysis," Kiel Institute Working Paper No. 1143. January 2003.

Caviglia, Giacomo, Gerhard Krause, and Christian Thimann (2002). In Thimann, Christian (2002), "Financial Sectors in EU Accession Countries," European Central Bank, August.

Claessens, Stijn, Daniel Oks, and Rossana Polastri (1998). "Capital Flows to Central and Eastern Europe and Former Soviet Union" World Bank Working Paper No. 1976, Washington, D.C., September.

———, Simeon Djankov, and Daniela Klingebiel (2000), "Stock Markets in Transition Economies," World Bank Financial Sector Discussion Paper No. 5, Washington, D.C., September.

Cook, T.D. (1993). A Quasi-Sampling Theory of the Generalization of Causal Relationships. In Denzin, N. and Lincoln, Y. (Eds.), *The Sage Handbook of Qualitative Research* (3rd ed.), Thousand Oaks, Cal.: Sage Publications.

Creswell, J. W. (1998). *Qualitative Inquiry and Research Design: Choosing Among Five Traditions*. Thousand Oaks, Cal.: Sage Publications.

———, and Clark, V.P. (2007). *Designing and Conducting Mixed Methods Research*. Thousand Oaks, Cal. Sage Publications, Inc.

Czech Ministry of Industry and Trade (2007). Foreign Trade. Retrieved April 12, 2007 from http://www.mpo.cz/en/foreign-trade/

Czech National Bank (2007). Balance of Payments Statistics retrieved April 12, 2007 from http://www.cnb.cz/www.cnb.cz/en/statistics/bop_stat/fdi/fdi_flows_2006/index.html

Deichmann, Joel (2001). "Distribution of Foreign Direct Investment Among Transition Economies in Central and Eastern Europe," *Post Soviet Geography and Economics*, 42 (2); 142-152.

———, Eshghi, A., Haughton, D., Sayek, S., Teebagy, N. & Topi, H. (2003). "Geography Matters: Kohonen Classification of Determinants of Foreign Direct Investment in Transition Economies," *Journal of Business Strategies*, 20 (1). P. 23.

Denzin, N. and Lincoln, Y. (Eds.), (2005). *The Sage Handbook of Qualitative Research* (3rd ed.), Thousand Oaks, Cal.: Sage Publications.

Depken, C. A., LaFountain, C. and Butters, R. (2006) "Corruption and Creditworthiness: Evidence from Sovereign Credit Ratings" (April 19, 2006). Available at SSRN: http://ssrn.com/abstract=899414

Dickey, D. and Fuller, W. (1979). "Distribution of the Estimators for Autoregressive Time Series with a Unit Root," *Journal of the American Statistical Association*, 74: 427-431.

———, (1981). "The Likelihood Ratio Statistics for Autoregressive Time Series with a Unit Root," *Econometrica*, 49: 1057-1072.

Dockery, E., and Vergari, F. (2001). "An Investigation of the Linkages Between European Union Equity Markets and Emerging Capital Markets: The East European Connection," *Managerial Finance*, 27 (1/2): 24-39.

Ebeling, R. (2004). "From the President: 1914 and the World We Lost," *The Freeman*, 54 (6).

The Economist (2007). "Charlemagne – A cool peace." March 3, 2007.

———, (2010). "Culture Creep." March 13, 2010.

Economist Intelligence Unit (EIU). Taken from Nova Southeastern University library website on 14 June 2006 http://0-wwwa4.secure.alacra.com.novacat.nova.edu/cgi-bin/alacraswitchISAPI.dll#

Edwards, R.D. and Magee, J. (1966). *Technical Analysis of Stock Trends*. (5th ed.). Boston: John Magee Publishers, Inc.

Eichengreen, B. (2006). "The Next Tsunami? Preparing for a Disorderly Correction of Global Imbalances?" Presented to the Asian Economic Panel, Seoul, March 2006.

Eichengreen, Barry, and Omar Choudhry (2005). "Managing Capital Inflows: Eastern Europe in an Asian Mirror," European Integration Studies Conference Paper on Macroeconomic Policies for EU Accession. Turkish Central Bank. Ankara, May 2005.

Engle, R. (1982). "Autoregressive Conditional Heteroskedasticity with Estimates of the Variance of UK Inflation," *Econometrica*, 50 987-1008.

——— and C.W. Granger (1987). "Cointegration and Error Correction: Representation, Estimation, and Testing," *Econometrica*, 55; 251-276.

Eller, M., Haiss, P., and Steiner, K. (2005). "Foreign Direct Investment in the Financial Sector: The Engine of Growth for Central and Eastern Europe?" University of Economics and Business Administration, Vienna. EI Working paper No. 69. December 2005.

Erb, Claude B., Campbell R. Harvey, and Tadas E. Viskanta (1996), "Expected Returns and Volatility in 135 Countries," *The Journal of Portfolio Management*, 21 (Spring): 46-58.

———, (1996b), "The Influence of Political, Economic and Financial Risk on Expected Fixed-Income Returns," *Journal of Fixed Income*, (June): 7-31.

———, (1996), "Political Risk, Economic Risk, and Financial Risk," *Financial Analysts Journal*, 52 (6): 29-46.

———, (1999), "New Perspectives on Emerging Market Bonds," *Journal of Portfolio Management*, 25 (2): 83-92.

———, (2000), "Understanding Emerging Market Bonds," *Emerging Markets Quarterly*, 4 (10): 7-23.

Fama, Eugene F. (1965), "The Behavior of Stock Market Prices," *Journal of Business*, 38 (1): 34-105.

———, (1970), "Efficient Capital Markets – A Review of Theory and Empirical Work," *Journal of Finance*, 25 (2): 383-417.

———, (1991), "Efficient Capital Markets: II," *Journal of Finance*, 46 (5): 1575-1617.

——— and Kenneth R. French (1992), "The Cross Section of Expected Stock Returns," *Journal of Finance*, 47 (2): 427-465.

———, (1998). "Value Versus Growth: The International Evidence," *Journal of Finance*, 53 (6); 1975-1999.

———, (2004). "The Capital Asset Pricing Model: Theory and Evidence," CRSP Working Paper No. 550; Tuck Business School Working Paper No. 03-26. January 2004.

Feig, Professor Konnilyn, Foothill College, Los Altos Hill, California, on 4 April 2007 http://www.omnibusol.com/easteurope.html#Slovenia

Ferragina, A., Giovannetti, G. and Pastore, F. (2006). "FDI Potential and Shortfalls in the Med: Determinants and Diversion Effects," Paper presented at the European Assoc. for Comaprative Economics Studies (EACES) 9th Bi-annual Conference. University of Brighton, UK. September 2006.

Financial Times, Various issues and special sections, 2005-2007.

Fitch Ratings (2006). Emerging Europe Sovereign Review – 2006. May 2006.

Foundation for Economic Education, November 23, 2005 from http://www.fee.org/

Fratzscher, Marcel (2002). "Financial Market Integration in Europe: On the Effects of EMU on Stock Markets," *International Journal of Finance and Economics*, 7 (3): 165-193.

Gabb, S. (1992, July). Czecho-Slovakia Rejoins the West. *The Freeman*, 42 (7). Retrieved 4 April 2007, from http://www.fee.org/publications/the-freeman/article.asp?aid=2093.

Glasser, B. & Strauss, A. (1967). Discovery of Grounded Theory. Chicago: Aldine Press. In Strauss, A. & Corbin, J. (1998). *Basics of Qualitative Research: Techniques and Procedures for Developing Grounded Theory*. (2nd ed.). Thousand Oaks, Cal.: Sage Publications.

Goldberg, L. S. (2007)."Financial Sector FDI and Host Countries: New and Old Lessons," *Federal Reserve Bank of New York Economic Policy Review*, March 2007.

Gourieroux, C. and Jasiak, J. (2001). *Financial Econometrics: Problems, Models, and Methods*. Princeton: Princeton University Press.

Gourinchas, Pierre-Olivier and Rey, Helene M. (2005). "International Financial Adjustment" UC Berkeley Center for International and Development Economic Research Working Paper No. C05-139.

Graham, B. & Dodd, D. L. (1951). *Security Analysis*. (3rc ed.). New York: McGraw Hill.

Granger, C.W.J. (1981). "Some Properties of Time Series Data and Their Use in Econometric Model Specification," *Journal of Econometrics*, 121-130.

———, (1983). "Co-Integrated Variables and Error-Correcting Models," unpublished UCSD Discussion Paper 83 - 13.

Gwartney, J. D.& R. Lawson (2005). *Economic Freedom of the World 2005 Annual Report*. Vancouver, British Columbia: The Fraser Institute. Retrieved November 17, 2005 from http://www.cato.org/pubs/efw/efw2005/efw2005title.pdf.

Harvey, Campbell R. (1991). "The World Price of Covariance Risk," *Journal of Finance*, 46 (1): 111-157.

———, (2004). "Country Risk Components, the Cost of Capital, and Returns in Emerging Markets," NBER abstract 620710. Cambridge, Mass.

Hauner, David, Jonas, Jiri and Kumar, Manmohan (2007). "Policy Credibility and Sovereign Credit – The Case of New EU Member States" (January 2007). IMF Working Paper No. 07/01 Available at SSRN: http://ssrn.com/abstract=956766.

Heinemann, Friedrich, and Viktor Winschel (2001). "Public Deficits and Borrowing Costs: The Missing Half of Market Discipline," Zentrum fur Europaische Wirtschaftsforschung (ZEW) Discussion Paper No. 01-16.

Houthakker, H.S. (1965). "New Evidence on Demand Elasticities," *Econometrica,* 33 (2); 277-288.

International Monetary Fund (IMF). Retrieved June 12, 2006 from http://dsbb.imf.org/Applications/web/sddscountrycategorylist/?strcode=CZE

———, International Financial Statistics and Balance of Payments data, 1995-2006.

Janicki, Hubert, P., and Phanindra V. Wunnava (2004). "Determinants of Foreign Direct Investment: Empirical Evidence from EU Accession Candidates," *Applied Economics*, 36 (5); 505-509.

Jaros, R.E. (1992). *Sokol – Gathering in the New World.* Kennett, Pa: KNA Press.

Johansen, S. (1988). "Statistical Analysis of Cointegration Vectors," *Journal of Economic Dynamics and Control*, 12: 231-254.

———, (1991). "Estimation and Hypothesis Testing of Cointegration Vectors in Gaussian Vector Autoregressive Models," *Econometrica,* 59: 1551-1580.

———, (1995a) "Likelihood-based Inference in Cointegrated Vector Auto-regressive Models," Oxford University Press, New York.

Kaminski, Bartlomiej (2001). "How Accession to the European Union Has Affected External Trade and Foreign Direct Investment in Central European Economies," World Bank Policy Research working Paper No. 2578. April 2001.

Kaminsky, Graciela, and Sergio L. Schmukler, 2002, "Emerging Market Instability: Do Sovereign Ratings Affect Country Risk and Stock Returns?," *The World Bank Economic Review*, 16 (2): 171.

Kim, Suk-Joong and Wu, Eliza (2006). "Sovereign Credit Ratings, Capital Flows and Financial Sector Development in Emerging Markets" Available at SSRN: http://ssrn.com/abstract=921263

Kejzar, K. (2006). "The Role of Foreign Direct Investment in the Firm Selection Process in a Host Country: Evidence from Slovenia," William Davidson Institute Working Paper No. 841 September 2006.

Kinoshita, Y. and Campos, N. (2003). "Why Does FDI Go Where It Goes? New Evidence From The Transition Economies," William Davidson Institute at the University of Michigan Business School. Working Paper No. 573. June 2003.

Kocenda, Evaen (2001). "Macroeconomic Convergence in Transition Economies," *Journal of Comparative Economics,* 29 (1); 1-23.

Krkoska, L. (2001). "Foreign Direct Investment Financing of Capital Formation in Central and Eastern Europe," EBRD Working Paper No. 67 December 2001.

Kutan, Ali M., and Taner M. Yigit (2002). "Nominal and Real Stochastic Convergence within the Transition Economies and to the European Union: Evidence from Panel Data," ZEI Working Paper B21, Center for European Integration Studies, Bonn, Germany.

———, (2004). "Nominal and Real Stochastic Convergence Within the Transitional Economies: Panel Evidence," *Journal of Comparative Economics*, 32: 23-36.

———, (2005). "Real and Nominal Stochastic Convergence: Are New EU Members Ready to Join the Eurozone?" *Journal of Comparative Economics*, San Diego, 33 (2): 387416.

Kvale, S. (1996). InterViews: An Introduction to Qualitative Research Interviewing. In Babbie, E. (2001). *The Practice of Social Research.* (9th ed.). Belmont, Cal.: Wadsworth/Thompson Learning.

Kyrkilis, D. and Pantelidis, P. (2006). "European Union Entry and Foreign Direct Investment Flows into Central and Eastern Europe," Paper presented at the European Association for Comparative Economics Studies (EACES) 9th Annual Conference: Development Strategies – A Comparative View. September 2006.

LaPorta, Rafael, Florenceio Lopez-de-Silanes, Andrei Shleifer, and Robert Vishny (1999). "Investor Protection and Corporate Valuation," NBER Working paper 7428, National Bureau of Economic Research, Cambridge, Mass.

Lemmen, Jan, J.G., and Charles A.E. Goodhart (1999), "Credit Risks and European Government Bond Markets; a panel Data Econometric Analysis," *Eastern Economic Journal*, 25 (1); 77-107.

Levine, Ross, Norman Loayza, and Thorsten Beck (2000). "Financial Intermediation and Growth: Causality and Causes," *Journal of Monetary Economics, Amsterdam*, August, 46 (1): 31.

Lewis, J. (2007). "Hitting and Hoping? Meeting the Exchange Rate and Inflation Criteria During a Period of Nominal Convergence," CESifo Working Paper Series No. 1655 Available at SSRN: http://ssrn.com/abstract=886492

Lintner, John (1965). "The Valuation of Risk Assets and the Selection of Risky Investments in Stock Portfolios and Capital Budgets, " *Review of Economics and Statistics*, 47, 13-37.

Lloyd, J. (2006, June 3). Let's just stick to the issues. *The Financial Times*, p. W3.

Ludwig von Mises Institute, on November 23, 2005 from http://www.mises.org/content/about.asp.

Lutkepohl, H. (2005). "Structural Vector Autoregressive Analysis for Cointegrated Variables," European University Institute Working Paper No. 2005/2. San Domenico, Italy.

McGee, R.W. (2003). "Foreign Direct Investment in Southeastern Europe," Andreas School of Business Working Paper Series at Barry University. December, 2003.

Mackie, J.L. (1974). The Cement of the Universe. Oxford, UK. Clarendon Press. In Denzin, N. and Lincoln, Y. (Eds.), (2005). *The Sage Handbook of Qualitative Research* (3rd ed.). Thousand Oaks, Cal.: Sage Publications.

Maiden, Ben, and Thomas Williams (2001). "Central Europe's Rough Road to the EU," *International Financial Law Review*," 20 (11): 49-53.

Markowitz, Harry (1952), "Portfolio Selection," *The Journal of Finance*, 7 (1): 77-91.

Maxwell, J.A. (1996). Working paper , Harvard Project on Schooling and Children, Harvard University. In Denzin, N. and Lincoln, Y. (Eds.), (2005). *The Sage Handbook of Qualitative Research* (3rd ed.), Thousand Oaks, Cal.: Sage Publications.

Merlevede, B. and Schoors, K. (2004). "Reform, FDI and Economic Growth: Tale of the Tortoise and the Hare," William Davidson Institute Working Paper No. 730. November.

———, (2004). "Gradualism versus Big Bang: Evidence from Transition Countries," Ghent University Working paper. April 2004.

———, (2006). "How to Catch foreign Fish? FDI and Privatisation in EU Accession Countries," William Davidson Institute Working paper No. 785. July.

Mishkin, Frederic S. (1999), "International Experiences with Different Monetary Regimes," *Journal of Monetary Economics*, 43 (3): 579-606.

———, (2000), "Inflation Targeting in Emerging-Market Countries," *The American Economic Review*, 90 (2): 105-109.

Mody, Ashoka, Mark P. Taylor, and Jung Yeon kim (2001). "Modelling Fundamentals for Forecasting Capital Flows to Emerging Market," *International Journal of Finance & Economics*, 6(3): 201-216.

Murphy, J. J. (1986). *Technical Analysis of the Futures Markets: A Complete Guide to Trading Methods and Application*. New York: New York Institute of Finance/Prentice Hall.

Nguyen, D.K. and Fontaine, P. (2006). "Stock Market Liberalization and Informational Efficiency in Emerging Markets: New Consideration and Tests," *Bank & Markets*, No. 84, 2006. Taken on May 6, 2007 from: http://papers.ssrn.com/sol3/papers.cfm?abstract_id=975260.

Obsterfeld, M. and Rogoff, K. (2005). "Global Current Account Imbalances and Exchange Rate Adjustment," Brookings Papers on Economic Activity 2005 (1) (Spring): 67-123.

Orlowski, Lucjan T. (2003). "Monetary Convergence and Risk Premiums in the EU Accession Countries," *Open Economies Review Dordrecht*, 14 (3): 251-278.

———, (2005), "Monetary Convergence of the EU Accession Countries to the Eurozone: A Theoretical Framework and Policy Implications," *Journal of Banking and Finance, Amsterdam*, 29 (1): 203.

Partners for Financial Stability (PFS) Program, on 3 April 2007, http://www.pfsprogram.org/capitalmarkets_research.php.

Pring, M. (1985). *Technical Analysis Explained*. (2nd ed.). New York: McGraw Hill.

Reinhart, Carmen, M. (2002). "Default, Currency Crises, and Sovereign Credit Ratings," *The World Bank Economic Review*, 16 (2): 151-170.

Reininger, Thomas, Franz Schardax, and Martin Summer (2002). "The Financial System in the Czech Republic, Hungary and Poland After the First Decade of Transition," Oesterreichische Nationalbank.

Reisen, Helmut, and Julia von Maltzan (1998). "Sovereign Credit Ratings, Emerging Market Risk and Financial Market Volatility," *Intereconomics*, 33 (2): 73-82.

Rocha, Katia, and Francisco A. Alcaraz Garcia (2005). "The Term Structure of Sovereign Spreads in Emerging Markets," *The Journal of Fixed Income*, March 2005, 45-56.

Roland, Gerard (2002). "The Political Economy of Transition," *Journal of economic Perspectives*, 16 (1): 29-50.

Royal Swedish Academy of Sciences (2003). "Time-Series Econometrics: Cointegration and Autoregressive Conditional Heteroskedasticity," Retrieved February15, 2007 from http://nobelprize.org/nobel_prizes/economics/laureates/2003/public.html

Rubin, J.L. (2004). "Cointegration and Antitrust: A Primer," *Economics Committee Newsletter*, 4 (1): 10-19.

Schadler, S., Mody, A., Abiad, A., and Leigh, D. (2006). Growth in the Central and Eastern European Countries of the European Union. International Monetary Fund Occasional Paper No. 252. Washington, D.C.

Schwammenthal, D. (2006, September). The Socialist Nationalist. *The Wall Street Journal*, September 17, 2006. Retrieved September 23, 2006, from http://online.wsj.com/article/SB115801113121659806.html

Serbu, S.G. (2005). "FDI flows towards CEECs: an analysis on Romania, Hungary, and Slovenia's performance," University of Orleans, France and Babes-Bolyai University in Romania. October 2005.

Sharpe, William F. (1964). "Capital Asset Prices: A Theory of Market Equilibrium Under Conditions of Risk," *Journal of Finance*, 19 (3): 425-442.

Sims, C.A. (1980) "Macroeconomics and Reality," *Econometrica,* 48: 1-48.

Sobol, Dorothy M. (1996). "Central and Eastern Europe: Financial Markets and Private Capital Flows," Federal Reserve Bank of New York, Research Paper # 9626.

Solnik, Bruno (1974). "The International Pricing of Risk: An Empirical Investigation of the World Capital Market Structure," *Journal of Finance*, 29 (2): 48-54.

Stake, R. (1995). The Art of Case Study Research. Thousand Oaks, Cal. Sage Publications. In Strauss, A. & Corbin, J. (1998). *Basics of Qualitative Research: Techniques and Procedures for Developing Grounded Theory.* (2nd ed.). Thousand Oaks, Cal.: Sage Publications.

Steiner, Manfred, and Volker G. Heinke (2001). "Event Study Concerning International Bond Price Effects of Credit Rating Actions," *International Journal of Finance and Economics*, 6 (2): 139.

Strauss, A., and Corbin, J. (1998). *Basics of Qualitative Research: Techniques and Procedures for Developing Grounded Theory.* (2nd ed.). Thousand Oaks, Cal.: Sage Publications.

Thimann, Christian (2002). "Financial Sectors in EU Accession Countries," European Central Bank, August.

Tille, C. and Eric van Wincoop (2007). "International Capital Flows," Federal Reserve Bank of New York Staff Reports, no. 280, March 2007.

Thornton, D. (2006). "Tests of the Expectations Hypothesis: Resolving the Campbell-Schiller Paradox," *Journal of Money, Credit, and Banking*, 38 (2).

Tupy, M. (2006). "The Rise of Populist Parties in Central Europe – Big Government, Corruption, and the Threat to Liberalism." Cato Institute Center for Global Liberty & Prosperity. November 8, 2006. No. 1.

von Boehm-Bawerk, E. (1884). *The Positive Theory of Capital.* Translated by William A. Smart. London: Macmillan & Co.

von Hagen, Jurgen, and Boris Hofmann (2004). "Macroeconomic Implications of Low Inflation in the Euro Area," *North American Journal of Economics and Finance,* 15: 5-23.

von Mises, L. (2007). *Principles of Economics.* Auburn, Ala. Ludwig von Mises Institute.

Wade, Jared (2005). "Political Risk in Eastern Europe," *Risk Management*, 52 (3): 24-30.

Walker, M. (2007). Europe Competes for Investment with Lower Corporate Tax Rates, report says. *The Wall Street Journal*, p. A12.

Webber, A. and Beck, G. (2005). "Price Stability, Inflation Convergence and Diversity in the EMU: Does One Size Fit All?," Center For Financial Studies, Frankfurt. CFS Working paper No. 2005/30. November 2005.

Wooster, Rossitza B., "The Strategic Interdependence of Foreign Direct Investment and Economic Reform in Transition Economies: An Evolutionary Game-Theoretic Approach" (March 2007). Available at SSRN: http://ssrn.com/abstract=976539

Yatrakis, P. (2005). "Japanese Candlestick Chart Patterns: An Apparent Anomaly in the Weak Form of the Efficient Market Hypothesis," version 2. Huizenga School of Business, Nova Southeastern University. December 2005.

Yildirim, H. and George Philippatos (2007). "Efficiency of Banks: Recent Evidence from the Transition Economics of Europe – 1993-2000," *European Journal of Finance*, 13 (2); 123-143.

Zagreb Stock Exchange taken 1 November 2006 http://www.zse.hr/history.php?sessionId=5d828ea44fe2ab96cf11c244d903cb6c

Zapal, Jan and Schneider, Ondrej (2006). "What are their Words Worth? Political Plans and Economic Pains of Fiscal Consolidations in New EU Member States" CESifo Working Paper Series No. 1655 Available at SSRN: http://ssrn.com/abstract=886492

Zhou, W (2007). *Slovak koruna hits record high after revaluation.* Retrieved March 19, 2007 from http://www.marketwatch.com/news/story/slovak-koruna-hits-all-time-high/story.aspx?guid=%7B502A8199%2DE763%2D412F%2DAC59%2DAB1A6AE175EB%7D

Index

Edward M. Jankovic

Dr. Edward M. Jankovic teaches international finance at Pace University in New York and Fairfield University in Connecticut. Dr. Jankovic holds a Doctor of International Business Administration degree from Nova Southeastern University. Before his teaching career, he was a broker for Merrill Lynch International, developing commodities business in Central and South America. He is a registered commodities broker and Commodity Trading Advisor.

Dr. Jankovic specializes in emerging markets finance and economies in transition. He has covered South America, Europe, and the Balkans in his business and academic work, and deals with organizations that need to handle business, political, financial, and market risks. He also has contact with cultural and language aspects at Marine Corps Intelligence.